FROM PLIGHT
TO SOLUTION

SUPPLEMENTS TO
NOVUM TESTAMENTUM

VOLUME LXI

FROM PLIGHT TO SOLUTION

*A Jewish Framework for Understanding
Paul's View of the Law
in Galatians and Romans*

BY

FRANK THIELMAN

E.J. BRILL
LEIDEN · NEW YORK · KØBENHAVN · KÖLN
1989

Library of Congress Cataloging-in-Publication Data

Thielman, Frank.
  From plight to solution.

  (Supplements to Novum Testamentum, 0167-9732;
v. 61)
  Includes bibliographical references.
  1. Bible. N.T. Galatians—Criticism, interpretation,
etc.   2. Bible. N.T. Romans—Criticism, interpretation,
etc.   3. Law (Theology)—Biblical teaching.   4. Paul,
the Apostle, Saint-Contributions in theology of Law.
I. Title.   II. Series.
BS2655.L35T45   1989   227'.106   89-17404
ISBN 90-04-09176-9

                    ISSN   0167-9732
                    ISBN   90 04 09176 9

PRINTED IN THE NETHERLANDS BY E. J. BRILL

For
Abby
ὁ γάρ ἀγαπῶν τὸν
ἕτερον νόμον πεπλήρωκεν

CONTENTS

PREFACE

More ink has flowed in the service of Paul's understanding of the Jewish law in recent years than perhaps any other topic in New Testament studies. Some restless voices are calling for a halt, and some may bemoan the appearance of yet another monograph on the subject. This is no time to turn back, however, for much progress has been made. Readings of Paul which necessitated a pejorative attitude toward first century Judaism have been laid to rest, the understanding of Paul's letters as contingent rather than systematic writings has been firmly established, and tensions within Paul's view of the law have been identified and explored rather than ignored. It is arguable that scholarship is in a better position now than at any time in the last century to understand what Paul meant when he said that faith rather than works of the law justify.

I have no illusions that the present study will produce a break-through in the understanding of that concept. Scholars far more experienced at reading Paul than I have produced weightier studies than this, and yet the full significance of the phrase remains an enigma. My modest hope is that this book will contribute usefully to the on going debate. It represents an experiment in understanding Paul from the perspective of Jewish eschatology—an experiment, it must be said, which many believe has already been weighed and found wanting. I attempt to argue below, however, that the failure of this method in the hands of Montefiore, Schweitzer, and others was due to an underestimation of the complex nature of first-century Judaism. When the Judaisms of late antiquity are allowed a voice in the debate on Paul, Paul appears as less a renegade than a reformer.

Heikki Räisänen has said, sensibly, that when we speak of Paul's relationship to Judaism we must not speak in absolute terms about his continuity or discontinuity with the faith of his fathers. Rather, "it would be more meaningful to try to establish the *relative* continuity *and* discontinuity that Paul shows with regard to Judaism...*in comparison with other contemporary Jews....*"[1] The argument below must not be taken to conclude that there was no discontinuity between Paul and Judaism. It is only an attempt to show that in his basic attitude toward the law Paul stands in continuity with parts of the Hebrew scriptures and with many Jewish contemporaries.

This experiment would not have been possible without the help of many. Julian Deahl, editor at E. J. Brill, guided me skillfully through the process of putting the manuscript in publishable form. Gregory D. Jordan, Kathleen Madigan, and Ursula Weibert, all of King College, cheerfully read parts of the

---

[1] "Galatians 2.16 and Paul's Break with Judaism," *NTS* 31 (1985):549.

manuscript and made available computers and a laser printer. D. Moody Smith, George Washington Ivey Professor of New Testament at Duke University, supervised my doctoral dissertation on Paul's view of the law, and any word of thanks to him would be inadequate. He rescued me from several errors, helped to clarify my thinking, and, by his winning manner and careful scholarship, made research a pleasure. This book would never have appeared without the enthusiastic support of my family. My parents have been excited about the research from the first, and my father not only provided useful suggestions along the way but, as always, gave me free rein within his excellent library at the Montreat Presbyterian Church. My brothers Samuel and Nathan, both in the middle of busy medical practices, offered encouragement and invaluable advice on using the computer to its fullest advantage. Most helpful of all, however, has been my wife Abby. Her provision of a happy environment in which to work, her readiness to help at a moment's notice, her delightful sense of humor, and her gentle reminders of what is important have enriched my study and my life immeasurably. She has gone a long way toward that fulfillment of the law of which Paul spoke in Rom. 13:8.

Frank Thielman
Pentecost Sunday, 1989

CHAPTER ONE

PAUL, TORAH, AND JUDAISM
IN RECENT DEBATE

Introduction

What does Paul mean when he says that a person is justified apart from works of the law? Has he pinpointed the Achilles heel of the entire Jewish religion? Has he reacted against a cold and unforgiving sector of Judaism? Has he sought to universalize his own religious experience? Or has he, in the heat of argument, inaccurately accused the Jews of holding a teaching which they did not in fact hold?

Until recently much Protestant, and especially Lutheran, scholarship believed that he had identified the chief weakness of the Jewish religion: Jews thought that by keeping the law they would attain salvation; but Paul knew that no one could keep the law in its entirety and therefore that all stood condemned before God. Jewish scholarship has always taken exception to this idea, claiming that no Jew believes the law must be kept in its entirety in order to attain salvation. The very law itself, these scholars protest, provides means of atonement for those who sin, and even when those means prescribed by the law are not followed God frequently forgives the sinner anyway out of his abundant mercy.

In recent years a consensus has been forming that Jewish interpreters were correct in their protests: the Judaism of Paul's letters is not the Judaism which most Jews during the second temple period experienced. This conclusion leaves the interpreter with a thorny problem, however. If Paul somehow misrepresented Judaism to lend weight to his argument that all must be saved through faith in Christ, he must have thought Judaism and its law wrong-headed and obsolete, and yet this is not the picture of either Judaism or the law which emerges from Paul's letters. Paul frequently proves his arguments from the law, and quotes scripture most prolifically precisely when he addresses the problem of the law. "Tell me, you who want to be under law," he says to the Galatians, "do you not hear the law?" (Gal. 4:21). At other times he appears anxious to claim that "the gifts and the call of God" to the Jewish people "are irrevocable" (Rom. 11:29). Thus, according to many, a tension exists in Paul's letters between his desire to stand in continuity with Judaism on one hand and his attempt to ascribe to it a position of works-righteousness which it did not hold on the other. The recent history of research on Paul's view of the law is to a large extent the history of the attempt to explain this tension. Some interpreters believe that Paul's statements about

the law can be explained on Jewish presuppositions of one type or another and
that the statements which seem to place Paul outside of Judaism should be read in
light of those other statements in which his continuity with Judaism appears
firm. Most interpreters, at least in the last decade, have concluded that Paul's
view of the law can only be explained if we assume that he had abandoned
Judaism and looked back on his "former manner of life," including his devotion
to the law, wholly from the standpoint of his experience with Christ. They have
concluded, in the words of Hyam Maccoby, that Paul was not the purveyor of
Jewish ideas but the maker of myths largely alien to Judaism.[1]

From Montefiore to Schoeps:
the Demise of Jewish Backgrounds

Claude G. Montefiore was one of the first of Paul's interpreters to attempt an
explanation of how Paul could say what he did about the law within a Jewish
context and expect to be understood, and the three positions which Montefiore
took on the problem illustrate well its confusing character. His first essay on
Paul anticipated the results of several later studies by other scholars almost
uncannily.[2] Here he compared the intelligibility of Jesus to the Jewish mind with
that of Paul and concluded that whereas Jesus' view of the law is perfectly understandable to the Jew, Paul's critique is "utterly unintelligible." Paul and the Jew
of his day moved "on different planes."[3] Moreover, Paul's conception of the law
is self-contradictory and differs according to the different questions posed to him.[4]
It is, he says, "an absolute *bouleversement* of the Jewish conception not to be
explained by any influence of Hellenism. It is purely due to the daring genius of
its author."[5]

Seven years later (1901), however, Montefiore published another article on
Paul.[6] Here, although the same insistence appears that Paul "while dealing with
Judaism, is inexplicable by Judaism,"[7] it is accompanied by an admission of the

---

[1] *The Mythmaker: Paul and the Invention of Christianity* (New York: Harper & Row,1986).
Maccoby's position is that Paul was never a Pharisee but was instead a Hellenistic adventurer who
invented the idea that Jesus of Nazareth was a divine being. Maccoby's evidence for this claim is
as weak as the claim is astonishing. Nonetheless, Maccoby is attempting to answer a problem
which many interpreters of Paul find in his letters: Paul claims to have been a Pharisee, but the
world of his epistles seems anything but Pharisaic.

[2] "First Impressions of Paul," *JQR* 6 (1894): 428-474.

[3] Ibid., p. 429.

[4] Ibid., pp. 432-435. Cf. Heikki Räisänen, *Paul and the Law* (Tübingen: J. C. B. Mohr [Paul
Siebeck], 1983), pp. 264-269 and E. P. Sanders, *Paul, the Law, and the Jewish People*
(Philadelphia: Fortress, 1983), pp. 3-4.

[5] Ibid., pp. 437-438.

[6] "Rabbinic Judaism and the Epistles of St. Paul," *JQR* 13 (1900-1901): 161-217.

[7] Ibid., p. 167.

variegated nature of Judaism in Paul's day and the possibility that "Hellenism refracted through a Jewish medium" could have influenced Paul's thought.[8]

Finally, in 1914, Montefiore published a study which represented a *volte face* from his first essay.[9] This article maintained that Paul's attitude toward the law could be explained by two premises: 1) Paul's ignorance of the gracious religion of the Palestinian Rabbis and 2) the influence upon him of religious conceptions which were not Jewish at all.[10] Paul's religion, said Montefiore,

> must have been, in many important points, very unlike the religion of a representative Rabbinic Jew of the year 500. But that does not make him unintelligible. For the question of the relation of the Rabbinic Judaism of 500 to that of 50 remains over. Moreover, there were other branches of Judaism existing in 50 over and above the purist Rabbinic type.[11]

It was one of these "other branches," specifically Diaspora Judaism, to which Montefiore attributed Paul's extreme pessimism about the ability of the Jew to keep the law.

At several points in this last essay on Paul, Montefiore also advanced the idea that Paul's pre-conversion Judaism was not only the "poorer" religion of Hellenistic Judaism but was "influenced by the Apocalyptic school of thinkers or dreamers."[12] Here he comes close to the thesis suggested by Albert Schweitzer in 1911 and again in 1930 that Paul's religion could be explained on the basis of apocalyptic Judaism and bore little resemblance to the Judaism of the Rabbinic literature.[13] Two important differences remain, however, between Schweitzer and Montefiore in their theories on the origin of Paul's teaching about the law. First, Schweitzer appealed to the apocalyptic literature as a possible background for Paul's view of the law not because of its pessimism, but because of a supposed similarity between Paul and the apocalyptic literature on the disappearance of the law in the Messianic age.[14] Paul's doctrine of justification by faith apart from the law with its accompanying pessimism was merely a convenient polemic against his Galatian opponents and was of no great importance to his theology.[15] Second, Schweitzer maintained, unlike Montefiore, that Paul's Judaism was not essentially different from the apocalyptic Judaism of Jesus and many other Palestinian Jews of the first century. It was certainly not, as Montefiore

---

[8] Ibid., p. 166

[9] *Judaism and St. Paul: Two Essays* (London: Max Goschen,Ltd., 1914), pp. 1-129.

[10] Ibid., p. 66.

[11] Ibid., pp. 17-18

[12] Ibid., p. 92. Cf. p. 95.

[13] *Paul and His Interpreters: A Critical History*, trans. W. Montgomery (New York: Macmllian Publishing Company, 1951), pp. 48-50.

[14] *The Mysticism of Paul the Apostle*, trans. W.Montgomery (New York: Seabury, 1968), pp. 205-226. Cf. William Wrede, *Paul*, trans. Edward Lumis (London: Philip Green, 1907), pp. 124-137.

[15] Schweitzer, *Interpreters*, p. 227.

(following the "comparative religions school") thought a Judaism heavily influenced by Hellenism:

> One error of the students of Comparative Religion deserves particular mention, for it is typical. In consequence of the parallelism which they maintain between the Mystery-religions and Paulinism, they come to ascribe to the Apostle the creation of a "religion." Nothing of the kind ever entered into his purpose. For him there was only one religion: that of Judaism. It was concerned with God, faith, promise, hope, and law. In consequence of the coming, the death, and the resurrection of Jesus Christ, it became its duty to adjust its teachings and demands to the new era thus introduced, and in the process many things were moved from the shadow into the light and others from the light into the shadow. "Christianity" is for Paul no new religion, but simply Judaism with the centre of gravity shifted in consequence of the new era. It professes to be nothing else than the true Jewish religion, in accord both with the time and with the Scriptures.[16]

Thus, whereas Montefiore saw Paul's teaching that no one would be justified by works of the law as a revolt against a certain type of Judaism (Hellenistic) with which Paul wanted nothing further to do, Schweitzer regarded it as the logical outcome of the teachings of a certain type of Judaism (apocalyptic) with which Paul saw himself in full sympathy.

By this time, however, another scholar had entered the debate on the side of discontinuity between the post-conversion Paul and Judaism. In 1927 George Foot Moore published his description of Judaism in the First Centuries of the Christian Era and lent his great scholarly weight to a position not far from that expressed in Montefiore's first article on Paul. Like the early Montefiore, Moore maintained that the Judaism of Paul's day was characterized by grace and sincere devotion to God not by striving for merit and boasting in achievement. Also like the early Montefiore, Moore considered Paul's statements about the law to be a travesty of the true Jewish position:

> The prejudice of many writers on Judaism against the very idea of good works and their reward, and of merit acquired with God through them, is a Protestant inheritance from Luther's controversy with Catholic doctrine, and further back from Paul's contention that there is no salvation in Judaism, for "by the works of the law shall no flesh be justified in his sight." Paul's assertion is

---

[16] *Interpreters*, p. 227. Schweitzer did not consider Paul's upbringing in the diaspora a threat to the thesis that Paul remained free of Hellenistic influences "Although he lived in the middle of Hellenism, it is possible that Paul absorbed no more of it than a Catholic parish priest of the twentieth century does of the critical theology, and knew no more about it than an Evangelical pastor does of theosophy,"p. 87.

the corollary of his first proposition, that the one universal and indispensible condition of salvation is faith in the Lord Jesus Christ.[17]

Moore goes on to explain that every Israelite was promised a place in the world to come "on the ground of the original election of the people by the free grace of God.... These facts are ignored when Judaism is set in antithesis to Christianity, a 'Lohnordnung' over against a 'Gnadenordnung.'"[18] If grace is operative in Christianity, says Moore, it is equally operative in Judaism.[19]

Moore's account of Paul's relationship to Judaism began to appear almost immediately in the works of American and English scholars. In 1930, for example, Morton Scott Enslin claimed that

> much that is said in criticism of Judaism may be true, but the artificial explanations of the Jew's strict keeping of Torah are false, and arise in no small measure from reading our conception of the law, namely, a product of legislators' ingenuity—often unjust—back into the term Torah; a view which would have scandalized any Jew....[20]

Paul, therefore, did not give an accurate picture of Judaism in his polemic against it; in fact, he distorted it. He came to his position as a result of years of fighting for his gospel against Jewish detractors, not as the result of clear-headed thinking.[21] M. E. Andrews, writing in 1934, claims similarly that it would have been possible for Paul to have an entirely satisfying experience within Judaism—other Jews did not labor under the "burden" of the law as Paul did—had he not been imbalanced:

> The indubitable evidence that Paul willingly persecuted the Hellenistic Christian group shows that he was abnormal. Psychologists classify this tendency to cruelty as sadism.... That Paul was temperamentally unfitted for a satisfying religious experience in Judaism is no fair criterion, of course, by which to judge its efficacy for other Jews.[22]

Again, in 1936 the Englishman James Parkes published his popular monograph *Jesus, Paul and the Jews*.[23] He claimed that Jews had always found Paul's

---

[17] *Judaism in the First Centuries of the Christian Era: The Age of the Tannaim*, 3 vols. (Cambridge, Mass.: Harvard University Press, 1927), 2:93-94.

[18] Ibid., p. 95

[19] Cf. Montefiore, "Rabbinic Judaism," p. 176 and *Judaism* p. 44.

[20] *The Ethics of Paul* (New York: Harper & Brothers Publishers, 1930), p. 5.

[21] Ibid., pp. 13-14.

[22] *The Ethical Teaching of Paul: A Study in Origin* (Chapel Hill: University of North Carolina Press, 1934), p.148. Cf. the similar thesis of Donald W. Riddle, "The Jewishness of Paul," *JR* 23 (1943): 240-244.

[23] London: Student Christian Movement Press, 1956.

opposition of "Law" and "Messiah" a "stumbling block" while "Christians have always maintained that the opposition was just.... Both sides have exaggerated," he said, "but from the point of view of scholarship it would appear that Jewish scholars are right."[24] He goes on to claim, appealing to Montefiore, that the Judaism which Paul opposed could not have been rabbinic Judaism and must, therefore, have been the unorthodox Judaism of the Diaspora.[25] Moore's volumes feature in the documentation of all three of these works.

The impact of Moore's study was, however, largely limited to North America and England. In fact, by 1930 some studies on the relationship between Paul and Judaism in Germany had begun to take a sinister turn. "Die Judenfrage" was a major theme of German religious scholarship[26] and during the 1930's a host of publications appeared alternately berating Paul for importing Judaism into Christianity or denying the "adulterating" influence of Judaism upon him.[27] Hans Windisch's *Paulus und das Judentum*[28] is one of the more important books on the subject during this era and offers a good indication of how German scholarship handled the problem of Paul's relationship to Judaism. It is pockmarked with references to "Rassenforschung" and, although Windisch was unwilling to side with those who appealed to research on Paul's Hellenistic background as evidence that he was conceptually (or even physically[29]) unjewish, he was eager to divorce Paul from "orthodox" Judaism. He thus accepted Montefiore's theory that Paul's religious-historical background should be located in "unorthodox" Hellenistic Judaism[30] and went on to investigate four areas of Paul's teaching in this light: "die Christlehre, die Lehre vom Teufel, den Sündenpessimismus und die Rechtfertigungslehre."[31] In each case he decided that Paul's ideas differed significantly from the rabbinic Judaism of his day. In the first three areas he concluded with Montefiore that Paul's teaching derived from the "unorthodox" doctrine of the Jewish Diaspora. When Windisch came to Paul's "Rechtfertigungslehre," however, he asserted against Montefiore that while "das Judentum kennt eine Rechtfertigung, kennt eine Vergebung," it nonetheless "kennt nicht und kaum nicht kennen und anerkennen die Rechtfertigung des als radikalen Sünders erkannten Menschen (die justificatio impii). Das Judentum kennt nicht die radikale Ausschaltung aller Werke bei dem Aussprechen der Rechtfertigung." The Jew, like Johannan ben Zakkai in Berakot 28b, therefore,

---

[24] Ibid., p. 124.

[25] Ibid., pp. 124-125.

[26] See, for example, Gerhard Kittel, *Die Judenfrage* (Stuttgart: Verlag von W. Kohlhammer, 1933).

[27] See Hans Windisch's summary of the positions of J. B. Schairer and H. St. Chamberlain in *Paulus und Judentum* (Stuttgart: Verlag von W. Kohlhammer, 1935), p.3.

[28] See note 26.

[29] Windisch, *Paulus*, p. 39.

[30] Windisch, *Paulus*, pp. 35-40. See also Erik Beijer, "Hans Windisch und seine Deutung für die neutestamentlicheWissenschaft," *ZNW* 47 (1956): 39.

[31] Windisch, *Paulus*, p. 40.

fears God's verdict on his life at death.[32] Paul, on the other hand, preached a gospel of freedom from death, the law, and sin, and thus from fear of God. He announced a new form of existence which means

> die Überwindung des Judentums und der jüdischen Frömmigkeit. Wenn das paulinische Christentum die Religion der Erlösung und der Freiheit ist, dann ist das Judentum die überwundene Religion der Sklavenseligkeit und der ständigen Furcht vor Gott.[33]

Pauline Christianity was, therefore, "die Aufhebung des Judentums."[34] Thus, according to Windisch, whatever combination of influences came together to produce Paul—and it is likely that they were largely Hellenistic—his doctrine of justification by faith was an accurate exposure of and antidote to the rabbinic Judaism of his day.

There were, of course, notable exceptions to the anti-Semitic tone of works like Windisch's, and Rudolf Bultmann is undoubtedly the most important. Bultmann did not write extensively on the relationship between Paul and Judaism, but what he did say shows that he took a position close to G. F. Moore's. In his 1930 article on Paul for *Religion in Geschichte und Gegenwart*[35] Bultmann emphasized that Paul's conversion was no reaction to the oppression of Judaism nor to the anxiety caused by the Torah,[36] but the simple abandonment of one way of salvation (works) for another (faith).[37] Romans 7, he said, was not autobiographical,[38] but the presentation of "the situation of the Jew under the law in the light of the real meaning of that situation as it is disclosed to the eye of faith."[39] Paul's conversion was the realization that by permitting the Messiah to suffer crucifixion, God "had destroyed the Jewish way of salvation and had thereby passed judgment against everything human, which had reached its highest point in Judaism."[40] Paul's theology could be catagorized under the headings of "man prior to the revelation of faith" and "man under faith"; but "it must be noted...that the being of man prior to faith first becomes visible in its true lineaments only from the standpoint of faith itself and that it is from this perspective alone that it

---

[32] Ibid., p. 53.

[33] Ibid., p. 55.

[34] Ibid., p. 56.

[35] "Paulus," vol. 4, 2d ed., (Tübingen: J. C. B. Mohr, 1930), pp. 1019-45. For an English translation see "Paul" in *Existence and Faith: Shorter Writings of Rudolf Bultmann*, trans. and ed. Schubert M. Ogden (New York: Meridian Books, Inc., 1960), pp. 111-146.

[36] "Paul," p. 115.

[37] Ibid. See also "Romans 7 and the Anthropology of Paul," in *Existence and Faith*, p. 147 and *Theology of the New Testament*, 2 vols., trans. Kendrick Grobel (New York: Charles Scribner's Sons, 1951-55), 1:187-89.

[38] Ibid., p. 114.

[39] Ibid., emphasis mine.

[40] Ibid., p. 115. See also "Romans 7," pp. 148-50 and *Theology,* 1:188.

can be understood."[41] Like Moore, therefore, Bultmann believed that Paul's thinking worked backwards from his pre-determined solution to a certain view of Judaism and the law. Paul's perspective on the law was only possible from the vantage point of faith. Bultmann, of course, was sympathetic with Paul, whereas Moore was not; but both saw Paul's view of the law as a product of his experience with Christ.[42]

Other German contributions to the problem of Paul's view of the law, while seldom as anti-Semitic as Windisch's study, continued to preserve the picture of Judaism as a self-striving and meritorious religion to which Paul provided the antidote. W. Grundmann, for example, published an important article in 1933 which took issue with Schweitzer's theory that Paul's doctrine of justification by faith was a "subsidiary crater" in his theology.[43] Grundmann claimed in the course of his argument that in the rabbinic Judaism of Paul's day righteousness before God, and hence salvation, came through doing the law.[44] The average Jew did not labor under the guilt of having offended God in small ways but thought that if he were more or less righteous, God would acquit him at the time of judgement. In contradistinction to this concept of sin, however, Paul saw every sin as serious—and deadly—in God's eyes. Sin became a sinister force for him and thus the law began to take on the character of revealer of sin rather than antidote to it. The law then became the guarantee of the curse rather than the guarantee of salvation.[45] Similarly, in 1941, Peter Bläser produced a study of *Das Gesetz bei Paulus* which, although free of anti-Semitism, explained Paul's view of the law against the background of a Judaism laboring not only under bondage to the pentateuchal Torah but to the numerous rabbinical additions to it.[46] Judaism, claimed Bläser, went from bad to worse as it first held the pentateuchal laws to be binding, then added to them other laws which it considered equally binding, and finally, in some cases, held the additional laws to be more important than the original, God-given ones. The basic difference between these concepts and Paul's teaching on the law, he said, is the difference between the law of Moses and the law of Christ.[47] The law of Moses is characterized by the letter—a list of outward prescriptions, powerless to enable one to please God—whereas the law of Christ is characterized by the Spirit, and thus by a life-giving relationship between the believer and the one he is to obey:

---

[41] Ibid., p. 128.

[42] Ibid., p. 120. The comparison between Bultmann and Moore extends only to their views on Paul's relationship to Judaism. When speaking of Judaism generally or of Jesus' relationship to Judaism, Bultmann could talk of "Jewish legalism" in a manner with which Moore had no sympathy. See *Primitive Christianity in Its Contemporary Setting*, trans. R. H. Fuller (New York: World, 1956) and *Theology*, 1:11-22.

[43] "Gesetz, Rechtifertigung und Mystik bei Paulus: Zum Problem der Einheitlichkeit der paulinischen Verkundigung," *ZNW* 32 (1933): 52-65.

[44] Ibid., pp. 59-60.

[45] Ibid., p. 57.

[46] Munster: Aschendorffsche Verlagsbuchhandlung, pp.1-38.

[47] Ibid., pp. 234-243.

Das Gesetz des Moses enthält die Gerechtigkeitsforderung in der Form des nur fordernden und darum totenden Buchstabens, das Gesetz Christi aber in der Form des lebendigmachenden Geistes.[48]

Thus, although both Grundmann and Bläser are free from anti-Semitic sentiment, they both claim that Paul's doctrine of the law is specifically formulated against the dismal character of first century rabbinic Judaism.[49]

Shortly after the end of World War II, W. D. Davies published his influential volume *Paul and Rabbinic Judaism*. The work represented a new approach to the problem of Paul's relationship to his Jewish heritage, for on one hand it refused to accept the idea that Paul revolted against a self-striving and meritorious religion (whether Palestinian or Hellenistic), and on the other it denied Moore's thesis that Paul's attitude toward the law was simply the "corollary" to his Christianity. Davies began his work with a threefold criticism of Montefiore's thesis. First, he argued that Montefiore's skeptical attitude toward the picture of Paul in Acts was unjustified. Montefiore had said that the claim in Acts (22:3) that Paul was a Pharisee in good standing with such great representatives of rabbinic religion as Gamaliel could not be correct.[50] Davies, however, appealed to Paul's own statements concerning his Jewish background in 2 Cor. 11:22 and Phil. 3:5-6 as evidence that the picture of Paul in Acts, at least on this subject, was accurate.[51] Second, Davies claimed that Montefiore had been too facile in his identification of fourth century rabbinic Judaism with first century Judaism. "We cannot," he said, "without extreme caution, use the Rabbinic sources as evidence for first-century Judaism."[52] Finally, and most importantly, Davies contended that Montefiore placed a wall between Palestinian Judaism and Diaspora Judaism which did not exist. Not only had Palestine been dominated by Hellenistic overlords from 333 B. C. until 63 B. C.,[53] but frequent wars had so greatly diminished the population of Palestine "that the Jews were reduced to a tiny political unit about the city of Jerusalem."[54] Moreover, there was frequent interaction between the Jews of Jerusalem and the Jews of the Diaspora.[55]

In place of Montefiore's picture of the relationship between Paul and Judaism, Davies proposed that Paul's most important theological concepts could be explained on the premise that he was a rabbi for whom the messiah had

---

[48] Ibid. p. 242

[49] See also Christian Maurer, *Die Gesetzeslehre des Paulus nach ihrem Ursprung und in ihrer Entfaltung dargelegt* (Zurich: Evangelischer Verlag, 1941) and W. Gutbrod, "νόμος" in *Theologisches Wörterbuch zum Neuen Testament*, ed. Gerhard Kittel, 10 vols. (Stuttgart: Verlag von W. Kohlhammer, 1942), 4:1046-1050.

[50] Montefiore, *Judaism*, pp. 90-91

[51] *Paul and Rabbinic Judaism: Some Rabbinic Elements in Pauline Theology* (London: S.P.C.K., 1948), pp. 2-3.

[52] Ibid., p. 3.

[53] Ibid., p. 5.

[54] Ibid., p. 6.

[55] Ibid., pp. 6-8.

come.[56] In a way reminiscent of Schweitzer, Davies both regarded Paul's view of
the law as an application by a loyal Jew of the Jewish principle that in the
Messianic Age the law would be modified[57] and considered Paul's teaching on
justification by faith to be a "convenient polemic" developed during the Judaizing
controversy.[58] Thus Davies maintained that Paul was not at odds with Judaism
either in its Hellenistic or rabbinic form; his belief in Christ was a fulfillment of
his Jewish heritage. Consequently, his critique of the law came not out of
dissatisfaction with meritoriousness and self-striving but both from a conviction
that with the messianic age a new law would become operative and from a
temporary argument with certain agitators at Galatia.

In 1950, two years after the publication of Davies' volume, Hans Joachim
Schoeps published his collection of essays *Aus frühchristlicher Zeit*[59] in which
for the first time he advanced his theory on Paul's view of the law. His thesis,
although apparently developed independently, reads like a pastiche of the ideas of
Montefiore, Schweitzer, and Davies. One chapter of the book, "Paulus als
rabbinischer Exeget: Zwei Studien,"[60] immediately identifies Schoeps as one
who, like Davies, is interested in explaining Paul's theology from the standpoint
of his rabbinic background. The first section of the chapter seeks to explain
Paul's view of the law both by reference to rabbinic and apocalyptic passages
which speak of the "Aufhören der Gesetzgeltung" at the coming of the messianic
age and by reference to the "distorted" (*verzerrtes*) picture of the law current in the
Jewish Diaspora.[61] Thus, in the first and longest part of this section Schoeps
agrees with Schweitzer that much of what Paul says about the law can be
explained by his belief that he was living in the messianic age when the law
would cease to operate. In the last part of the section, however, Schoeps departs
significantly from both Schweitzer and Davies and expresses an idea similar to
Montefiore's many years earlier: Paul's extremely negative statements about the
law can be explained by his background in the type of Judaism seen in the
Septuagint and in Philo. Paul, like the Hellenistic Judaism out of which he
came, saw only the ethical-normative side of the law and did not understand, "dass
das Gesetz des Moses *Bundes-gesetz* ist, in der *berith* Gottes mit Volke
gründet...."[62] Paul reduced the *tora qodascha* to its ethical demands and claimed
that the law could not make people righteous, since they were sinful. Paul
therefore began with a Hellenistic distortion of the role of the law and, not surprisingly, concluded that the law was a source of death and sin rather than life.

----

[56] Ibid., p. 71.

[57] Davies formulated his theory more carefully than Schweitzer, claiming that the law, rather
than becoming inoperative in the Messianic age, would be replaced by a new law. See *Paul and
Rabbinic Judaism*, p. 72.

[58] Ibid., p. 222.

[59] The work is subtitled *Religionsgeschichtliche Untersuchungen* (Tübingen: Verlag J. C. B.
Mohr [PaulSiebeck], 1950).

[60] Ibid., pp. 221-238.

[61] Ibid., pp. 228-229.

[62] Ibid., p. 229.

In his later book on Paul, published in 1959, Schoeps expanded this assessment of Paul's teaching on the law to include a dialogue with Montefiore, whose hypothesis "had much to be said for it."[63] He also included new sections on Gal. 3:10-13, Romans 7, Jewish "counter-positions" to Paul's insistence on the connection between the law and sin, and "faith and works."[64] Paul's "fundamental misapprehension" about the law, however, remained his "failure to appreciate the *berith* as the basis of the fulfilling of the law—a failure which was part of Paul's fateful inheritance."[65]

Thus, like Schweitzer and Davies, Schoeps claimed that Paul's belief in the cessation of the law as it was previously known was simply the application of an apocalyptic and rabbinic idea to what Paul believed to be the messianic age. Like Montefiore, however, Schoeps said that Paul's pessimism about the law was not a critique of Palestinian, and therefore, rabbinic Judaism; rather it can only be understood against the grey background provided by the Hellenistic Judaism of the Diaspora.

Schoeps's account of Paul's view of the law was not destined to endure, however, and with its demise came the eclipse of the theories of Montefiore, Schweitzer, and Davies. First, critics attacked the idea that the origin of Paul's view of the law lay in a supposed Jewish concept of the termination or modification of the law in the messianic age.[66] They maintained that no such teachings are found either in the apocalyptic literature (as Schweitzer maintained) or in the relevant rabbinic literature (as Davies argued). Critics claimed, for example, that B. Sanhedrin 97a—a text frequently cited as evidence that the Torah would not be present in the age to come—could only yield the sense which this theory requires if it is distorted: its purpose was to date the Messiah's coming, not to restrict the validity of the Torah.[67] Furthermore, said the critics, Paul's letters themselves do not support such a theory. Paul nowhere refers to the idea that the law would become obsolete in the coming age, although he had occasion to do so if such an

---

[63] Ibid., *Paul: The Theology of the Apostle in the Light of Jewish Religious History*, trans. Harold Knight (Philadelphia: Westminster, 1961), p. 25. Schoeps criticized Montefiore, however, for regarding rabbinic religion as too homogeneous and for neglecting the importance of apocalyptic in the study of Paul; see pp. 25-26.

[64] Ibid., pp. 175-183; 183-193; 193-200; and 200-213.

[65] Ibid., p. 214.

[66] Davies himself offered a study of the law in the messianic age which found scant evidence from Paul's time for the idea that the messiah would establish a new law. He concluded that the most persuasive evidence was that early Jewish Christians made a place for a new torah in their teaching. See *Torah in the Messianic Age and/or the Age to Come*. JBL Monograph Series, no. 7 (Philadelphia: Society of Biblical Literature, 1952), pp. 90-91.

[67] B. Sanhedrin 97a describes the history of the world in eight stages and, while it mentions the Torah in the third and fifth stages, it does not mention its continued existence in the final stage when the messiah will come. Both Samuel Sandmel, *The Genius of Paul: A Study of History* (New York: Farrar, Straus, and Cudahy, 1958), p. 40 and Ernst Bammel, "NOMOS CHRISTOU," *SE* 3 (1964): 124-125 took issue with the interpretation of this text which claimed that it taught the cessation of the law in the messianic age.

idea had been available to him.[68]   Moreover, for Paul the messianic age had not yet fully come in any case, for Christ had not yet returned.[69]

Second, what Davies had said about Montefiore's simple division between "Hellenistic Judaism" and "rabbinic Judaism" was also applicable to Schoeps. Davies had found the air-tight compartments of Palestinian Rabbinic Judaism and Hellenistic Diaspora Judaism to be mythical long before the 1959 publication of Schoeps' *Paulus*, and thus one of Schoeps' major contentions was doomed from the start.   The publication of Martin Hengel's massive study on the interaction between Judaism and Hellenism in Palestine from the fourth to the first centuries B. C. made Davies' conclusions about Montefiore's thesis even more certain.[70] Hengel demonstrated decisively the extent to which Greek culture influenced not only those Jews in Palestine who collaborated willingly with their Macedonian, Ptolemaic, and Seleucid overlords but also those who tried to insulate themselves from Greek influences.   From the impeccable Greek which Pseudo-Aristeas claimed for the famous seventy-two Palestinian Jewish translators of the Septuagint, to the Greek names by which many of the Maccabees were known, to the concept of free association among the Qumran covenanters and the Essenes, Hengel showed how Hellenistic language, culture, and philosophy had penetrated Jewish Palestine.[71]   Montefiore's ideas and their restatement in Schoeps had breathed their last.

Although the demise of Montefiore's specific theory was now certain, the idea that Paul had employed a current Jewish belief about the law in the messianic age continued to influence scholarship for several more years. Thus between 1959 and 1977 several attempts were made to navigate between the Jewish Paul of Schweitzer and Davies, the individualistic Paul of Moore, Enslin, and Andrews, and the Lutheran Paul of the principally German exegetes. Moore's theory, however, was destined to triumph.

---

[68] Sandmel, *Genius*, p. 41; Bammel, "NOMOS CHRISTOU,"pp. 124-125.

[69] Sandmel, *Genius*, p. 41. See also E. P. Sanders, *Paul and Palestinian Judaism: A Comparison of Patterns of Religion* (Philadelphia: Fortress Press, 1977), pp. 479, 497, and Räisänen, *Law* pp. 236-240.

[70] See Martin Hengel, *Judaism and Hellenism: Studies in their Encounter in Palestine during the Early Hellenistic Period*, 2 vols. (Philadelphia: Fortress Press, 1974) and the reviews of *Paulus: Die Theologie des Apostels im Lichte der jüdischen Religionsgeschichte* by W. D. Davies in *NTS* 10 (1963-1964): 295-304; P. Benoit in *RB* 67 (1960): 290; and F. W. Young in *Theology Today* 20 (1963-1964): 555.

[71] *Judaism and Hellenism*, 1:1-309 and Martin Hengel, *Jews Greeks and Barbarians: Aspects of the Hellenization of Judaism in the Pre-Christian Period* (London: SCM Press, 1980), pp. 110-126.

From Wilckens to Sanders:
the Rise of Christology

Shortly after the publication of Schoep's volume, Ulrich Wilckens published a study of Paul's conversion which was an omen of things to come. Wilckens developed the thesis that in his view of the law Paul had simply shifted Christ into the place in salvation-history which the law had previously occupied in his Jewish apocalyptic heritage. Wilckens maintained against Schoeps that Paul's understanding of the law could not be explained by appeal to the Jewish doctrine that the law would end when the messianic age dawned.[72] Instead, said Wilckens, Paul's understanding of the law was an apocalyptic and therefore a unified understanding. The law was not, in his thinking, a series of commands and proscriptions but a unified entity which God had given to his elect people.[73] It had "eine spezifische heilsgeschichtliche Funktion."[74] As an apocalyptist, the pre-christian Paul considered the proclamation of salvation in Christ alone in the early church to be wholly incompatible with the law's salvation-historical function. After his conversion, said Wilckens, Paul still thought as an apocalyptist; but Paul now excluded the law *in toto*, on the basis of his conviction that salvation was available only in Christ.[75] Thus although Wilckens sought to explain Paul's view of the law on the basis of a Jewish religious-historical background,[76] like Moore and Bultmann before him, he also acknowledged the importance of christology to a right understanding of Paul's teaching. Paul's convictions about Christ, said Wilckens, necessarily excluded salvation by means of the law.

In 1964 Richard N. Longenecker's *Paul, the Apostle of Liberty*[77] produced an answer to the question of the relationship between Paul's religious-historical background and his view of the law which bucked the current of christological explanations and went back to a Jewish solution to the problem. Longenecker attempted to join three concepts which in previous studies had been considered incompatible. First, he sought to take seriously Moore's picture of Judaism and thus remained sensitive to the criticism that Paul's statements about the law did not address the Jewish understanding of it. Second, he attempted to

---

[72] "Die Bekehrung des Paulus als religionsgeschichtliches Problem," *ZTK* 56 (1959): 273-293, reprinted in *Rechtfertigung als Freiheit: Paulusstudien* (Neukirchener Verlag, 1974), pp. 11-32. References are to the latter edition.

[73] "Die Bekehrung des Paulus," pp. 20-25.

[74] Ibid., p. 22.

[75] Ibid., pp. 22-23. Cf. Karl Kertelge, *Rechtfertigung bei Paulus: Studien zur Struktur und zum Bedeutungsgehalt des paulinischen Rechtfertigungsbegriffs*, NTAbh, no. 3 (Munster: Verlag Aschendorff, 1967), pp. 203-204.

[76] Wilckens, in the later edition of his essay, accepted the distinctions made between rabbinic and apocalyptic Judaism by D. Rössler, *Gesetz und Geschichte: Eine Untersuchung zur Theologie der jüdischen Apokalyptik und der pharisäischen Orthodoxie*, WMANT, no. 3 (Neukirchen Kreis Moers: Neukirchener Verlag, 1962).

[77] The work is subtitled *The Origin and Nature of Paul's Christianity* (New York: Harper & Row Publishers, 1964).

retain the centrality of Paul's doctrine of justification by faith apart from the law. Finally, he tried to show that Paul's thinking about the law was not incompatible with his Jewish background. Thus Longenecker maintained that Paul's conversion was not the result of a life of frustration under the burden of keeping the whole law; nor, he claimed, could it be said that Paul, if he were a typical Jew, did not take sin seriously before his conversion. How, then, could Paul's conversion be explained? Longenecker gave a two-fold answer. First, it originated in the common Jewish conviction of man's inability to do God's will when left to himself. This, claimed Longenecker, is the subject of Romans 7. Here "Paul is writing approximately a quarter-century after his conversion, and all his words bear the Christian stamp. But this does not require us to view all his expressions as exclusively Christian."[78] He then cites 1QH 1.21-23, 3.24-36, 5.5-40, 1QS 11.9-10, and 4Ezra 8:31-36 as examples of a similar conviction from the Judaism of Paul's era. In direct continuity with this Jewish tradition, Paul believed that the law showed people their need of God's grace.

Second, Paul's post-conversion convictions about the law and its purpose came from his position that the law in its "contractual aspect"—the aspect of obligation to adhere to "a prescribed form of religious expression and ethical guidance"[79]—had come to an end with the coming of Christ.[80] Christ was able to bring this aspect of the law to an end by fulfilling the contractual obligation to the law in "His death and His life, in His sacrifice and His obedience."[81] Again, Longenecker contended that Paul's insight in this regard was not particularly original, and certainly was not the necessary result of a Christian position to which he was already committed.[82] In a way similar to Davies, Longenecker argued that the idea of a modified Torah in the messianic age was common in Paul's day. Thus in both his doctrine of justification by faith apart from works of the law and in his teaching that with the coming of the messiah the law would cease to function in its usual way, Paul stood in direct continuity with Judaism and remains comprehensible within its framework.[83]

---

[78] Ibid., p. 115.

[79] Ibid., p. 125.

[80] Ibid., p. 128.

[81] Ibid., p. 148.

[82] Ibid., p. 128. Longenecker makes this statement against the contention of W. L. Knox, *St. Paul and the Church of Jerusalem* (Cambridge: Cambridge University Press, 1925), p. 28, n. 65 that "St. Paul's arguments are only thought out in order to justify a step to which he was irrevocably committed."

[83] Longenecker's study bears several similarities and dissimilarities to the well known study of "St. Paul and the Law" by C. E. B. Cranfield which also appeared in 1964 (*SJT* 17: 43-68). First, like Longenecker, Cranfield claims that there was in Paul's thought a right use of the law and a wrong use ("legalism," pp. 47 and 55). Unlike Longenecker, however, Cranfield does not seem to think that it was possible for Jews outside of Christ to avoid legalism (p.53). Second, whereas for Longenecker Paul sees even the right use of the law ("nomism" or the doing of "ethical obligations") as excluded by the coming of Christ (pp. 128-155), Cranfield sees the new age of the Spirit as the time in which the law is truly established (pp. 65-68). Finally, both Longenecker (pp. 147-153) and Cranfield (pp. 48-52) agree that Christ fulfilled the law by keeping it himself and vicariously fulfilling its demands for those who were unable to keep it.

In 1968, Andrea van Dülmen produced a study of *Die Theologie des Gesetzes bei Paulus* which made its way through the maze of scholarly opinion in a way different from Longenecker and closer, in its emphasis on christology, to Wilckens. Her thesis was that Paul's statements about the law are christologically oriented rather than anthropologically oriented—they derive from his conviction that the law cannot be kept outside of Christ and has been replaced by Christ. Although she formulates her thesis primarily against Bultmann's idea that the human plight is not simply a matter of transgression but of doing the law as a means of boasting before God,[84] she and Bultmann are one in their conviction that Paul's christology dethrones the law. Christ and law, she says, exclude one another in Paul's thinking. Thus in Galatians Paul sees two mutually exclusive forces operative in history: faith, which can be traced from Abraham to Christ, and works of the law, which became operative with Moses.[85] The same exclusivity appears in Rom. 10:3 which seems to say that "wenn in Christus Gottes Gerechtigkeit offenbar wurde, dann muss alle andere Gerechtigkeit nur Schein, ja sogar Ungerechtigkeit sein."[86]

In subsequent years, the emphasis on the importance of Paul's christology for a proper understanding of his view of the law went from strength to strength. By 1976 Friedrich Lang could say that

> In der Paulusforschung hat sich ziemlich allgemein die Erkenntnis durchgesetzt, dass die Rechtfertigungslehre des Apostels und sein Verständnis des Gesetzes sachgemäss nur von der Christologie aus erfasst werden können.[87]

Lang's own article is a good example of the direction of scholarship during this period. He maintained that Paul's radical opposition of the New Covenant to the Law had no parallel in either the pre-pauline church or in Judaism.[88] Moreover, Paul's appeal to the Old Testament as a witness to justification by faith was an attempt to maintain continuity with Judaism without maintaining continuity with the Law.[89] Thus Paul's prior conviction about Christ led him to his unique stance on the place of the law.

---

[84] SBM, no. 5 (Stuttgart: Verlag Katholisches Bibelwerk, 1968). Van Dülmen consciously formulates her thesis in opposition to Bultmann and Schlier, whose existential interpretations she considers backwards. See esp. pp. 248-257.

[85] Van Dülmen, p. 174. See also Ulrich Luz, *Das Geschichtsverständnis des Paulus*, BEvT, no. 49 (Munich: Chr.Kaiser Verlag, 1968), pp. 216-222. Luz also believes that Paul's statements about the law can only be explained by his christological convictions. He claims, however, that these convictions were not original with Paul but were part of his heritage from the early Jewish Christian community. Cf. Johannes Munck, *Paul and the Salvation of Mankind*, trans. Frank Clarke (London: SCM, 1959), pp. 122-129 and 247-55.

[86] Ibid., p. 178.

[87] "Gesetz und Bund bei Paulus" in *Rechtfertigung: Festschrift für Ernst Käsemann*, ed. Johannes Friedrich, Wolfgang Pohlmann, and Peter Stuhlmacher (Tübingen: J. C. B.Mohr [Paul Siebeck] and Göttingen: Vandenhoeck und Ruprecht, 1976), p. 305.

[88] Ibid., pp. 309-312.

[89] Ibid., pp. 319-320.

The christological interpretation of Paul's view of the law achieved its climax, however, in 1977 with the publication of E. P. Sanders's *Paul and Palestinian Judaism*. The first part of the book is a comprehensive refutation of the view that first century Judaism was a meritorious religion devoid of grace and forgiveness. It begins with a close examination of the pattern of soteriology within Tannaitic Judaism and concludes that Moore's treatment of the subject is accurate. It then goes far beyond Moore to examine the Dead Sea Scrolls, the Apocrypha, and the Pseudepigrapha. In each body of literature Sanders discovers the same pattern of "covenantal nomism" whereby salvation was assumed until flagrant violation of the covenant placed one outside of God's elect people. Forgiveness for sin was generously provided by atoning sacrifices and by God's merciful character, and salvation was never based on toting up deeds or on human effort.[90]

In the second part of his book Sanders applied these insights about first century Judaism to the interpretation of Paul's letters. Since Judaism was not a meritorious and self-striving religion in Paul's day, Sanders said, any attempt to explain Paul's thought as a critique of Jewish legalism was doomed to failure.[91] Paul's thought, he said, was less rooted in Judaism than in the conviction that Christ was the savior of the world.[92] Thus Paul did not criticize Judaism from within—claiming that it pursued the correct goal (righteousness) in the wrong way (works)—but from without—claiming that it began at the wrong place (the law) and arrived at the wrong goal (righteousness by the law). Paul argued that the correct place to begin was participation in Christ and the correct goal to reach was righteousness by faith in Christ.[93]

To prove all of this Sanders relied heavily upon his carefully argued thesis that Paul's soteriology depends upon participationist rather than on juristic categories.[94] Sanders considered this so important because he felt that the view of Judaism commonly reproduced in New Testament scholarship was derived from the idea that the center of Paul's thought was justification by faith apart from works of the law. This was the view, said Sanders, that the most influential interpreters of Paul held. Martin Luther claimed that Paul's thinking was centered in justification by faith alone and was designed to refute the supposedly Jewish belief that one must keep a certain number of the law's requirements to be saved. Luther's view of Judaism was perpetuated in Ferdinand Weber's influential account of the Jewish religion, and both Luther and Weber influenced Rudolf Bultmann's interpretation of Paul. Bultmann, in turn, passed this perspective to much of modern scholarship. Against this idea Sanders proposed not only that the Lutheran-Weberian account of Judaism was hopelessly skewed but that the

---

[90] Sanders, *Paul*, pp. 1-428, esp. pp. 419-428.

[91] Sanders, ibid., pp. 33-59, traced to Ferdinand Weber the wide distribution of the view that Paul's teaching on justification by faith offered a piercing critique of Judaism.

[92] Ibid., p. 474, esp. n. 2.

[93] Ibid., pp. 505-506.

[94] Ibid., pp. 434-442 and 497-508.

source of Paul's thinking was his doctrine of participation in Christ. The center of Paul's religion was not a critique of Jewish soteriology but the assertion of his own new convictions about Christ.[95] For Paul, salvation occurred when one participated in Christ, not when one was declared righteous by God. Thus, the locus of salvation was not a righteousness attained by justification despite legal transgressions, but participation in Christ.[96]

Nowhere does the christological source of Paul's religion appear more clearly, according to Sanders, than in Phil. 3:4-12. Here the reader sees the real argument that Paul has with Judaism, for Paul acknowledges two righteousnesses, one based on works of the law and one—the correct one—based on faith in Christ. It is not that the Jew fails to work his or her way to God by attaining righteousness; the Jew in fact has a righteousness—one which Paul himself attained.[97]   The problem, rather, is that the Jew is not "in Christ." Thus, says Sanders, Paul argues from solution to plight, not from plight to solution. He does not claim that Jews cannot keep the law and therefore need Christ's atoning death to attain righteousness. Rather, Paul says that because Christ is savior of the world, everyone needs the salvation which Christ offers.[98]

According to Sanders, therefore, Paul's view of the law cannot be explained as a misunderstanding of Judaism (as Montefiore and Schoeps had believed), nor as in any way connected with his Jewish background (as Davies and Schweitzer had maintained). "It is the Gentile question and the exclusivism of Paul's soteriology which dethrone the law, not a misunderstanding of it or a view predetermined by his background."[99]

As we have seen above, this was not a new insight. George Foot Moore had made a similar observation many years before, and others had at least registered their dissent from the picture of Judaism as a meritorious religion. It is curious that Sanders does not perceive that Bultmann too, whatever his thoughts about justification by faith being the center of Paul's religion, wholeheartedly endorsed the view that Paul's religion could only be understood from the perspective of his experience with Christ.

Despite these predecessors, however, Sanders's book had a sweeping impact on pauline scholarship. Many acclaimed it as a significant achievement,[100] and one of the most important reviews placed it beside the works of Schweitzer, Davies, Bultmann, and Munck in importance.[101] Two criticisms, however, regularly appeared in the reviews, corresponding, not unnaturally, to the two parts of

---

[95] Ibid., pp. 499-500.

[96] Ibid., pp. 502-504.

[97] Ibid., pp. 442-447, 497-502.

[98] Ibid., p. 493.

[99] Ibid., p. 497.

[100] The book was hailed as "a major work" (N. A. Dahl, *RelSRev* 4 [1978]: 153), "monumental" (G. B. Caird, *JTS* 29 [1978]: 543), and a "very considerable achievement" (W. Horbury, "Paul and Judaism," *Exp Tim* 89 [1977-1978]: 118).

[101] Dahl, review, p. 153.

the book. First, several reviewers balked at Sanders's assessment of Palestinian Judaism. Although ready to acknowledge that it was not, generally speaking, a religion centered around merit and devoid of mercy and forgiveness, these critics questioned whether Sanders had adequately dealt with evidence that some Palestinian Jews, notably the Qumran covenanters, viewed the "proper" keeping of the law as the path to salvation and excluded even other Jews from salvation as long as they did not keep the law in the way which the sect prescribed.[102] Second, critics also charged Sanders with severing Paul from his Jewish background and his Jewish Christian contemporaries so thoroughly that his efforts to relate belief in Christ to Judaism in Romans 9-11 become inexplicable and his form of Christianity eccentric and historically improbable.[103] Paul, with his emphasis on participationist eschatology and Judaism, with its concern for Torah, guilt, atonement, and forgiveness, to quote William Horbury, "pass like ships in the night."[104]

In view of these criticisms, Sanders produced another book in 1983 which sought to "expand and clarify, and sometimes correct, the account of Paul's view of the law which was sketched in *Paul and Palestinian Judaism*."[105] *Paul, the Law and the Jewish People*, therefore, set out to show why Paul says what he does about the law and to give Paul's statements some historical plausibility in view of the pictures of Paul and Judaism drawn in *Paul and Palestinian Judaism*.

Sanders's basic thesis in this monograph was that Paul's statements about the law can only be understood if they are seen from the vantage of Sanders's contention in Paul and Palestinian Judaism that Paul thought not from plight to solution, but from solution to plight. Paul's central conviction was that Christ was savior of the world. His statements about the law, therefore, do not provide reasons *why* Christ is savior of the world, but a variety of *arguments* that this is in fact the case.[106] Paul's central conviction that Christ is universal savior remains constant, but the arguments he uses to defend it vary considerably and are sometimes contradictory. The direction of these arguments depends on the question that Paul is trying to answer at any given time. When asked about the purpose of the law, he can produce three incompatible answers in the space of a few verses (Rom. 5:20f., 7:7-13, 7:14-25).[107] When asked whether the law should be fulfilled by Christians he can answer both that it should be fulfilled

---

[102] Ibid., p. 155. Cf. Caird, review, p. 540 and Horbury, review, p. 116.

[103] J. C. Beker, *Paul the Apostle, the Triumph of God in Life and Thought* (Philadelphia: Fortress, 1980), p. 237 is typical of Sanders's critics. He claims that Sanders's thesis is irenic for it denies that Paul's critique of the law has much to do with Judaism and is instead based on christological presuppositions. But, says Beker, the consequence of this approach is that the scholar is not allowed to raise the vital issue of the interface between Paul and Judaism. Cf. Dahl, review, p. 156; Caird, review p. 540; and Davies, *Paul and Rabbinic Judaism*, 4th ed. (Philadelphia: Fortress, 1980), pp. xxxii and xxxv-xxxvii

[104] Review, p. 116.

[105] *Law*, p. ix.

[106] Ibid., p. 4.

[107] Ibid., p. 75.

(Gal. 5:14; 6:2; Rom. 13:8-10) and that no one is made righteous by doing the law (Gal. 2:15-3:18).[108] Finally, in Romans 2, he can actually extend the possibility of salvation by works in a convoluted argument that all have sinned and therefore all need to be saved by Christ.[109] These observations occupy Sanders in chapters 2 and 3 and in an appendix on Romans 2.

Perhaps the most important parts of his book for meeting the criticisms levelled at his first volume, however, are chapters 1 and 4. There he seeks to dispel any misconception that the differences between Paul and Judaism detailed in *Paul and Palestinian Judaism* rendered Paul's view of the law enigmatic and inexplicable. Thus he seeks to refute the idea, based on Galatians 2-3, Gal. 5:3, Romans 3-4, and Romans 9-11, that Paul conceived of the law as an impossible standard which no one could keep or that he considered "doing" the law to be an evil activity which, by its nature, leads man to make claims upon God.[110]

Sanders claimed that in Galatians doing the law is not considered wrong (he called attention to 6:15).[111] Paul was not arguing against Jews who thought that everyone must quantitatively do the law in order to be saved but Jewish Christians who wanted to institute the requirements of the law (i.e., the means by which one becomes Jewish) as entrance requirements for Christianity.[112] Sanders recognized that this reading of the situation contradicted the commonly accepted reading of Gal. 3:10, 5:3, and 6:13.[113] But, he said, not only does that reading ignore the lack of meritoriousness in first century Judaism, it also turns a blind eye to other passages in Paul's letters (Phil. 3:6, 1 Thess. 3:13, 1 Thess. 5:23, and 1 Cor. 1:8) which show that, both before and after his conversion, Paul considered it more or less possible to keep the whole law.[114]

Similarly when Sanders turned to Romans he claimed that Romans 3-4 and 9-11 show no more than Paul's concern that all people, Jews as well as Gentiles, be regarded as acceptable before God on the basis of faith in Christ.[115] Boasting in works before God is not the issue in these passages. They speak rather about the acceptance of the Gentiles into the people of God without making the law an entrance requirement.[116] Thus, according to Sanders, Paul nowhere argues against Judaism as a legalistic religion, which is only what we would expect since Judaism was not a legalistic religion.

---

[108] Ibid., pp. 93-122.

[109] Ibid., pp. 123-135.

[110] Ibid., pp. 17-64.

[111] Ibid., p. 20.

[112] Ibid., p. 18.

[113] Sanders directs his attack on this position most frequently at Hans Hübner's thesis that in Galatians Paul wrote from the presuppositions of his former Shammaite training. Like a Shammaite, says Hübner, Paul believed that an infraction of the least of the law's commands was equivalent to breaking all of the law's commands. See *Law in Paul's Thought*, trans. James C. G. Greig (Edinburgh: T&T Clark, 1984), pp. 15-50, especially pp. 22-23 and Sanders, *Law*, pp. 28-29.

[114] *Law*, pp. 29-43.

[115] *Law*, p. 23.

[116] Ibid., p. 33.

Sanders considered his argument clinched by Paul's statements in 2 Cor. 3:4-18 and Phil. 3:3-11.[117] In neither passage, said Sanders, does Paul depict life under the law as one of striving for an unattainable goal or of asserting individual merit against God. Rather, in 2 Corinthians 3 the former dispensation is considered "glorious" and in Philippians 3 Paul claims that before his conversion he possessed legal righteousness. Thus, Paul cannot be used as evidence that first century Judaism was a legalistic religion, nor can Paul be charged with misrepresenting Judaism as legalistic. His polemic against the law is neither that it leads to legalistic self-righteousness nor that the law is impossible to keep, but derives from his thinking from solution to plight. His christological convictions meant that entrance into salvation by accepting the yoke of the Torah was excluded by faith in Christ.

The Reaction to Sanders:
In Search of a Historical Basis for Exegesis

Sanders's two books effected something of a revolution in studies on the relationship between Paul's Jewish background and his teaching on the law. They laid out the issues clearly, soundly refuted several long held positions, and placed the christological interpretation of Paul's statements on a firmer basis than ever. Nonetheless, interpreters of Paul felt that even after the clarifications of his second book, fundamental problems remained in Sanders's theory.

According to Heikki Räisänen, Sanders correctly drew attention to the arbitrary and contradictory nature of Paul's statements about the law but failed to recognize that these statements misrepresent Judaism and would have drawn blank stares from the Jewish Christians to whom they were addressed. Räisänen finds himself in sympathy with Sanders in all but this one respect:

> The conclusion is hard to avoid that Paul tears apart, not without violence, what belonged together in 'genuine' Judaism. It is he who drives a wedge between law and grace, limiting 'grace' to the Christ event. He pays no attention to the central place of God's free pardon to the penitent and the role thus accorded to repentance in Judaism. *It should not have been possible to do away with the 'law as the way to salvation' for the simple reason that the law never was that way.*
> Here my assessment of Paul's position differs from that of E. P. Sanders, if I understand him correctly. What Sanders regards as an *incorrect* formulation of the issue, seems to me a quite *correct* statement: 'Paul agreed on the *goal*, righteousness, but saw that it should be received by grace through faith, not achieved by works....'
> ...I cannot avoid the strong impression that Paul actually does give his readers a distorted picture of Judaism. He comes to misrepresent Judaism by

---

[117] Ibid, pp. 137-141.

suggesting that, within it, salvation is by works and the Torah plays a role analogous to that of Christ in Paulinism.[118]

Why did Paul distort the Jewish view of the law so radically? Räisänen suggests that part of the explanation lies in Paul's own struggle with the law before his conversion[119] and part in the problems encountered in his "missionary experience."[120] Whatever the origin of Paul's view of the law, however, Paul's reliance on intuition rather than logic led him into incoherence, and thus Christian interpreters of Paul should give up the idea that what he had to say about the law was an "invaluable accomplishment."[121]

Hans Weder, in a way similar to Räisänen and Sanders, claimed that Paul's view of the law could not be explained on the basis of Judaism, but unlike Räisänen, considered Paul's insights profound. Paul, he said, broke through to a new understanding of both sin and the law. This new understanding appears most clearly in Rom. 5:12-21. There Paul separates sin and righteousness from law. All people are sinners, regardless of their legal deeds; and all are made righteous regardless of their ability to do the law:

> Der hier festzustellende qualitative Sprung im Denken des Paulus besteht also darin, dass er die quantitative Aussage des Sünderseins einiger (vielleicht vieler) übersteigt durch die qualitative Aussage, dass schlechthin alle Menschen Sünder sind. Daraus ergibt sich die These, dass Paulus die Sünde gar nicht mehr durch das Gesetz definiert sein lässt. Daraus folgt wiederum, dass Sünde nicht mehr ausschliesslich ein Tatphänomen ist, auch wenn Paulus den Tataspekt ganz und gar nicht ausschliesst. Der Tatsache, dass die Sünde unabhängig vom Gesetz begriffen wird, entspricht der andere Tatsache, dass die Gerechtigkeit ebenso unabhängig vom Gesetz verstanden wird.[122]

Thus, although Paul expressed the deepest concern over the relationship of his gospel to the Jewish faith, his criticism of the law broke the bonds of his Jewish background.

Weder sustained this idea throughout his article by comparing Paul's view of the law to that in 4 Ezra. Ezra is still bound to the idea that righteousness is obtained by doing. This concept is the source of his despair. Paul, on the other hand, goes beyond the idea of the person as a "doer." In the salvation which Christ brings, the tension between obedience and disobedience no longer exists.

---

[118] *Law*, pp. 187-188.
[119] Ibid., pp. 229-236.
[120] Ibid., pp. 256-263.
[121] Ibid., pp. 268-269. Räisänen does not believe, however, that Paul's thinking was confused or muddled. Paul was, in Räisänen's view, honestly attempting to wrestle with both the continuity and discontinuity of Christianity with Judaism. See "Galatians 2.16 and Paul's Break with Judaism," *NTS* 31 (1985):548-550 and *Paul and the Law*, 2d ed. (1987), p. xxv.
[122] "Gesetz und Sünde: Gedanken zu einem qualitative Sprung im Denken des Paulus," *NTS* 31 (1985): 362.

Thus, "der Gehorsam des Christus erfordert nicht den Gehorsam der Menschen, sondern erbringt ihre Gerechtigkeit."[123]   To be in Christ is to be a "receiver" rather than a "doer." To Weder, therefore, the question of whether Paul has distorted mainstream Judaism is not important. Far more important is that his teaching about the law represents an original insight which corresponds to human experience.[124]

A third type of reaction to Sanders's assessment of Paul's view of the law is represented by James D. G. Dunn. In a series of articles published between 1983 and 1985 Dunn claimed that Paul's polemic against "works of the law" in Galatians was directed against the attempt of the Judaizers to impose the "nationalistic badges" of circumcision, Sabbath keeping, and food laws upon Gentiles. It is only against the idea that one must display these banners of Judaism in order to become a Christian that Paul speaks when he argues against "works of the law." Dunn first developed this thesis in his article "The Incident at Antioch (Gal. 2:11-18)."[125]   There he contended that Paul's encounter with Peter in Antioch first sparked the Pauline antithesis between faith in Christ and covenantal nomism. This incident, said Dunn, was the "crossroads" of Christianity, the point at which Paul decided that justification through faith and covenantal nomism were not compatible but contradictory. Paul's belief that "justification through faith must determine the whole of life and not only the starting point of discovering (or being discovered) by God's grace " began here.[126] Thus, the incident at Antioch explains why Paul answers the Galatian agitators in the way he does despite the Jewish doctrine of "God's electing and forgiving grace" and the Jewish belief in "justification through faith."[127]   Paul is concerned not with the Lutheran idea of justification by faith but "with the relation between Jew and Gentile."[128]   His basic assertion is that faith in Christ is the all important ground of acceptance before God and thus abolishes national and racial distinctions made on the basis of circumcision, food laws, and Sabbath observance.[129]

In a second article, published in 1985, Dunn developed this thesis in opposition to Sanders's work. He began by acknowledging his debt to Sanders's picture of Judaism in Paul and Palestinian Judaism but quickly turned to criticism of the portrait of Paul which Sanders painted there. Sanders, he said, decided too quickly that

---

[123] Ibid., p. 367.
[124] "Wahrheitskriterium für die Entdeckung des Paulus kann keineswegs sein, ob sie sich mit dem Selbstverständnis des jüdischen (oder eines sonstigen) Gesetzes verträgt," p.370.
[125] *JSNT* 18 (1983): 2-57.
[126] Ibid., p. 41.
[127] Ibid., p. 40.
[128] Ibid., p. 5.
[129] Dunn tries to show that Jews in Antioch were particularly careful to observe these nationalistic rituals in an effort to maintain their religious and national sanctity, "Incident," pp. 5-11.

Paul's religion could be understood only as a basically different system from that of his fellow Jews. ...The Lutheran Paul has been replaced by an idiosyncratic Paul who in arbitrary and irrational manner turns his face against the glory and greatness of Judaism's covenant theology and abandons Judaism simply because it is not Christianity.[130]

Sanders's second volume, he said, was equally weak at this point. He

still speaks of Paul breaking with the law, he still has Paul making an arbitrary jump from one system to another and posing an antithesis between faith in Christ and his Jewish heritage in such sharp, black-and white-terms, that Paul's occasional defense of Jewish prerogative (as in Rom. 9:4-6) seems equally arbitrary and bewildering....[131]

Against these alleged defects in Sanders's scheme, Dunn advanced his own theory. He observed that justification by faith is the common ground between Paul and Jewish Christianity ("we who are Jews know," 2:16)[132] not the bone of contention between them (contra Luther, et al.). The problem is rather the place of "works of the law," which Dunn defines as circumcision, Sabbath keeping, and food restrictions. Since these aspects of the law are at issue in Galatians according to Dunn, the problem is not grace versus merit, or faith versus works in the Lutheran sense, but the desire of the Galatian agitators to look upon these observances as badges of covenant status with God. What Paul opposes is "that God's justification depends on 'covenantal nomism,' that God's grace extends only to those who wear the badge of the covenant."[133]

Thus, said Dunn, Paul does not disparage the law as such, but only certain aspects of the law which identify Christianity with the Jewish nation. This insight, he contended, explains why Paul evaluates the law positively on occasion and why he could say what he did in Galatians without breaking entirely from Judaism. Had Sanders read Galatians in this way, "he would have been able to give a more adequate account of Paul's more positive attitude toward the law elsewhere."[134]

---

[130] "The New Perspective on Paul," *BJRL* 68 (1985): 100-101.
[131] Ibid., p. 102.
[132] Ibid., p. 104-106.
[133] Ibid., p. 110.
[134] Ibid., p. 121. Karl Kertelge, "Gesetz und Freiheit im Galaterbrief," *NTS* 30 (1984): 382-394 heartily endorses Dunn's approach. Parallels to Dunn's sociological analysis of Paul's view of the law can be found in William Wrede, *Paulus* (Tübingen: J. C. B. Mohr [Paul Siebeck], 1906), pp. 72-74; George Howard, *Paul: Crisis in Galatia: A Study in Early Christian Theology* SNTSMS, no. 35 (Cambridge: Cambridge University Press, 1979); Roman Heiligenthal, *Werke als Zeichen: Untersuchungen zur Bedeutung der menschlichen Taten in Frühjudentum, Neuen Testament und Früchristentum*, WUNT 2.9 (Tübingen: J. C. B. Mohr [Paul Siebeck], 1983), idem., "Soziologische Implikationen der paulinischen Rechtfertigungslehre im Galaterbrief am Beispiel der 'Werke des Gesetzes'," *Kairos* 26 (1984): 38-51, and Francis Watson, *Paul, Judaism and the*

Although Räisänen, Weder, and Dunn have all sought to offer an alternative to Sanders's position in light of its inadequacies, their own positions contain clear weaknesses. Räisänen's thesis does not commend itself because of its appeal to the "last resort" of incoherence and self-contradiction.[135] Ancient writers could and did contradict themselves, sometimes as a result of carelessness, sometimes because their rhetoric outran their logic, and sometimes for reasons that were probably psychological. But before coming to these kinds of conclusions about Paul's statements on the law, it seems fair to give Paul the opportunity to speak coherently as long as avenues for understandng him as a coherent thinker remain open. I hope to follow one such avenue below.

Although Dunn's theory offers many helpful insights into the historical and sociological context of Paul's statements about the law, it does not account for all that Paul says about the law. Thus while Dunn has usefully pointed out that circumcision, Sabbath observance, and food laws are in the center of Paul's argument in Galatians, it is not possible to limit Paul's critique of the law in either Galatians or Romans only to those "nationalistic badges." In Gal. 5:2-3, for example, Paul singles out circumcision as a particular problem in Galatia but then goes on to connect that particular problem with the problem of the law in general.[136] In Rom. 3:20 Paul says that "works of the law" do not justify because their purpose is to bring knowledge of sin. Yet it is difficult to see how the three "nationalistic badges" could function in this capacity. Paul apparently means by "works of the law" in this context the law's prohibitions of deceit (vv. 13-14), murder (vv. 15-17), and blasphemy (v. 18). Circumcision, food laws, and Sabbath keeping are nowhere mentioned.[137] Thus Dunn's thesis, although helpful, does not fully explain Paul's thinking about the law.

Gentiles: A Sociological Approach, SNTSMS, no. 56 (Cambridge: Cambridge Universtiy Press, 1986), pp. 23-48.

[135] Räisänen locates the source of Paul's supposedly contradictory statements about the law in the psychological tension set up within Paul by his rejection of his Jewish background. Others have found the explanation in Paul's rhetorical skill. See, for example, Hans Dieter Betz, *Galatians: A Commentary on Paul's Letter to the Churches in Galatia*, Hermeneia (Philadelphia: Fortress, 1979), p. 275 and Jerome Hall, "Paul, the Lawyer, on Law," *The Journal of Law and Religion* 3 (1985):1-49. Betz believes that Paul's rhetoric has led to self-contradiction when Paul attempts to reintroduce a favorable attitude toward the law in Gal. 5:14 after his negative statements in the first part of the letter. Hall, similarly, believes that Paul has contradicted himself when speaking of the law in Galatians and Romans not by carelessness but by design. "He had a lawyer's job to do," says Hall, p. 38, "and one can only admire the skill and subtlety with which he did it." It seems best, however, in dealing with Paul to follow Michael E. Stone's advice. In discussing 4 Ezra Stone says that it "is more than merely possible that some ancient writers wrote incoherent and contradictory statements, and even whole books. This assumption should be, however, a hypothesis of the last resort, and will be strongest when supported as well by other features of the writing than conceptual 'inconsistencies,'" "Coherence and Inconsistency in the Apocalypses: The Case of 'the End' in 4 Ezra," *JBL* 102 (1983): 243.

[136] Hans Hübner responds to E. P. Sanders with a similar argument in *Law*, p. 152.

[137] Rom. 7:7-25 gives an account of how the law brings knowledge of sin and here again the three "nationalistic badges" do not appear.

Weder's position correctly points out that simply because Paul cannot be explained on Jewish presuppositions does not mean that his thinking about the law is banal. But Dunn's criticism of Sanders is also applicable to Weder. Simply to bracket the question of Paul's relationship to Judaism makes Paul such a solitary figure in the history of earliest Christianity that he becomes an enigma. This picture of Paul is not impossible, but every avenue should be explored before it is pronounced the most probable.

In summary, although these interpreters of the relationship between Paul's Jewish background and his view of the law have identified weaknesses in Sanders's scheme, they have failed to provide a viable alternative to it. "The new perspective on Paul" is still searching for a historical basis.

The Debate from Montefiore to Dunn: A Summary

Prior to Sanders, studies of the relationship between Paul's view of the law and the teaching on the law in first century Judaism produced basically four explanations. Some claimed that Paul's statements of humankind's inability to do the law and to be justified by works of the law attacked the cardinal doctrine of Jewish soteriology: works-righteousness (Windisch, Grundmann, Bläser). Others claimed that Paul's statements were unintelligible on the basis of rabbinic soteriology but could be explained by Paul's background in the pessimism of Hellenistic Judaism (Montefiore, Parkes). A third group maintained that Paul's view was the logical development from his knowlege of Jewish eschatology and either his temporary quarrel with Judaizing opponents (Schweitzer, Davies) or his familiarity with the pessimism of Hellenistic Judaism (Schoeps). A final group broke with the idea that Paul's view of the law was intelligible against a Jewish background and said that Paul's statements could only be explained on the basis of his prior conviction that Jesus was the universal savior (Moore, Enslin, Andrews, Bultmann, Wilkens, van Dülmen, Lang). As problems with the first three explanations began to multiply, the fourth one—which I have called the "christological" explanation—gained the ascendency, and reached a climax in the publication of E. P. Sanders book, Paul and Palestinian Judaism.

Sanders succeeded in reorientating studies on the relationship between Paul's Jewish background and his view of the law by exposing the view of Judaism as a cold and legalistic religion as bogus, by engaging in a learned critique of the three other explanations of Paul's view of the law, and by arguing that Paul's christological convictions caused him to reject the law with a set of less than consistent arguments. Although most critics accepted, with occasional modification, Sanders's picture of Judaism, problems remained with his formulation of Paul's view of the law. Räisänen felt it had not gone far enough; Weder and Dunn felt it had gone too far. These critics, however, proposed solutions to the problem which themselves fell short of a full explanation of the relationship between Paul's Judaism and his statments about the law.

The current debate on the relationship between Paul's view of the law and his Jewish background has therefore come to a bewildering variety of conclusions based on various backgrounds, whether Hellenistic, apocalyptic, rabbinic, sociological, christological, or even psychological.[138] The need for firm historical and exegetical ground on which to stand is acute.

A Proposal for a Return to Paul's Jewish Heritage

As we have seen above, attempts to explain Paul's view of the law in terms of his Jewish background, especially appeals to supposedly common Jewish eschatological notions, have been widely criticized.[139] Schweitzer, Schoeps, and Davies did not convince most scholars that Paul's attitude toward the law was the logical outcome of the eschatological ideas which he had inherited from Judaism, for, as Davies himself said in 1952, the literary evidence for belief in any modification of the Torah in the messianic age was distressingly scant.[140]

Since the writings of these three scholars, however, the picture of Judaism in Paul's era has undergone considerable changes. Pseudepigraphic material has been re-edited, newly translated, and made readily accessible,[141] the extensive interchange between Judaism and Hellenism has been further documented and evaluated,[142] and the place of Old Testament eschatology within the New Testament generally and within the pauline epistles especially has received extensive attention.[143] In light of this new information about Judaism in Paul's era it is appropriate to re-examine the possibility that Paul's view of the law

---

[138] Gerd Theissen, *Psychological Aspects of Pauline Theology*, trans. John P. Galvin (Philadelphia: Fortress, 1987).

[139] Sanders, *Paul*, pp. 479-80; Räisänen, *Law*, pp. 236-40, especially p. 239. For an exception to the negative attitude toward understanding Paul's thinking with the help of Jewish eschatology see Beker, *Paul*, pp. 144-45.

[140] *Torah*, pp. 90-91.

[141] See, for example, James H. Charlesworth, ed. *The Old Testament Pseudepigrapha*, 2 vols. (New York: Doubleday, 1983-85) and *The Old Testament Pseudepigrapha and the New Testament: Prolegomena for the Study of Christian Origins* (Cambridge: Cambridge University Press, 1985).

[142] See, for example, Martin Hengel, *Judaism and Hellenism* and J. J. Collins, *Between Athens and Jerusalem: Jewish Identity in the Hellenistic Diaspora* (New York: Crossroad, 1983).

[143] See, for example, James A. Sanders "Torah and Christ," *Int* 29 (1975): 372-90; Harmut Gese, "The Law" in *Essays on Biblical Theology*, trans. Keith Crim (Minneapolis: Augsburg Publishing House, 1981), pp. 60-92; Peter Stuhlmacher "The Law as a Topic of Biblical Theology" in *Reconciliation, Law, and Righteousness*, trans. Everett R. Kalin (Philadelphia: Fortress, 1986), pp. 110-133; A. Feuillet, "Loi de Dieu, loi du Christ et loi de l'Esprit d'après les épîtres pauliniennes: Les rapports de ces trois lois avec la Loi Mosaique," *NovT* 22 (1980): 29-65; Craig A. Stephens, "Paul and the Hermeneutics of 'True Prophecy': A Study of Romans 9-11," *Bib* 65 (1984): 560-70.

owes its origin to an eschatological pattern common within some expressions of Judaism at the time he wrote.

In the following chapters I hope to make an initial attempt to re-read Paul in this way. To this end, chapter two investigates a common eschatological pattern within the Old Testament and second temple Judaism, and chapters three and four seek to show how Paul uses this pattern in Galatians and Romans, the two epistles in which he discusses the law most extensively. This re-examination of Paul in light of his Jewish heritage will, I believe, show that he neither distorts Jewish soteriology nor provides evidence that first century Judaism was generally a meritorious religion, but that he applies to Christ's death and the coming of the Spirit a common concept within ancient Judaism. I hope, therefore, that this re-reading will offer a corrective to the picture of Paul the renegade or solitary colossus and locate him, somewhat more plausibly, within the complicated interplay of Jewish and Hellenistic forces which colored the environment of many first century Jews.

CHAPTER TWO

FROM PLIGHT TO SOLUTION
IN ANCIENT JUDAISM

Introduction

In chapter one we saw how scholarship of roughly the past century has
sought to explain the enigma of Paul's view of the law. Those who favored an
approach based on Paul's "former manner of life in Judaism" confronted such difficulties that in recent years most scholars have argued that Paul's unique
experience with Christ accounts for his attitude toward the law. By the end of
chapter one, however, signs of restlessness with what I have called the
"christological interpretation" began to appear, and the way seemed open to renew
the investigation of the Old Testament and the Jewish literature of the second
temple period as a means of elucidating Paul's view of the law.

In this chapter I hope to begin that process by examining one of the angles
from which the law and the covenant are viewed in the Hebrew scriptures of
Paul's time and in representative pieces of non-canonical Jewish literature from
the second temple period.[1] More specifically, I hope to demonstrate that within
this literature authors sometimes spoke of Israel's failing in terms of disobedience
to the law and of Israel's redemption in terms of God's intervention on her behalf
to enable her to keep the law. Israel, these writers frequently said, had become
entangled in a web of sin from which only God could extract her, and God *would*
rescue her at some future time. In later chapters I hope to show how this pattern
of thinking about Israel's plight and God's solution to it lies behind much of what
Paul says about the law and its place both in the human plight and in
eschatological redemption.

---

[1] The notion that law and covenant became separated in later Judaism with the result that
Judaism evolved into a religion of "works-righteousness" was advocated most notably by Julius
Wellhausen, *Prolegomena to the History of Ancient Israel with a Reprint of the Article "Israel"
from the "Encyclopaedia Britannica"*, trans. Mr. Menzies and Mr. Black (Cleveland and New York:
The World Publishing Company, 1957), pp. 423-25 and Martin Noth, "The Laws in the
Pentateuch: Their Assumptions and Meaning" in *The Laws in the Pentateuch and Other Essays*,
trans. D. R. Ap-Thomas (Edinburgh and London: Oliver & Boyd, 1967), pp. 1-107. The idea has
met with such heavy weather, however, in W. Zimmerli, *The Law and the Prophets: A Study of the
Meaning of the Old Testament*, trans. R. E. Clements (Oxford: Basil Blackwell, 1965), pp. 46-60;
Meinrad Limbeck, *Die Ordnung des Heils: Untersuchungen zum Gesetzesverständnis des
Frühjudentums* (Düsseldorf: Patmos-Verlag, 1971); and Sanders, *Paul*, pp. 419-28 that it is no
longer tenable.

Humanity's Inclination toward Sin
as a Topic of Old Testament Theology

The idea that humanity is inescapably tainted with sin is repeated frequently in the Hebrew Bible and in the Septuagint.[2] It is prominent in "the Law," appears thematically in "the Prophets," and recurs occasionally in "the Writings." The Pentateuch begins on a pessimistic note about humanity's ability to avoid rebellion against God. Thus the sin of the first man and woman leads to the pain of child bearing and of tilling the soil (Genesis 3). It also, however, begins a story of murder (Genesis 4) and lust (Gen. 6:1-6) so insidious and widespread that eventually God decides to "blot out man whom I have created from the face of the ground...." (Gen. 6:7). Gerhard von Rad summarizes the theme of the primal history thus:

> With man's stepping out of the simplicity of obedience to God, and with the knowledge obtained by disobedience, a movement began in which man pictures himself as growing more and more powerful, more and more titanic. ....But this evolution and slow rise to cultural greatness is accompanied by an ever-growing estrangement of man from God that was bound to lead to catastrophe.[3]

---

[2] Statements such as this have been debated often, but usually with reference to "original sin" and Adam's role in the problem of evil. The question addressed here is distinct from these issues since my concern is to establish that parts of the Old Testament view humanity as inescapably sinful apart from God's intervention, not that the Old Testament traces the origin of man's sinful tendency back to Adam. There are those, however, who dispute the idea that within the Old Testament humanity is seen as inevitably sinful. Egon Brandenburger, *Adam und Christus: Exegetisch-religionsgeschichtliche Untersuchung zu Röm. 5:12-21 (1. Kor. 15)*, WMANT, no. 7 (Neukirchen: Neukirchener Verlag, 1962), pp. 15-20, followed by Alden Lloyd Thompson, *Responsibility for Evil in the Theodicy of IV Ezra: A Study Illustrating the Significance of Form and Structure for the Meaning of the Book*, SBLDS, no. 29 (Missoula, Montana: Scholars Press, 1977), pp. 14-20, claims that the Old Testament nowhere speaks of humanity as "tainted" with sin. Both writers point to Job 33:9, Psa. 18:24, and 2 Sam. 22:24 (Brandenberger, p. 19; Thompson, p. 24) to demonstrate that the Old Testament could conceive of individuals as "blameless." In the course of his discussion Thompson does draw attention to a series of texts in which evil is depicted as universal: Jer. 17:9, Job 4:17, 14:4, 15:14-16, 25:4, 1 Kgs. 8:46, 2 Chr. 6:36, Psa. 53:2-3, Prov. 20:9, and Eccl. 7:20, but claims that the five passages within this list which say that no one has remained sinless (1 Kgs. 8:46, 2 Chr. 6:36, Psa. 53:2-3, Prov. 20:9, and Eccl. 7:20) are only being "realistic about the poverty of man's native abilities," and "stop short of making excuses or shifting the blame to an inherited taint" (p. 16). That righteousness and blamelessness were relative terms, however, was understood. On this see Moore, *Judaism*, 1:494-96 and note 15 below. Thus Thompson's references to texts where the author regards himself or another as blameless do not mitigate the force of the (more numerous) references to humanity's sinfulness and frailty.

[3]*Old Testament Theology*, 2 vols., trans. D. M. G. Stalker (New York: Harper & Row), 1:160. See also Claus Westermann, *Elements Of Old Testament Theology*, trans. Douglas W. Stott (Atlanta: John Knox, 1982), p. 119 and Walther Zimmerli, *Old Testament Theology in Outline*, trans. David E. Green (Atlanta: John Knox, 1978), pp. 167-74. Translations of the Masoretic text in this chapter and in the following chapters are taken from the Revised Standard Version.

This theme of the human tendency to rebel against God again appears in the "historical narratives" of Genesis. Genesis 12-50 is the story of how God accomplished his purposes despite Abraham's impatience (Genesis 16), Jacob's cunning (Gen. 25:27-34; 27; 30:25-43) and familial dissension and intrigue (Genesis 34, 37, and 38.)[4] In Exodus-Numbers, Israel is under the guiding hand of Yahweh, but repeatedly shows herself unwilling to participate in God's purpose for deliverance from Egypt and settlement in Canaan (Exod 5:20-21, 14:10-12, 16:3, 17:3-4, Num 11:4-6, 14:2-4, 16:12-14, 20:2-5).[5] Leviticus and Deuteronomy seem to hold out obedience as a real possibility for Israel, and indeed demand it as the pathway to life, but both books predict the eventual punishment of Israel for her disobedience to the law. Lev 26:14-45 outlines the curses which will come upon Israel for disobeying the law, and the list looks like a brief history of Israel from the establishment of the monarchy to the deportations and exiles under Assyria and Babylon. Much the same can be said of Deut 29:19-29 and 30:14-29. The story of disobedience and curse predicted in these passages is chronicled in Joshua, Judges, Samuel, and Kings, the first four books of the prophets in the ancient Hebrew canon.[6]

The theme achieves its most poignant expression in the literature of the "writing prophets." Amos indicts all Israel with a long history of disobedience. Neither famine, drought, blight, pestilence, nor war, he says, were effective in bringing Israel to her senses, and thus Yahweh will visit her with judgment (4:6-12).[7] Hosea charges Israel with possessing "no faithfulness or kindness, and no knowledge of God" (4:1). Instead "there is swearing, lying, killing, stealing, and committing adultery; they break all bounds and murder follows murder" (4:2). Thus no man can "contend" and "none accuse, for with you is my contention, O priest" (RSV, translating the MT, וְעַמְּךָ כִּמְרִיבֵי כֹהֵן). The Septuagint applies the fault to all Israel. Because of rampant cursing, lying, murder, theft, and adultery, says the Septuagint text, the land will mourn together with all that dwells in it, the beasts of the field, reptiles of the earth, the birds of the heavens, and the fish of the sea, "...in order that no one should judge and no one accuse. But *my people* are like an obstinate priest" (Hosea 4:4, LXX). Hosea also pictures Israel and Judah as so permeated by "the spirit of harlotry" that they cannot obey God:

> Their deeds do not permit them to return to their God. For the spirit of harlotry is within them, and they know not the Lord. The pride of Israel testifies to his face; Ephraim shall stumble in his guilt; Judah shall stumble with them. With their flocks and herds they shall go to seek the Lord, but they will not find him; he has withdrawn from them (Hosea 5:5-6).

Translations of the Septuagint are my own. Translations of the New Testament in the following chapters are chiefly mine, but I have on occasion quoted the Revised Standard Version.

[4] Zimmerli, *Outline*, pp. 174-75.

[5] Ibid., pp. 175-76.

[6] Westermann, *Elements*, pp. 121-122.

[7] Von Rad, *Theology*, 2:136-37.

Isaiah begins with a pessimistic statement of Israel's insistance on rebellion. The nation is "laden with iniquity" and is "utterly estranged" from God (1:4).[8] Israel has been so rebellious, in fact, that God himself proposes to harden her heart in judgment through his prophet (6:10). Speaking of the eighth century prophets, von Rad says that they passed the verdict of failure upon all of salvation history up to their own time.[9]

With Jeremiah and Ezekiel the theme of human inability to avoid sin reaches its climax. Jeremiah complains that Judah's sin is so ingrained that lye and soap cannot remove it (2:22); that she has never obeyed God "whole-heartedly" (MT, בְּכָל-לִבָּהּ, LXX, ἐξ ὅλης τῆς καρδίας, 3:10); that she can no more do good than an Ethiopian can change his skin or a leopard his spots (13:23); and, finally, that her sin is engraved on "the tablet of her heart" with a pen of iron (17:1). It is no wonder that the prophet holds out as Judah's only hope the promise that God will write his law on her heart (31:33).[10]

In a similar but more vivid way Ezekiel demonstrates the inability of God's people to obey God. In chapters 16, 20, and 23 he gives accounts of how throughout Israel's history she has responded to God's grace and mercy toward her with rebellion. Thus in chapter 16 she is depicted as an abandoned child, lovingly rescued from death by Yahweh but who, when grown, thoughtlessly plays the harlot. Chapter 20 provides a brief summary of God's saving acts in Israel's history which, in Ezekiel's hands, becomes a stark reminder of her incessant rebellion against her God.[11] From the days of their slavery in Egypt to Ezekiel's own day, he says, Israel has pursued a course of idolatrous rebellion against her God:

> I gave them my statutes and showed them my ordinances, by whose observance man shall live. Moreover I gave them my sabbaths, as a sign between me and them, that they might know that I the Lord sanctify them. But the house of Israel rebelled against me in the wilderness; they did not walk in my statutes but rejected my ordinances, by whose observance man shall live; and my sabbaths they greatly profaned.... And I said to their children in the wilderness, Do not walk in the statutes of your fathers, nor observe their ordinances, nor defile yourself with their idols.... But the children rebelled against me.... In this again your fathers blasphemed against me..., wherever they saw any high hill or any leafy tree, there they offered their sacrifices and presented the provocation of their offering....

---

[8] See also Isa. 5:1-7 where the history of God's dealings with Israel is seen as "completely fruitless," von Rad, *Theology*, 2:151.

[9] *Theology* 2:181, 395-97.

[10] On the connection between Jer. 2:22, 3:10, 13:23, 17:1, and 31:33 see Harry D. Potter, "The New Covenant in Jeremiah 31:31-34," *VT* 33 (1983): 347-57. On the theme of Jeremiah's attitude toward human sinfulness see R. E. Clements, *Prophecy and Covenant*, SBT, no. 43 (Naperville, Illinois: Alec R. Allenson, Inc., 1965), pp. 112-113 and von Rad, *Theology*, 2:216.

[11] Von Rad, *Theology*, 2:226.

When you offer your gifts and sacrifice your sons by fire, you defile yourselves
with all your idols to this day (Ezk 20:10-13, 18, 21, 27-28, 31).[12]

Likewise chapter 23 casts Samaria and Jerusalem in the roles of Yahweh's wives
Oholah and Oholibah who played the harlot from their days in Egypt down to
Ezekiel's own time. Von Rad aptly summarizes the difference between the eighth
century prophets on one hand and Jeremiah and Ezekiel on the other. He says that
whereas the eighth century prophets concentrate on Israel's disobedience to single
commandments and on her ingratitude in response to God's saving acts in history,
Jeremiah and Ezekiel measure "Israel against the whole body of Jahweh's will, and
to this degree they recognize Israel's complete incapacity to obey."[13]

Finally, some mention should be made of the theme of human sinfulness in
the "writings." Psalms 78 (LXX 77), 105 (104), 106 (105), 130 (129), and 143
(142), speak of the proclivity of Israel, and humanity in general, for sin.   Psalm
78, in outlining the history of Israel down to the reign of David, paints a picture
of unfaithfulness and rebellion.[14]   Psalms 105-106 similarly trace the history of
Israel's disobedience to God and lament its result—the curse of exile (106:40-46).
Psalm 130 thanks God for his willingness to forgive since no one could with-
stand his scrutiny if he kept a record of sins, and Psalm 143 likewise pleads with
God not to judge the psalmist, since nothing living is righteous.[15]

The Chronicler also shows how the monarchy in Judah moved inexorably
toward disaster as a result of sin. In 1 and 2 Chronicles one evil king after
another fails to heed the warnings of God's messengers, and 2 Chronicles ends
with the claim that the calamaties of the Assyrian and Babylonian captivities were
punishments from God for the persistent disobedience of his people.

---

[12] Some scholars, most notably Zimmerli, *The Law and the Prophets*, p. 82 and *A Commentary on the Book of the Prophet Ezekiel*, 2 vols., trans. Ronald E. Clements (Philadelphia: Fortress, 1969), 1:412 and von Rad, *Theology*, 2:402, have considered 20:25 ("I gave them statutes that were not good and ordinances by which they could not have life....") relevant to Paul's view of the law. Räisänen, *Law*, p. 160, however, correctly observes that to make Ezekiel say that the law actually brings about sin is to read too much into this verse, "In other passages in Ezekiel, the sacrifice of children is mentioned in plain words as a sin of Israel,without any indication that a mysterious statute of God was being carried out (16:20f.). There is no sense of a divine mystery in these verses; the tone is one of outright condemnation."

[13] Ibid., p. 269-70, 398-99.

[14] See also Dan. 9:4-20 and Song of the Three Children, 1-9.

[15] Cf. Psa. 53:3-4. These statements must, of course, be balanced with others which assert the blamelessness of the Psalmists: 7:9; 17:3-5; 18:21-25, 33; 26:11; 101:2. The Psalmists' protestations of blamelessness often occur, however, in contexts where the writer is comparing his faithfulness to God with the blatant wickedness of his enemies. In any case, the claim of blamelessness does not exclude a consciousness of sin. See, for example, 2 Chr. 15:17-16:14 where the statement that Asa was blameless before the Lord is followed by a chronicle of his sins.

Violation of the Law as
Evidence of Humanity's Inclination toward Sin

Of special significance for Paul's understanding of the law, however, is that the sections of the Old Testament discussed above often do not simply indict Israel and Judah for sin in general terms, but frequently bind the sin of God's people specifically to violation of his law. In the Septuagint text of the prophets, the text which Paul apparently used,[16] Israel and Judah are reprimanded twenty-one times for forgetting, dealing impiously with, rejecting, not desiring to obey, and not keeping God's law. Amos prophesies against Judah that "because they repudiated the law of the Lord" God will send "a fire" upon them (2:4-5). Moreover, the Septuagint text of Hos 4:4-6 frames its indictment of Israel precisely in terms of the law which, it says, Israel has "forgotten." Similarly, Isaiah binds together Israel's distress and her transgression of the law: the reason that Judah's root will be as chaff and her flower will go up in dust is that "they did not desire the law of the Lord" (5:24).[17] Habakkuk likewise complains that the law is "frustrated" (1:4) and Zephaniah that not only have the priests "profaned" the law (3:4), but that all of Judah has rebelled against God (3:11). The same connection between judgment and violation of God's law appears throughout Jeremiah, especially in the Septuagint text,[18] and the poignant expressions of Israel's complete inability to avoid sin in Jeremiah and Ezekiel are linked with the law. In Jer 2:22, 13:23, and 17:1 the words תּוֹרָה and νόμος do not appear, but Jer 31:33, which is thematically linked to these passages,[19] describes Israel's deliverance from sin as deliverance from disobedience to the law. Similarly, in Ezekiel 16, 20, and 23, the words תּוֹרָה and νόμος are absent, but 16:59-63 makes clear that the chapter has been dealing with violations of the בְּרִית (LXX, διαθήκη) and in chapter 20 the refrain that Israel has broken God's commandments (חֹק, πρόσταγμα), ordinances (מִשְׁפָּט, δικαίωμα), and sabbaths (שַׁבָּת, σάββατα) appears frequently.[20]

Together with this explicit connection between the prophets' pronouncement of judgment and the law, the canonical or literary connection between the two should be mentioned. Fourteen times the New Testament refers to the Hebrew scriptures as "the law and the prophets," "Moses and the prophets," or "the law of Moses and the prophets." Paul demonstrates his familiarity with this designation

---

[16] D. Moody Smith, Jr., "The Use of the Old Testament in the New" in *The Use of the Old Testament in the New and Other Essays: Studies in Honor of William Franklin Stinespring*, ed. James M. Efird (Durham, N. C.: Duke University Press, 1972), pp. 39-40; Richard N. Longenecker, *Biblical Exegesis in the Apostolic Period* (Grand Rapids: Eerdmans, 1985), p. 113.

[17] Cf. 24:5; 30:9-14; 42:24-25 where the same connection appears.

[18] See 6:19, 8:9; 9:12-16; 16:11-13; 23:23-40; 33:6 and 51:23.

[19] See Potter, "New Covenant."

[20] See Clements, *Covenant*, pp. 69-85 and von Rad, *Theology* 2:269.

in Rom. 3:21.[21]   First century readers of the Hebrew Bible, therefore, assumed that the preaching of the prophets was based on the Torah.[22]   Thus, regardless of specific connections between the law on one hand and sin and judgment on the other, the shape of the canon in the first century suggested to those who read it that when the prophets spoke of Israel's proclivity toward sin, they were speaking of Israel's inability to perform "the Law."

Finally, some mention should be made of four Psalms which connect Israel's penchant for rebellion with her continued violation of the law. Throughout the picture of Israel's disobedience in Psalm 78, the psalmist defines Israel's sin in terms of her continued violation of God's law (vv. 1 and 5, תּוֹרָה, νόμος), statutes (vv. 5 and 6, עֵדוּת, νόμος) and covenant (vv. 10 and 37, בְּרִית, διαθήκη). Psalms 105-106 define Israel's sin as rebellion against God's "words" and "counsel" (105:28, cf. 106:13, MT, דְּבָרוֹ;   LXX, τοὺς λόγους αὐτοῦ).[23]   Psalm 130 also expresses the inability of humanity to do God's will, and although it does not mention law, covenant, statutes or God's word specifically, in the LXX it describes sin as ἀνομία   (vv. 3 and 8, MT, עָוֹן).

Eschatological Salvation as a Solution
to the Plight of Israel in the Old Testament

Despite its heavily pessimistic outlook on human ability to please God, the Old Testament does not typically abandon Israel to its sinful inclination. Often, the same contexts which express pessimism about humanity's rebellious tendency, contain a note of optimism about God's historical plans for the plight of his people. Thus von Rad maintains that "the end of the Biblical primeval history is...not the story of the Tower of Babel; it is the call of Abraham in Gen. 12:1-3...."[24]   If that is true, then the story of mankind's rebellious beginnings ends on the hopeful note that God has a historical plan for the relief of humanity's plight. The so-called Deuteronomic history, at least according to some interpreters, also demonstrates hope for Israel despite her disobedience. The account of Johoiachin's release from prison by Evilmerodach (2 Kings 25:27-30), say these interpreters, seems to hold out the possibility of the fulfillment of the promise to

---

[21] Cf. the prologue of Ecclesiasticus which refers to "the reading of the law and of the prophets and of the other books of the fathers" and Philo,Vita 25 which speaks of "laws, oracles from God spoken through the Prophets, Psalms, and the other writings." On the question of the structure and order of the Hebrew canon in the first century see Smith, "Use," pp. 4-20 and Roger Beckwith, The Old Testament Canon of the New Testament Church and Its Background in Early Judaism (Grand Rapids: Eerdmans, 1985), pp. 110-234.

[22] On this see R. E. Clements, Old Testament Theology (Atlanta: John Knox, 1978), pp. 124-26. Since we are concerned with how the prophets were read in Paul's era we need not delay over the idea that the law came after the prophets, an idea which has, in any case, found few supporters in recent discussion. See Zimmerli, The Law and the Prophets, pp. 17-60.

[23] In Deuteronomy דָּבָר is frequently used to signify the law. See note 45 below.

[24] Theology, 1:164.

David that his throne would endure.[25] Similarly, the Septuagint version of Psalm 130 (LXX 129), despite its pessimism concerning human righteousness, demonstrates hope in God's future deliverance. The psalmist asks, "If you kept track of lawlessness, O Lord, who would stand?" and the answer comes back in terms of hope that God would "redeem" his people from their "lawlessness."

The prophets, at least in their first century form, clearly express this plight to solution pattern. Even in the middle of his warning of impending doom because of Israel's incessant sin, Amos extends the possibility that if Israel seeks "good, and not evil...it may be that the Lord, the God of hosts will be gracious to the remnant of Joseph" (5:14-15).[26] The conclusion of Amos also sounds a strong note of hope:

> In that day I will raise up the booth of David that is fallen and repair its breaches, and raise up its ruins, and rebuild it as in the days of old... (9:11).[27]

Hosea too, despite his pessimism, expresses hope. He looks forward to a new exodus in which Israel will return to seek her God (Hos. 3:4-5) and God will, in response, "speak tenderly" to his people in the wilderness (2:14).[28] Like Hosea, the book of Isaiah speaks not only of Israel's plight but of a new exodus (Isa. 42:13, 48:21, and 52:12),[29] and the conclusion to Isaiah both decries the lack of righteousness in Israel (Isa. 64:6-7) and proclaims the restoration of the created world (65:8-25, 66:5-23).

Jeremiah and Ezekiel bring the theme of deliverance from a rebellious heart into sharp focus. As we saw above, Jeremiah 31:31-34 says that one day God will write his law upon the hearts of his people. This future action provides the solution to Israel's incorrrigibly rebellious heart, which, either implicitly or explicitly, has been the object of Jeremiah's prophecies of doom in 3:10, 2:22, 13:23, and 17:1.[30]

Ezekiel too shows that God does not intend to abandon his people to their tendency to rebel against his law. After his lengthy description in chapter 20 of Israel's repeated violation of the law, he prophesies that a time is coming when Israel will return to God's holy mountain and offer sacrifices which God will accept (20:40-41). Then, God says, "you shall loathe yourselves for all the evils

---

[25] Von Rad, *Studies in Deuteronomy*, STB, no. 9, trans. David Stalker (London: SCM), pp. 89-91. Zimmerli, *Outline*, p. 179, thinks that the idea is "not impossible." Hans Walter Wolff, "The Kerygma of the Deuteronomistic Historical Work," in Walter Brueggemann and Hans Walter Wolf, *The Vitality of Old Testament Traditions* (John Knox: Atlanta, 1978), pp. 83-100, however, claims that it is not valid and proposes instead that the editor of the Deuteronomic History simply meant to call his people to repentance and thus did not assert any specific future for them.

[26] Again, since our concern is with the first century form of this book, there is no need to discuss the possibility that either this passage or 9:11-15 were added by a later hand.

[27] See Clements, *Covenant*, pp. 103-18; Zimmerli, *The Law and the Prophets*, pp. 68-69.

[28] Clements, *Covenant*, pp. 110-11; Zimmerli, *The Law and the Prophets*, p. 72.

[29] Von Rad, *Theology*, 2:246.

[30] See Potter, "New Covenant" and Clements, *Covenant*, pp. 112-14.

that you have committed. And you shall know that I am the Lord..." (20:43-44).
In Ezekiel 16, after a long and severe indictment of Israel for breaking her
covenant with God, the prophet turns to the future when God will establish an
everlasting covenant with his people (v. 60) and forgive them of all they have
done (v. 63). The theme of God's intervention in the future to cure the sinfulness
of his people continues in 36:26-32 where God promises to supply Israel with

> a new heart and a new spirit and I will remove the heart of stone from your flesh
> and I will give to you a fleshly heart. I will give my spirit to you and I will make
> it so that you will walk in my just commandments and both keep and perform my
> judgements (36:27 LXX).

Thus Jewish scripture during Paul's day, especially in the Greek form in
which Paul knew it, viewed the history of God's people largely as a history of
failure to do God's will. Often this failure was expressed in terms of Israel's
continual violation of God's law or covenant. Many of the same passages in
which this failure was expressed, however, also extended the hope that at some
future time God would intervene to destroy the vicious cycle of sin and rebellion
and produce a people who would obey him from their hearts.

The Plight-Solution Pattern in the
Literature of the Second Temple Period

The Old Testament as it existed in Paul's day was not alone in defining the
human plight in terms of disobedience to God's law and redemption in terms of
renewed obedience to it. This same pattern appears in writings which were
themselves composed during Paul's time. In this section we will look at
representative documents from the second temple period and shortly thereafter,
particularly those from the Qumran community, in which the plight-solution
pattern appears.

A) The Pattern in the Dead Sea Scrolls[31]

Like the Old Testament, certain writings of the Qumran covenanters express
clearly both a pessimistic view of human ability to please God and confidence

---

[31] The translation used in quotations from the scrolls below is that of Geza Vermes, *The Dead Sea
Scrolls in English*, 2d ed. (Harmondsworth, Middlesex, England: Penguin, 1975), hereafter cited
as "Vermes." References in parentheses are to the Hebrew text of the scrolls as it is found in
Eduard Lohse, *Die Texte aus Qumran: Hebräisch und Deutsch mit masoretischer Punktation,
Übersetzung, Einführung und Anmerkungen* (Munich: Kösel-Verlag, 1964).

that in the eschaton God will purify his people from their sins. Also like the Old Testament passages discussed above, the first part of this plight-solution pattern defines sin, at least implicitly, in terms of the law.[32] The pattern as it is found at Qumran, however, differs from the Old Testament pattern discussed above in one significant way: it assumes that the second half of the pattern—God's intervention to purify his people from sin—has been at least partially realized.[33]

In several places in the Qumran literature a markedly pessimistic view of human ability to escape sin is coupled with an expression of confidence in God's compassion and mercy. Thus in 1QH 1:21-23 the author says that he is

> a ground of shame and a source of pollution, a melting-pot of wickedness and an edifice of sin, a straying and perverted spirit of no understanding.

The question, therefore, naturally arises,

> What shall a man say concerning his sin? And how shall he plead concerning his iniquities? And how shall he reply to righteous judgment (1QH 1.25-26)?

These questions are answered several lines later:

> By Thy mercies and by Thy great goodness, Thou hast strengthened the spirit of man in the face of the scourge and hast purified [the erring spirit] of a multitude of sins (1QH 1.32).

---

[32] Ulrich Wilckens, "Was heißt bei Paulus: 'Aus Werken des Gesetzes wird kein Mensch gerecht'?," in *Rechtfertigung als Freiheit: Paulusstudien* (Neukirche: Neukirchener Verlag, 1974), pp. 90-91 and *Der Brief an die Römer*, EKKNT, no. 6, 3 vols. (Zurich and Neukirchen-Vluyn: Benziger Verlag and Neukirchener Verlag, 1978-82) vol. 1, pp. 173-74 and N. A. Dahl, "The Doctrine of Justification: Its Social Function and Implications," *Studies in Paul: Theology for the Early Christian Mission* (Minneapolis, Minn.: Augsburg Publishing House, 1977), pp. 104-106 argue that the Qumran covenanters, like Paul, believed in universal sinfulness, but, unlike Paul, did not consider the law to be the means by which sin became known. Neither scholar, however, defends his contention with extensive reference to the Qumran texts.

[33] The definitive work on the partially realized eschatology of Qumran is Heinz-Wolfgang Kuhn, *Enderwartung und gegenwärtiges Heil: Untersuchungen von Qumran mit einem Anhang über Eschatologie und Gegenwart in der Verkündigung Jesu*, SUNT, no. 4 (Göttingen: Vandenhoek & Ruprecht, 1966). See also Annie Jaubert, *La notion d'alliance dans le Judaïsme aux abords de l'ère Chrétienne* (Paris: Editions du Seuil, 1963), pp. 236-37; David Edward Aune, *The Cultic Setting of Realized Eschatology in Early Christianity*, NovTSup, no. 28 (Leiden: E. J. Brill, 1972), pp. 29-44; George W. E. Nicklesburg, Jr., *Resurrection, Immortality, and Eternal Life in Intertestamental Judaism*, HTS, no. 26 (Cambridge, Mass.: Harvard University Press, 1972), pp. 152-56 and *Jewish Literature between the Bible and the Mishnah: A Historical and Literary Introduction* (Philadelphia: Fortress, 1981), p. 142; and Paul Garnet, *Salvation and Atonement in the Qumran Scrolls* WUNT, no. 23 (Tübingen: J. C. B. Mohr [Paul Siebeck], 1977), pp. 84, 90-91. Dahl, "Justification," pp. 102-103 cautions against the idea that the Qumran literature contains a pronounced tension between the "now" and "not yet" since, unlike the Christian community, the Qumran covenanters could point to no historical event marking the beginning of the new age.

On a first reading it is tempting to interpret this final passage as a simple expression of God's willingness to forgive the truly penitent sinner, such as we find in the biblical Psalms, the Prayer of Manasseh, or indeed the scrolls themselves (1QH 7.30-31, 9.12-15, 13.16-18, and 16.11-15).[34] When the passage is read in the light of other less ambiguous ones, however, it becomes clear that the hymn-writer considered himself to be living, in some sense, in the eschatological age in which God has begun to purify his elect of sin. Thus in 1QH 3:21-22 the author claims

> Thou hast cleansed a perverse spirit of great sin that it may stand with the host of the Holy Ones, and that it may enter into community with the congregation of the Sons of Heaven.[35]

1QH 11.10-14 also speaks of the member of the Qumran community as a participant in God's eschatological purification of his people:

> For the sake of Thy glory Thou hast purified man of sin that he may be made holy for Thee, with no abominable uncleanness and no guilty wickedness; that he may be one with the children of Thy truth and partake of the lot of Thy Holy Ones; that bodies gnawed by worms may be raised from the dust to the counsel (of Thy truth) and that the perverse spirit (may be lifted) to the understanding (which comes from Thee); that he may stand before Thee with the everlasting host and with (Thy) spirits (of holiness), to be renewed together with all the living and to rejoice with them that know.[36]

1QH 11.19-27, however, clearly looks to a future eschatological day when "the [evil] inclinations of man, of his return [to dust, and of his leaning] towards sin and the sorrow of guilt" will be destroyed and God's truth will be revealed with its attendant glory and peace. And in 1QH 17.13-16 it is in the final day, when "the bases of the mountains shall melt and fire shall consume the deep places of Hell," that God will accomplish his promise to Moses and forgive

> trangression, iniquity, and sin...rebellion and unfaithfulness.... Thou wilt keep Thine oath and wilt pardon their transgression; Thou wilt cast away all their sins.

---

[34] See Menahem Mansoor, *The Thanksgiving Hymns Translated and Annotated with an Introduction* (Grand Rapids: Eerdmans, 1961), pp. 58-65.

[35] According to Kuhn, *Enderwartung*, pp. 44-52, the cleansing spoken of here is an eschatological purification in which the community sees itself already participating.

[36] Kuhn, *Enderwartung*, pp. 90-93 argues that "the holy ones" are not heavenly beings but the purified eschatological community of the apocalyptic literature. He points to Dan. 7:17-27; TLevi 18, 11:14; TDan 5:12, 1En 100:5; 1En 38:4, 48:4; 50:1; 51:1; 51:2; 58:3; 62:8; and Sib. 5.432 as evidence that a purified Israel was a common eschatological expectation during the period in which 1QH was written.

Thou wilt cause them to inherit all the glory of Adam and abundance of days (1QH 17.13-16).[37]

The hymn writer's hope is that the effects of the fall, especially the tendency of humanity to repeat Adam's sin, would be reversed and the glory of man without sin would be restored. Nonetheless, the writer shifts back to the idea that his eschatological hope has been realized in the present only one column later:

> My heart is astounded, for to the uncircumcised ear a word has been disclosed, and a heart [of stone has understood the right precepts]... For into an ear of dust [Thou hast put a new word] and hast engraved on a heart of [stone] things everlasting. Thou hast caused [the straying spirit] to return that it may enter into a Covenant with Thee, and stand [before Thee forever] in the everlasting abode...(1QH 18.20-29).

In language that echoes Jeremiah's prophecy of a new covenant which will be written on the hearts of his people (31:31-34) and thus replace "the sin of Judah...written with a pen of iron; with a point of diamond engraved on the tablet of their heart" (17:1), the hymn-writer claims that the day of purification from sin has arrived.

In both the Community Rule and the Damascus Rule a similar plight-solution scheme together with the tension between a realized and a future eschatology appears. In the Community Rule, for example, the author discusses the presence within all people of a good and an evil tendency (1QS 4.2-18) and then looks forward to a day when God's people will be purified from sin:

> But in the mysteries of His understanding, and His glorious wisdom, God has ordained an end for falsehood, and at the time of the visitation He will destroy it forever. Then truth, which has wallowed in the ways of wickedness during the dominion of falsehood until the appointed time of judgement, shall arise in the world for ever. God will then purify every deed of Man with his truth; He will refine for Himself the human frame by rooting out all spirit of falsehood from the bounds of his flesh. He will cleanse him of all wicked deeds with the spirit of holiness; like purifying waters He will shed upon him the spirit of truth [to cleanse him] of all abomination and falsehood. And he shall be plunged into the spirit of purification that he may instruct the upright in the knowledge of the

---

[37] Vermes's translation assumes that the text is oriented toward the future, and the talk of devouring fires and the netherworld lends weight to this position. The scroll is badly damaged at this point, however, and this text has therefore been construed in various ways; see, for example, Lohse, *Die Texte aus Qumran*, p.171. Despite these difficulties, the text clearly connects forgiveness of and cleansing from sin with an eschatological perspective. Some ambiguity also appears both in this text and in the texts quoted below which refer to "the glory of אדם." The writer could be referring to humanity generally (Lohse, *Qumran*, pp. 171 and 173) or to Adam (Vermes, pp. 100 and 198). Lohse's translation, however, is probably incorrect in view of the prominent "paradise regained" motif elsewhere in the hymns. See Aune, *Realized Eschatology*, pp. 37-42.

Most High and teach the wisdom of the sons of heaven to the perfect of way. For
God has chosen them for an everlasting Covenant and all the glory of Adam shall
be theirs (1QS 4.18-23, cf. 1QS 11:2-3 and 1QS 11:13-15).

This eschatological period when the effects of Adam's fall will be destroyed and
man's original purity will be restored has apparently not yet arrived and, accord-
ingly, provision is made within 1QS for community members who sin (1QS
6.24- 7.25, 8.21-9.2, 11.25).[38] Paradoxically, however, community members can
be described as "the perfect" (1QS 3.3), the purpose of the community can be
characterized as living "perfectly" before God (1QS 1.8), and the initiate to the
community is said to have been "cleansed from all his sins by the spirit of holi-
ness uniting him to His truth" (1QS 3.6-8).[39]

The situation is similar in the Damascus Rule. It uses the Old Testament
plight-solution pattern with the variation that in places the day of purification
appears to be present. Thus, in a way similar to Isaiah and Ezekiel, the
Damascus Rule gives a historical narrative of Israel's sin and concludes it with the
statement that God

> forgave them their sin and pardoned their wickedness; and he built for them a sure
> house in Israel whose like has never existed from former times until now. Those
> who hold fast to it are destined to live forever and all the glory of Adam shall be
> theirs (CD 3).

Here the writer expresses both the certainty that as a member of the eschatological
community[40] his sins are forgiven and the hope that when the final days are
complete man's glory before the primal sin will be restored.[41] In view of these
passages there can be little doubt that members of the Qumran Community
adopted the plight-solution pattern which we observed in the Old Testament with
the difference that they perceived the future hope for freedom from sin to have
been partially realized in their own community.[42]

---

[38] On this see Karl Georg Kuhn, "New Light on Temptation, Sin and Flesh in the New
Testament" in Krister Stendahl, ed. *The Scrolls and the New Testament* (New York: Harper & Row,
1957), pp. 106 and 110.

[39] See also 1QS 2.11-18, 1QS 3.7-12, 1QS 5.1-11, 1QS 8.21-23, and 1QS 9.7-9.

[40] The "sure house" is the Qumran community, the remnant of the house of Zadok. See Garnet,
Salvation, p. 90, who points to 1 Sam. 2:25 as the source for the description of the Qumran
community as the "sure house in Israel."

[41] Aune, *Realized Eschatology*, pp. 37-42.

[42] Jaubert, *Alliance*, pp. 236-237; Garnet, *Salvation*, pp. 84, 90-91; Nickelsburg, *Resurrection,*
pp. 152-56 and *Jewish Literature*, p. 142; Aune, *Realized Eschatology*, pp.29-44. Bernd Janowski
and Hermann Lichtenberger, "Enderwartung und Reinheitsidee: Zur eschatologische Deutung von
Reinheit und Sühne in der Qumrangemeinde," *JJS* 34 (1983):31-62 maintain that the Qumran
community saw itself as an eschatological community of pure priests who were atoning for the
sins of the rest of Israel shortly before the day of judgment. Jürgen Becker, *Das Heil Gottes:
Heils— und Sündenbegriffe in den Qumrantexten und im Neuen Testament,* SUNT, no. 3

The problem of the connection of this pattern with the law, however, still remains. Did the Qumran covenanters couple their pessimistic view of human ability to please God to the law? It is certainly true that, at least in their surviving literature, they never did this explicitly.[43] Yet it would not be true to say that universal sinfulness and the law are completely separated in the Dead Sea Scrolls. In the Community Rule, for example, the most basic difference between members of the eschatological community and those outside is that members of the community "no longer" (עוֹד...לוֹא) do evil but observe "God's precepts" (חֻקֵּי אֵל 1QS 1.6-8).[44] The community member is to transgress none of God's "words" (1QS 3.11), and when he enters the community is said to have "freely pledged" himself "to be converted from all evil and to cling to all His commandments" (צִוָּה כּוֹל אֲשֶׁר 1QS 5.1). Thus, as participants in the eschatological community, members were in some way free from the common lot of those outside who transgressed God's law. Likewise in the Hymns, deliverance from sin is described as the opening of the "uncircumcised ear" (1QH 18.20) or the "ear of dust" (1QH 18.27) so that it can hear God's "word" (דָּבָר), images that are reminiscent of the "shema" and of the frequent use of דָּבָר in Deuteronomy to designate the law of the covenant.[45] Finally, the hymn-writer can claim, as a member of God's eschatological community, to have the law engraved on his heart (1QH 4.10 and 18.20, 23, and 27; cf. 1QS 10.11). Thus, when the scrolls speak of universal sinfulness, and when individual authors speak of their own lack of righteousness, they are apparently defining sin in terms of the law.

B) The Pattern in Other Jewish Literature of the Second Temple Period

Other Jewish literature also contains the pattern we have identified in the Old Testament and Qumran. In these texts, the eschatological era will be a period of destruction both for the Satanic powers of the heavenly world and for the wicked who have despised God and blatantly violated his law.[46] It will also be a time, however, in which God's elect will be purified from sin, temptation to sin will be removed, and God's Spirit will enable his people to keep the law from their

---

(Göttingen: Vandenhoeck & Ruprecht, 1964), pp. 67 and 71 claims that certain hymns within 1QH can be assigned to the Teacher of Righteousness because they do not see humanity as radically sinful.

[43] Ulrich Wilckens, "Was heißt bei Paulus," p. 91; *Römer*, pp. 173-174; Dahl, "Justification," pp. 102-03.

[44] The definition of "precepts" in this context is those statutes God "commanded by the hand of Moses and all His servants the Prophets" (1QS 1.3).

[45] דָּבָר is used twice in Deuteronomy to signify the ten commandments (4:13 and 10:4), and frequently appears in the plural to refer to the law (6:6; 12:28; 17:19; 27:3; 27:26; 28:58; 29:1, 9 [8], 19 [18], 29 [28]; 31:12; 31:24; 32:46).

[46] See Paul Volz, *Jüdische Eschatologie* (Tübingen and Leipzig: J. C. B. Mohr [Paul Siebeck], 1903), pp. 352-53.

hearts. Several examples of this pattern within the pseudepigrapha and the targums will be sufficient to illustrate its wide currency.

The first example comes from 1 Enoch where, at the end of his introductory speech, Enoch tells "the sinners and wicked ones" (1:9) of their lot and of the lot of the righteous in the final day of judgment. Among the blessings given to the righteous is freedom from sin:

> And then wisdom shall be given to the elect. And they shall all live and not return again to sin, either by being wicked or through pride; but those who have wisdom shall be humble and not return again to sin (5:8-9).[47]

Again, in Enoch's vision of the last days in chapter 10, God instructs the angel Michael to

> ...cleanse the earth from all injustice, and from all defilement, and from all oppression, and from all sin, and from all iniquity which is being done on the earth; remove them from the earth. And all the children of all the people will become righteous..." (10:20-21).[48]

Thus the eschatological era will be established not merely by destroying the wicked, but by purifying the "righteous" of all sin.

A similar statement, reminiscent of Jer. 31:31-34 and Ezek. 36:26-27, appears in Jub. 1:22-25 where after God prophesies the disobedience and punishment of Israel he predicts that she will return to him. At that time, God says, Israel's heart will be circumcised, God will give to Israel his Spirit, and she will never again disobey God's commandments. The theme is repeated in 5:12 where the writer claims that in the eschaton God will make

> for all his works a new and righteous nature so that they might not sin in all their nature forever, and so that they might all be righteous, each in his kind, always (cf. 50:5).[49]

Another lucid example comes from Psalms of Solomon 17. The theme of this Psalm is the movement from Israel's sin and subsequent punishment to her deliverance and restoration through the messiah. Israel's sins, says the author, resulted in her defeat by the Gentiles and exile into distant lands (vv. 1-20); but God will send his messiah who will purify Israel of all unrighteousness (vv. 26-

---

[47] *The Old Testament Pseudepigrapha*, 2 vols., ed. James H. Charlesworth (New York: Doubleday, 1983-85), hereafter, *OTP*, 1:15.
[48] Ibid., p. 18.
[49] *OTP*, 2:65.

27, 30-32) and restore her to her place of pre-eminence among the nations (vv. 30-46).

The Greek Apocalypse of Moses and 4 Ezra also provide clear examples of the plight-solution pattern from the second temple period and shortly thereafter. The Apocalypse of Moses looks toward a day when paradise will be regained and humanity will be free from sin:

> ...all flesh from Adam up to that great day shall be raised, such as shall be the holy people; then to them shall be given every joy of Paradise and God shall be in their midst, and there shall not be any more sinners before him, for the evil heart shall be removed from them, and they shall be given a heart that understands the good and worships God alone.[50]

4 Ezra expresses a similar thought when Uriel tells Ezra that in the end times those who have "despised the Most High," held his law in contempt, and forsaken his ways (8:56) will be destroyed (8:59); but those, who, like Ezra, have been righteous will have "the root of evil...sealed up from" them (8:53).[51]

Despite the swirl of controversy since the seventeenth century concerning the date and origin of the Testaments of the Twelve Patriarchs, they too can offer some evidence for the currency of the plight-solution scheme within Jewish circles of Paul's era.[52] Even if the Testaments come originally from a Jewish-Christian community rather than from a non-Christian Jewish community, they give evidence of how a Jewish group which flourished between the second century B. C. and the second century after Christ viewed the human plight and God's response to it. In six passages the Testaments speak of Israel's sin, God's punishment for her sin, and God's eventual deliverance of Israel from the plight of disobedience. TLevi 14-17 predicts that Israel, because of her sin, will be pun-

---

[50] The date of the composition lying behind the Apocalypse of Moses and the Life of Adam and Eve is uncertain; but M. D. Johnson, *OTP*, 2:252, makes a plausible case for a date between 100 B.C. and A. D. 200. The translation used here comes from Johnson, *OTP*, 2:275, and, although the portion of the text on which it is based is found in a small number of Greek manuscripts, it contains no overtly Christian features and is, therefore, probably genuine. See *OTP*, 2:275.

[51] When Uriel claims here that righteous Ezra will be freed from the evil tendency in the age to come, he implicitly agrees with Ezra's statement in 7:48 (cf. 7:68 and 9:36) that almost all, including himself, who have been created have sinned and transgressed the covenant. In doing so, however, Uriel seems to contradict his chief contention that Ezra is among the few completely righteous who will be saved (8:46-52).

[52] According to H. Dixon Slingerland, *The Testaments of the Twelve Patriarchs: A Critical History of Research*, SBLMS vol. 21 (Missoula, Montana: Scholars Press, 1977), the first Greek editor of the Testaments, J. E. Grabe, considered them to be Jewish rather than Christian; but the majority of scholars between the late seventeenth century and the mid nineteenth century regarded them as Christian in origin. Several scholars during this period even argued that they were heavily influenced by Paulinism. From the early twentieth century until M. de Jonge began publishing in this field in the 1950's, most scholars believed that the Testaments were Jewish documents, probably dating from the Hasmonean era, which had subsequently been edited by Christians. Today scholars are widely divided over the issue, and barring significant manuscript discoveries, no consensus appears possible.

ished with severe suffering; but, according to chapter 18 God eventually will raise up a new priest, presumably the Messiah. TLevi 18:9-12 says that

> In his priesthood will all sin come to an end, and the lawless cease to do evil; and the righteous will rest in him... and the spirit of holiness will be on them. And Beliar will be bound by him, and he will give power to his children to tread the evil spirits underfoot.[53]

TDan 5 contains a similar passage in which Dan predicts that in the "last days" Israel will give herself up to

> every kind of evil, doing all the abominable things the Gentiles do and wantonly pursuing the women of the lawless, while the spirits of error work in you every kind of wickedness (5:5).

Because of their sin, says Dan, God's people will be taken captive by the Gentiles and suffer greatly. But eventually God "will turn the hearts of the disobedient back to the Lord again; and he will give to them that call on him eternal peace" (5:11). Both of these passages are reminiscent of Lev. 26 and Deut. 29-30 in the way they recount the history of Israel as a story of disobedience and predict God's intervention to reconcile his people to himself.[54] They show that Lev. 26 and Deut. 29-30 were important to the self-perception and expectations of Judaism during Paul's era.

Those who translated the Hebrew scriptures into Aramaic also demonstrate an awareness of and interest in the plight-solution pattern as it is articulated in Lev. 26 and Deut. 29-30. The Palestinian Targum on Lev. 26 reveals that its authors knew that the curses of Lev. 26:14-39 had already fallen upon Israel in the form of her suffering under ungodly overlords from Babylon to Rome. But the Targum's rendering of Lev. 26:40-45 also shows that its authors believed God would deliver them from their punishment:

> Yet for all this I will have mercy upon them by My Word, when they are captives in the land of their enemies, I will not spurn them away in the kingdom of Babel; nor shall My Word abhor them in the kingdom of Madai, to destroy them in the

---

[53] I have used the translation of M. de Jonge in *The Apocryphal Old Testament*, ed. H. F. D. Sparks (Oxford: Clarendon Press, 1984), pp. 505-600.

[54] Israel's sin and punishment are also mentioned in TJudah 23:4-5, TIss 6:4, TNaph 4:5, and TAsher 7:6-7; but the remedy to Israel's plight in these texts is Israel's repentance rather than God's intervention.

kingdom of Javan (Greece), or to abolish My covenant with them in the kingdom of Edom (Rome); for I am the Lord in the days of Gog (Pal. Tg. Lev. 26:44).[55]

The Palestinian Targum on Deut. 29:19-30:10 also dutifully repeats what will happen when God's laws are violated but then holds out the hope that

> ...though you may be dispersed unto the ends of the heaven, from thence will the Word of the Lord gather you together by the hand of Elijah the great priest, and from thence will He bring you by the hand of the King Meshiha.... And the Lord your God will take away the foolishness of your heart, and of your children's heart; for He will abolish evil desire from the world, and create good desire, which will give you the dictate to love the Lord your God with all your heart and soul, that your lives may flow on for evermore (Pal. Tg. Deut. 30:6).

In the future, says the translator, God would not only show his faithfulness to his covenant with Israel, but would rectify the source of past problems. God would take away Israel's tendency to break his law and give her a new heart.

In summary, both canonical and non-canonical Jewish literature from the era in which Paul lived demonstrate familiarity with a pattern of thinking about God's dealings with Israel which runs from plight to solution. In some cases, the plight was conceived as the inability of Israel to obey God's law and the solution was conceived in terms of a future in which Israel would be free from sin. This was certainly not the only way of thinking of God's historical design for Israel in ancient Judaism; but it was one way, and it was current in the first century. It remains now for us to examine Paul's statements about the relationship between the law and universal sinfulness in light of the plight-solution pattern which we have found in both canonical and non-canonical writings of his day.

---

[55] In quotations from the Targums both here and below, I have used the translation of J. W. Etheridge, *The Targums of Onkelos and Jonathan ben Uzziel on the Pentateuch with the Fragments of the Jerusalem Targum, from the Chaldee*, 2 vols. (New York: KTAV, 1968). The date of the Targums is, of course, uncertain, and there is no guarantee that they come from the time of Paul. The passages cited here, however, probably *reflect* traditions current in the first century.

CHAPTER THREE

FROM PLIGHT TO SOLUTION
IN GALATIANS

Introduction

Galatians has for centuries been considered Paul's most unjewish epistle. Simon Magus apparently appealed to it for evidence that the God of the Hebrew scriptures was a lesser God; Marcion made use of Galatians in his case against the Old Testament; and the Gnostics had recourse to the epistle in their polemic against the Jewish "demiurge."[1] In more recent days, the same passages which appealed to Simon, Marcion, and the Gnostics have been criticized as nonsensical from a Jewish perspective and even, on occasion, as anti-Semitic. C. G. Montefiore's 1894 article, "First Impressions of Paul" claims that Galatians is "the epistle in which Paul's antagonism to the Jews is emphasised most strongly."[2] Similarly, on the basis of Gal. 3:10, George F. Moore concluded that Paul had ignored, "and by implication" denied, that Judaism possessed a doctrine of repentance. This denial, said Moore, is inexplicable from the Jewish point of view, and Paul could only have arrived at it from his "predetermined conclusion...that there is no salvation but by faith in the Lord and Saviour, Jesus Christ." Arguments such as those which Paul makes in Gal 3:10, Moore concludes, could hardly have been persuasive to Jews.[3] Scholars as theologically diverse as Rudolf Bultmann,[4] Ragnar Bring,[5] and Hans Joachim Schoeps[6] have also concluded that in Galatians Paul argues upon completely different premises from Judaism.

---

[1] For Simon Magus see *Pseudo-Clementine Homilies* 3.2.2- 3. I am indebted to Betz, *Galatians*, p. 172, n. 85 for drawing this reference to my attention. For Marcion, see Tertullian, *Adversus Marcionem* 5.4. And for the Gnostic use of Galatians see the numerous references in Elaine Hiesey Pagels, *The Gnostic Paul: Gnostic Exegesis of the Pauline Letters* (Philadelphia: Fortress Press, pp. 101-114.

[2] P. 432.

[3] *Judaism*, 3:150-51

[4] Theology, 1:263.

[5] *Commentary on Galatians*, trans. Eric Wahlstrom (Philadelphia: Muhlenberg Press, 1961), pp. 12, 35, 87, 120- 21, 128-34.

[6] *Paul*, pp. 175-83. Although Schoeps maintains that Galatians and Romans are equally antinomian, he bases his thesis that Paul misunderstood the relationship between Torah and covenant and therefore broke with Judaism largely on Paul's statements about the curse of the law in Gal. 3:10-13.

In the last twenty years, despite attempts to bring the Paul of Galatians back to his Jewish roots,[7] the separation between the "Christianity" of Galatians and Judaism has grown wider. Günther Klein is representative of others within the Bultmann school who carried on Bultmann's legacy of a stark separation between the salvation history of Judaism as contained in the Old Testament and Paul's concept of salvation.[8] Galatians was of great significance to Klein's thesis. Paul's argument in that epistle, he said, has nothing to do "mit einer Verheißungsstruktur des Judentums,"[9] rather, its idea of world history is attached to a concretely experienced "Individualgeschichte."[10] E. P. Sanders, although at great pains to distance himself from Bultmann on the details of Paul's view of the law, takes a position surprisingly similar to the Bultmann school on the wide chasm between Paul and Jewish covenantal nomism. As with Klein, one of the mainstays of his argument is the idea that Galatians, especially Galatians 2-3, demonstrates Paul's distance from Judaism.[11] More radical than the position taken by the Bultmann school and Sanders is the claim of Heikki Räisänen that Paul, especially in Galatians, distorted Jewish attitudes toward the law as he attempted to persuade his readers of his own religious convictions.[12]

Others have steered clear of Räisänen's conclusions by advancing various theories about the development of Paul's thinking. John Drane, for example, compared Galatians, 1-2 Corinthians, and Romans and concluded that Paul's thinking developed from a nearly gnostic antinomianism in Galatians to a legalistic stance in 1 Corinthians, and finally arrived at a moderating position in 2 Corinthians and Romans. In Romans, said Drane, Paul held together

> the teaching of Galatians, that Christ had abolished the Law once and for all, and his teaching in 1 Corinthians that the principle of law as such was necessary for

---

[7] Krister Stendahl, *Paul among Jews and Gentiles and Other Essays* (Philadelphia: Fortress Press, 1976); George Howard, *Crisis*; Dunn, "Incident" and "New Perspective"; Kertelge, "Gesetz"; Roman Heiligenthal, *Werke als Zeichen* and "Soziologische Implikationen."

[8] For Bultmann's position, see his essay "Prophecy and Fulfillment" in *Essays on Old Testament Hermeneutics*, 2nd ed. Claus Westermann, trans. James Luther Mays (Richmond, Va.: John Knox Press, 1964), pp. 50-75. Klein's position is expressed in "Römer 4 und die Idee der Heilsgeschichte," *EvT* 23 (1963):424-47 and "Individualgeschichte und Weltgeschichte bei Paulus: Eine Interpretation ihres Verhältnisses im Galaterbrief," *EvT* 24 (1964):126-65.

[9] "Individualgeschichte," p. 140.

[10] Ibid., p. 162.

[11] *Law*, pp. 17-29 and 65-70.

[12] *Law*, pp. 189-90; Recent commentaries on Galatians have not generally gone to Räisänen's extremes, but most have commented on the distance in the epistle between Paul and Judaism. See especially Heinrich Schlier, *Der Brief an die Galater übersezt und erklärt*, MeyerK, vol. 7 (Göttingen: Vandenhoeck & Ruprecht: 1949), pp. 53-58; D. Albrecht Oepke, *Der Brief des Paulus an die Galater*, THKNT, vol. 9 (Berlin: Evangelische Verlagsanstalt, 1957), p. 59; Bring, *Galatians*, pp. 9-17; Franz Mußner, *Der Galaterbrief*, HTKNT vol. 9 (Freiberg: Herder, 1974), pp. 167-175; Betz, *Galatians*, pp. 30-31; and F. F. Bruce, *The Epistle to the Galatians: A Commentary on the Greek Text* (Grand Rapids: Eerdmans, 1982), p. 140.

the Christian, so that while he may not be 'under law', he was 'under law to Christ' (1 Cor. 9.21).[13]

Hans Hübner advocated a similar thesis. He claimed that the Jerusalem apostles, with whom Paul had entered into an agreement at the Jerusalem council, were horrified at Paul's stance toward the law in Galatians and Paul, out of concern for the success of his collection for the Jerusalem church, modified his position in Romans.[14] Thus, says Hübner, Galatians assigns to the law the function of calling "forth sinful deeds" and advances the notion that the law was given by evil angels who wanted to trick people into sin (3:19); but in Romans the law merely brings knowledge of sin and, far from being demonic, is holy, just, and good (7:12).[15] In a more recent book, Hübner bolsters his thesis with the argument that Paul's supposedly negative attitude toward Judaism in 1 Thessalonians and Galatians shifts to a positive posture in Romans 9-11.[16]

J. Christiaan Beker's assessment of Romans and Galatians, although it does not suggest an evolution in Paul's thinking from one epistle to the other,[17] has similarities to the theories of Drane and Hübner. Beker says that because Paul believed the Galatians were falling away from the faith through adding legal observances to faith in Christ, Paul could not risk taking a carefully nuanced position on the law in his letter to them. The situation demanded, in Paul's view, that the Galatians see law and faith in black and white terms. Later, in Romans, says Beker, Paul had the leisure to reflect on the law's positive traits.[18] Like Drane and Hübner, then, Beker believes that Paul has moved from a negative attitude toward the law in Galatians to a relatively positive attitude in Romans.

---

[13] *Paul: Libertine or Legalist? A Study in the Theology of the Major Pauline Epistles* (London: SPCK, 1975), p. 133. For a slightly different arrangement see Charles Buck and Greer Taylor, *Saint Paul: A Study of the Development of His Thought* (New York: Charles Scribner's Sons, 1969) and C. H. Dodd, "The Mind of Paul I" and "The Mind of Paul II" in *New Testament Studies* (Manchester: University of Manchester Press, 1953), pp. 67-82 and 83-128.

[14] *Law*, pp. 60-65.

[15] Ibid., pp. 78-79.

[16] *Gottes Ich und Israel: zum Schriftgebrauch des Paulus in Römer 9-11*, FRLANT no. 146 (Göttingen: Vandenhoeck & Ruprecht, 1984), pp. 127-135. W. D. Davies, "Paul and the People of Israel" in *Jewish and Pauline Studies* (Philadelphia: Fortress Press, 1984), pp. 128-29 also argues that Paul's position on Israel in Galatians, when compared to his position on Israel in his other letters, stands closer to 1 Thess. 2:14-16 than to Romans. Nonetheless, says Davies, Paul's position on Israel in Galatians is not unwaveringly negative, as Gal. 6:15-16 demonstrates. Ulrich Wilckens also proposes a developmental theory of Paul's view of the law in "Statements on the Development of Paul's View of the Law" in *Paul and Paulinism, Essays in Honour of C. K. Barrett*, ed. M. D. Hooker and S. G. Wilson (Cambridge: Cambridge University Press, 1982), pp. 17-26. See also his "Zur Entwicklung des paulinischen Gesetzesverständnisses," *NTS* 28 (1982):154-90.

[17] Beker, *Paul*, pp. 11-19 prefers to speak of the "contingency" and the "coherence" of Paul's thought rather than its development. The coherent center of Paul's thinking is the triumph of God through the gospel; but this center is expressed in various ways under the exigencies of different situations.

[18] Ibid., p. 53.

Most scholars, therefore, see Galatians as conclusive evidence that Paul broke with Judaism in such a radical manner that his ideas shared little ground with his "former manner of life" and would have been unintelligible to Jews. They base this verdict almost exclusively on the attitude which Paul expresses in the epistle toward the law—the *sine qua non* of Judaism.[19] The reasoning runs that if Paul claims to have "died to the law" (2:19), has associated the law with a curse (3:10-14), has assigned the origin of the law to angels (3:19), compared its function to a "taskmaster" (3:23-4:2), and equated it with "enslaving evil spirits" (4:3, 9), he has abandoned Judaism's central religious symbol, leapt into another religious system, and looks back at Judaism through an entirely unjewish lens.

There are problems, however, with the position that the Paul of Galatians has become dissatisfied with and alienated from his Jewish origins. Paul begins the substance of his argument by classifying himself as a Jew: "We who are Jews by birth and not Gentile sinners," he says, "have ourselves believed in Christ Jesus because we know that a man is not justified by works of the law but by faith in Jesus Christ" (2:15-16). His subsequent argument contains ten quotations from Hebrew scripture, nine of which come from the Torah proper. And, as we shall see below, Paul assumes—to the consternation of many scholars—that his readers will fulfill "the whole law" by obeying Lev. 19:18, "You shall love your neighbor as yourself" (Gal. 5:4). Clearly Paul did not simply and unambiguously disassociate himself from Judaism or even from the Torah.[20]

Some, of course, would contend that this more Jewish side of Galatians simply springs from the contradictory nature of Paul's argument. Paul, this theory goes, only spoke negatively of the law when it was convenient for his argument to do so; in contexts where the law posed no threat to his own religious convictions, he was happy to use it to "prove" his argument or to provide a ready-made list of ethical requirements for new Gentile believers.[21] A careful reading of Paul's argument in Galatians, however, reveals that the law assumes an integral role in his theological thinking. For Paul the law is necessary not only as a guide to Christian ethics but as a definition of Israel's (and the Gentiles') failure to keep the covenant and therefore of their need for God's eschatological, saving intervention.

In this chapter I hope to show a way out of the difficulty which this seeming ambivalence creates for the interpreter by demonstrating that Paul's argument in

---

[19] On the law as the identity symbol of Judaism see, among others, J. Bonsirven, *Le Judaïsme palestinien au temps de Jésus Christ: sa théologie,* 2 vols. (Paris: Beauchesne, 1934-35) 1:247-48; Moore, *Judaism,* 1:235-80; W. D. Davies, *Torah.* Jacob Neusner, *Judaism in the Beginnings of Christianity* (Philadelphia: Fortress, 1984), p. 13.

[20] Although the meaning of Paul's benediction upon "the Israel of God" in Gal. 6:16 is disputed, it should probably also be listed here. See Davies, "Paul and the People of Israel," p. 129.

[21] See, for example, Sanders, *Law,* pp. 93-114. Räisänen, *Paul and the Law,* pp. 62-73; 113-119 sees Paul's statements about fulfilling the law as simple contradictions of his more negative statements. The source of Paul's ambiguity, he says, may lie within his psyche.

Galatians flows from the same eschatological presuppositions present in parts of the Old Testament and in certain non-canonical writings from the second temple period. I hope to demonstrate that although Paul says that the law cannot be kept in "the present evil age," that it "encloses" humanity under sin, and that it pronounces a curse upon humanity for its disobedience, he affirms that in the eschatological age of deliverance from sin, believers keep the law by walking in the Spirit. Thus Paul does not argue against the law as the codified will of God, but against life "under law"—under the curse which the law pronounces on sin. In sum, I hope to show that instead of casting aside the most important symbol of Judaism, Paul claims that a common eschatological hope within Judaism is being fulfilled: the age of the curse of sin is drawing to a close and the age of obedience to the law from the heart is beginning.

My method will be to attempt first to show that Paul's claim that Christians should fulfill the law in 5:14 cannot be adequately explained on the thesis that he simply abrogated the Jewish law, second to address the important question of the definition of the law in Galatians, and finally to demonstrate that the bulk of what the letter says about the law is not an attempt to abrogate it but an effort to say that the curse of the law on those who disobey it has been cancelled.[22]

Paul's Command to Fulfill the Law (5:14)

In at least one place in Galatians Paul clearly admonishes his readers to "fulfill" the law (5:14, cf. 5:23, 6:2). They should, he says, avoid using their freedom "as an opportunity for the flesh," but instead should serve one another in love. To lend weight to his advice Paul appeals to Lev. 19:18: "For ($\gamma\acute{\alpha}\rho$) the whole law is fulfilled in one word, 'You shall love your neighbor as yourself.'" The most obvious reading of this statement, of course, poses a problem for those who claim that Galatians abolishes the law in its every aspect or that Paul opposes Judaism, for Paul quotes from the Torah itself to summarize its precepts, formulates his summary of the law in a way common in Judaism, and counsels the Galatians to obey it.

Thus, at least three ways of coping with the statement on an "unjewish" or "antinomian" reading of Galatians have arisen, and it is important for us to consider these arguments.

1. The most uncomplicated way of explaining this verse in light of Paul's supposed abrogation of the law in 2:15-5:12 is to distinguish between the "doing" of the law in Judaism and the "fulfilling" of the law in 5:14 (and 6:2). In the first

---

[22] My purpose here is not to deny that Paul's experience with Christ radically changed his attitudes toward Judaism. Paul's talk of his "former manner of life in Judaism" (1:13, cf. 1 Cor. 9:19-21 and Phil. 3:4-8) is enough to show that a radical change had in fact occurred. My point is instead that what Paul says is, despite his change, still compatible with at least some expressions of first century Judaism and intelligible on Jewish eschatological presuppositions.

case, it is said, the emphasis is on performing as many of the 613 commandments of the law as possible, but in the second it is on freely doing "the good."[23]
Some advocates of this position claim that Paul distinguishes between "doing"
and "fulfilling" the law. The contrast between the negative tone of Paul's statement in 5:3 that "every man who becomes circumcised is obligated to do all the
law" and the positive tone of his claim in 5:14 that "the whole law is fulfilled" in
the one word of Lev. 19:18, it is said, demonstrates that Paul saw a difference
between the two ideas. On this view 5:3 looks at the law from the standpoint of
each of its individual demands and 5:14 sees it from the standpoint of its spirit
and intention.[24] Paul, on this view, is not suddenly saying that the law has a
place in Christian ethics (he has afterall just forbidden the Galatians from
practicing circumcision), but that Christian ethics overwhelm and, by
overwhelming, supercede the Jewish law.[25]

2. A second idea, proposed by Hans Hübner, is that if read at face value,
Paul's statement in 5:3 contradicts his injunction in 5:14; but if 5:14 is taken in
an ironic sense, then both statements are intelligible within the larger context of
the letter. 5:3, says Hübner, forbids the doing of the law, particularly circumcision. 5:14 would contradict this negative attitude toward the law if it meant
either that the law could be reduced to the one command of love for one's neighbor or that the law's particular requirements were summed up in this command
(cf. Hillel). But, by placing πᾶς in the attributive position in 5:14, Paul refers
to the totality of the individual commands of the law which he then, ironically,
sums up in a single command. The overall effect, according to Hübner, is to sat-
irize the concept of the law. Thus 5:14 is not a positive reference to the law at
all but a purposeful trivializing of it.[26]

3. A final explanation of 5:14 is offered by Heikki Räisänen who claims that
it is a positive reference and stands in contradiction to 5:3. Paul, says Räisänen,
was an unsystematic thinker who alternately supported and denied the validity of
the law in an effort to wrestle with the tension created by Christianity's roots in
Judaism on one hand and rejection of Judaism on the other.[27]

---

[23] Betz, *Galatians*, p. 275.

[24] Bruce, *Galatians*, p. 241-42.

[25] The most articulate and convincing spokesperson for this view is Stephen Westerholm,
Israel's Law and the Church's Faith: Paul and His Recent Interpreters (Grand Rapids: Eerdmans,
1988), pp. 201-205. The clarity, care, and humor with which Westerholm argues his position on
Paul's view of the law cannot be praised too highly. For this reason, and because Westerholm's
basic position differs from my own, I regret that I was unable to give his book the attention which
it so clearly deserves. Unfortunately, my manuscript was complete when this outstanding book
appeared. I have, nevertheless, attempted to interact with Westerholm here and in other places
where to do so seemed important enough to warrant a last-minute revision of my manuscript

[26] *Law*, pp. 36-42. See also Hübner's essay, "Das ganze und das eine Gesetz, zum Problem
Paulus und die Stoa," *KD* 22 (1976): 250-76.

[27] *Law*, pp. 62-64, 200-202 and "Galatians 2.16 and Paul's Break with Judaism," pp. 548-50;
Betz, *Galatians*, p. 275 believes that the problems Paul faced in trying to win the Galatian
churches back to his side forced him into a contradiction at this point. "If he wants to win his
churches back," Betz says, "he cannot ignore the issue that looms largest in their minds and that

None of these explanations of 5:14, however, carries conviction. Stephen Westerholm, a supporter of the first position, points out that when Paul speaks of "doing" and "fulfilling" the law he makes a clear distinction between Christians and those still "under law." Christians alone are said to "fulfill" the law, while those still "under law" are obligated to "do" it.[28] The difference between doing the law and fulfilling the law in Paul's letters, however, does not show that Paul thought Christians were no longer required to do the law because they had fulfilled its intention. To prove that point one would need to show that Paul *opposed* doing the law to fulfilling it, or that he used the word πληρόω in its eschatological sense of "bring to an end."[29] In fact he does neither. He never says that "doing" brings condemnation while "fulfilling" brings salvation, nor among the twenty-four times he uses πληρόω does he ever use it to mean "bring to an end". Paul does use the term, however, to mean "do completely" and can even couple it with the word ὑπακοή to mean "render complete obedience" (2 Cor. 10:6). Paul probably used πληρόω of the believer's relationship to the law because it possessed connotations of completeness and finality, connotations well suited to his eschatological convictions but which were missing from the more prosaic term ποιέω.

While Westerholm's case does demonstrate some difference between the concept of "doing" and "fulfilling" in Galatians, it is difficult to see any difference between "all the law" in 5:3 and "the whole law" in 5:14 as Hübner describes it. If no parallels to Paul's reduction of the law could be found in ancient literature, we might well suppose that he had made a startling and witty joke which proposed the shrinking of the many laws to one principle, thus demonstrating his contempt for the law. But such reductions were common in Hellenistic Judaism, especially as a concession to the non-jewish world,[30] and we can be sure that Paul was familiar with them. Thus, it is difficult to see any great difference between what Paul says in 5:14 and what Philo describes as the principle theme of sermons heard in the synagogues of "every city":

> But among the vast number of particular truths and principles there studied, there stand out practically high above the others two main heads: one of duty to God as shewn by piety and holiness, one of duty to men as shewn by humanity and justice... (*Spec. Leg.* 2.62-63[282]).[31]

---

is central to the theology of his opponents.... Therefore his argument in the parenetical section must integrate the concept of Torah in such a way that the Jewish (Jewish-Christian) concept of the opposition is eliminated, while the concern of the Galatians in regard to the ethical problems is taken care of." See also Wilckens, "Development," p. 23 and "Entwicklung," p. 179.

[28] *Israel's Law*, pp. 203-204.

[29] See, for example, *Herm Vis* 2.2.5.

[30] J. J. Collins, *Between*, pp. 162-63.

[31] I have used the translation of F. H. Colson in *Philo, with an English Translation*, trans., F. H. Colson, G. H. Whitaker, and R. Marcus, 9 vols., Loeb Classical Library (Cambridge: Harvard

Irony depends for its effectiveness on the unexpected, but as Philo shows us, such summaries as Paul provides were so common in the synagogues of the diaspora that 5:14 would have been unremarkable.

Are we then left with Räisänen's explanation of an inconsistent and largely incoherent Paul as the only possible option? Aside from the general objections to Räisänen's position registered in chapter one, a careful consideration of Paul's language in 5:2-3 militates against this view and allows a coherent reading of 5:2-3 and 5:14. It is clear that in 5:3 Paul argues against circumcision and warns the Galatians that if they submit to it, they are obligated to do the "whole law." Circumcision, at least to Paul's opponents, and for many other Jews, was not only part of the law, but a vitally important requirement, for it was the distinguishing mark of the Jew. Most interpreters have therefore viewed Paul's remarks in 5:2-3, especially since they come after what is frequently considered the most antinomian section of Paul's writings (2:15-5:1), as an argument against the "whole law." Paul, on this reading is saying, "If you accept circumcision, you are accepting the Torah and must obey it completely in order to be saved. That cannot be done. Thus the Torah in its entirety has been superceded." In fact, however, Paul in his other writings clearly distinguishes between circumcision and the law. In 1 Cor. 7:19 he can claim that "neither circumcision counts for anything, nor uncircumcision, but keeping the commands of God," and in Rom. 2:25-29 he asserts that the true Jew is one who is circumcised inwardly and thus keeps the law, even though he may not be circumcised physically. When Paul denies the continued validity of circumcision in 5:3, therefore, he by no means refers to the law in general. Instead he delivers a challenge to the Galatians to try to keep the "whole law" after transferring their allegience from the Spirit (3:1-5) to the rite of circumcision (5:2), with the implication that they would find it impossible to do so. It is not through accepting circumcision and becoming outwardly Jewish that one receives the hope of righteousness,[32] Paul says, but through the Spirit (5:4-5). He then asserts in 5:14 that those who walk in the Spirit keep the law. Thus, even when 5:3 and 5:14 are given their most obvious grammatical meaning, they do not stand in tension with one another. 5:3 is a challenge to keep the law without the Spirit (implying that it cannot be done) and 5:14, taken within its larger context, is an assertion that the challenge can be met by walking in the Spirit.

University Press, 1929-1953), 7:347. I am indebted to Collins, *Between*, p. 163, for bringing this reference to my attention.

[32] The righteousness of which Paul speaks here is not merely "forensic" but "ethical" as well. On this problem and for the recent trend among scholars of both Roman Catholic and Protestant persuasions to see ethical connotations to Paul's term "righteousness," see Ernst Käsemann, "The Righteousness of God in Paul" in *New Testament Questions of Today*, trans. W. J. Montague (Philadelphia: Fortress, 1969), pp. 168-82; Peter Stuhlmacher, *Gerechtigkeit gottes bei Paulus*, 2d ed. (Göttingen: Vandenhoeck & Ruprecht, 1966), and "The Apostle Paul's View of Righteousness," in *Reconciliation*; Karl Kertelge, *"Rechtfertigung"*; and John Ziesler, *The Meaning of Righteousness in Paul*, SNTSMS no. 20 (Cambridge: Cambridge University Press, 1972).

In summary, Paul clearly reserves a place for obedience to the law in his eschatological scheme. In fact, he claims that those who "walk" in the eschatological gift of the Spirit have the hope of attaining righteousness (5:5) and possess the ability to fulfill the law by love (5:14).

The Boundaries of the Law in Galatians

Paul's claim that circumcision does not matter (6:15) while fulfilling the law does (5:14) raises an important question. How can Paul distinguish between the love command on one hand and circumcision, food laws, and Sabbath keeping on the other? Are not the "ceremonial" commands of the law as much part of the law as the command to love? How could Paul have argued within the eschatological pattern of Judaism if he denied that circumcision, dietary restrictions, and the observance of "days and months and seasons and years" were part of the law which would be obeyed perfectly in the new age?[33] Is not this reduction of the law to Lev. 19:18 an indication that he is working with a unique definition of the law, one based on his presupposition that Christ is the savior of the world and therefore one which no first century Jew could possibly accept?[34]

Although there is no entirely satisfactory answer to these questions, it is important that any explanation of Paul's view of the law take into account the varied definitions of the law within second temple Judaism. There was considerable debate, particularly within the Diaspora, over which aspects of the law were most important, and some Jewish writers played down the importance of precisely those aspects with which Paul is most concerned in Galatians.[35] In the Letter of Aristeas, for example, the author records an interview with the Jewish High Priest Eleazar in which Eleazar attempts to explain those "passages in the law dealing with food and drink and animals regarded as unclean"—passages about which

---

[33] In Jubilees, for example, the "plight" of Israel is described primarily in terms of the "ceremonial" law. In 1:14 the Lord predicts that after Israel is scattered among the nations in punishment for her sins, "they will forget all of my laws and all of my commandments and all of my judgments, and they will err concerning new moons, sabbaths, festivals, jubilees, and ordinances," OTP, 2:53. Presumably, when the author speaks of the eschatological age as a period of obedience to the law in 1:22-25 he also has these commandments in view. The Dead Sea Scrolls exhibit similar concerns.

[34] Sanders, Law, p. 103 regards 1 Cor. 7:19 as "one of the most amazing sentences [Paul] ever wrote" because it supposedly demonstrates how he could, willy-nilly, accept some parts of the law as God's commands and reject others. See also Räisänen, Law, pp. 23-28, esp. p. 28.

[35] Although educated at the feet of Gamaliel (Acts 22:3), Paul was born in the Diaspora and conducted his missionary labors outside of Palestine. Research over the last forty years has discovered, in any case, that Palestinian Jewry could be as concerned as their kinsmen in the Diaspora about making their religion understandable to Hellenistic ways of thinking. See Davies, Paul, pp. 1-16 and Hengel, Judaism and Hellenism.

"most men feel some curiosity" (128).[36] Two aspects of Eleazer's apology demonstrate the embarassment of the author over the law's ceremonial aspects and his eagerness to define them in terms of common Hellenistic virtues. First, it is only after a lengthy proof that the Mosaic law teaches the unity, omnipotence, and omnipresence of God (132-34)[37] and a discourse on the foolishness of idolatry—ideas popular in Hellenistic philosophical thought—that Eleazar goes on to explain the reason for the more peculiarly Jewish commandments. Second, he explains these commandments as symbolic reminders of the virtues by which the people of God should seek to order their lives: justice, peace, and the contemplation of God (144-167). Again, these are virtues commonly praised in Hellenistic philosophical writing. The author of the Letter of Aristeas was clearly anxious to show that the parts of the Torah which were peculiarly Jewish were not at the center of Jewish religion and only pointed to deeper, more important, and more universally accepted ideas.[38]

Similarly, circumcision, food laws, and Sabbath keeping are conspicuously absent in some of the surviving ethical literature of Hellenistic Judaism. Pseudo-Phocylides, probably written by a Hellenistic Jew between 200 B. C. and A. D. 200,[39] consists of a long list of ethical injunctions, but concentrates on those places where Hellenistic and Jewish ethics intersect. The honor of God and parents (l. 8), the execution of justice (ll. 9-21), showing mercy to the poor and helpless (ll. 22-41), exercising moderation (ll. 59-69), and avoiding such sins as greed (ll. 42-47) and sexual immorality (l. 3, ll. 175-206) form the ethical center of this work. Aside from one reference to "purifications" (l. 228)—possibly an allusion to ritual washings—there is no mention of those parts of the law which are distinctively Jewish. For whatever reason the sentences of Pseudo-Phocylides were written to reconcile Jewish and Hellenistic culture, and those parts of the law considered expendable were precisely those parts which Paul considers expendable in Galatians: dietary restrictions, Sabbath and festival observances, and circumcision.

The Testaments of the Twelve Patriarchs, if they represent non-Christian Judaism at all, have perhaps been used too quickly as evidence that certain Jews distinguished between the "ethical" and the "ceremonial" aspects of the law.[40] The

---

[36] In quotations both here and elsewhere from the Letter of Aristeas I have used the translation of Moses Hadas, *Aristeas to Philocrates (Letter of Aristeas)*, Dropsie College Edition: Jewish Apocryphal Literature (New York: Harper & Brothers, 1951).

[37] Ibid., p. 153, n. 132.

[38] Philo undertakes a similar task on a massive scale in his *De Specialibus Legibus*. This treatise subsumes the laws of the Pentateuch under the ten headings provided by the "ten words" and attempts to define many of the "special laws" in terms of Hellenistic virtues.

[39] P. W. van der Horst follows what he describes as a "growing consensus" in dating Pseudo-Phocylides around the turn of the era. See *OTP* 2:567-68. W. Kroll, "Phokylides" in *Paulys Real-Encyclopädie der klassischen Altertumswissenschaft*, 24 vols., re-edited by Georg Wissowa (Stuttgart: J. B. Metzler, 1894-1963):20:1:505-510 similarly dates Pseudo-Phocylides to the first century of the common era.

[40] See the protest of Dixon Slingerland, "The Nature of *Nomos* (Law) within the *Testaments of the Twelve Patriarchs*," *JBL* 105 (1986): 39-48.

Testaments do afterall show some interest in cultic matters such as sacrifice (TRuben 6:8; TLevi 9:5-9, 14; TJudah 18:5, 21:5-6; TIss 3:6), fasting (TAsher 2:8-10), circumcision (TLevi 5:2-6), and clean and unclean animals (TLevi 9:13, TAsher 4:4-5). In spite of these interests, however, the Testaments see the essence of the law not in these particularly Jewish features but in the law's "ethical" requirements. In TIss 7, for example, Issachar concludes his testament with the claim that he has been a righteous man. In the process he gives a description of what it means to be upright:

> ...I am not aware of having committed a sin unto death. I have not had intercourse with any woman other than my wife, nor was I promiscuous by lustful look. I did not drink wine to the point of losing self-control. I was not passionately eager for any desirable possession of my neighbor. There was no deceit in my heart; no lie passed through my lips. I joined in lamentation with every oppressed human being, and shared my bread with the poor. I did not eat alone; I did not transgress boundaries; I acted in piety and truth all my days. The Lord I loved with all my strength; likewise, I loved every human being as I love my children (7:2-6).[41]

That Issachar makes no reference to the circumcision of his children, the dutiful performance of sacrifices, or the observance of food laws is significant. Similarly in TZeb 8 the criterion for receiving God's mercy on the last day is being careful to show mercy to others:

> You also, my children, have compassion toward every person with mercy, in order that the Lord may be compassionate and merciful to you. In the last days God will send his compassion on the earth, and whenever he finds compassionate mercy, in that person he will dwell. To the extent that a man has compassion on his neighbor, to that extent the Lord has mercy on him (8:1-4).[42]

This statement is remarkable in its offer of God's mercy to anyone, presumably including the Gentile, who is willing to show mercy to others.

The frequently quoted story of Izates' conversion to Judaism in Josephus' *Ant* 20.38-48 provides a final illustration of liberal attitudes toward the "ceremonial" aspects of the law. It is of particular importance to Paul's position on the law in Galatians because it demonstrates a "division of the house" within Judaism over the content of the law similar to the division represented by Paul and his opponents. In both situations missionaries attempt to persuade interested Gentiles to follow the God of Abraham; in both there is a disagreement between the missionaries over what a Gentile must do in order to be acceptable before God; and in both the disagreement revolves around whether or not Gentiles must accept circumcision. As Josephus tells the story, Izates, king of Adiabene, became

---

[41] The translation is that of H. C. Kee in *OTP*, 1:804.
[42] *OTP*, 1:807. See also TIss 5:2, 7:6; TZeb 5:1, 6:4, 6:7, 7:2, 8:1; and TBen 4:2.

interested in Judaism both through his mother's conversion and through the efforts of a Jewish travelling merchant named Ananias. Eventually he decided to undergo circumcision but reconsidered because of his mother's fears that his subjects would reject him if they discovered his attachment to foreign rites. Ananias agreed with Izates' mother and assured Izates that he

> could worship God even without being circumcised if indeed he had fully decided to be a devoted adherent of Judaism, for it was this that counted more than circumcision (20.41).[43]

He added that God would forgive him for not accepting the rite, if necessity compelled him to remain uncircumcised (20.42). Later, however, a Jew named Eleazar persuaded Izates that not to become circumcised was the "greatest offence against the law and thereby against God" (20.44), and Izates accepted circumcision. Although Josephus clearly favors Eleazar's position and even makes Ananias refer to abstinance from circumcision as a sin which needs God's forgiveness, his story betrays the existence among some Jews of the belief that one could be a "devoted adherent of Judaism" (ζηλοῦν τὰ πάτρια τῶν ' Ιουδαίων) and remain uncircumcized.

What light does all this shed on Paul's attitude toward circumcision, food laws, and Sabbath observance in Galatians? It must be admitted immediately that few scholars have been willing to see behind this literature a group of Jews who actually abandoned circumcision, food laws, and Sabbath observance.[44] As Hellenistic a Jew as Philo specifically refused to take the allegorization of the law to such extremes,[45] and liberties taken in apologetic literature, admittedly, should not be seen as normative for the actual religious practice of Hellenistic Judaism. Nevertheless, the literature referred to above does demonstrate a certain uneasiness over these peculiarly Jewish rites. "Just as Philo denied that the literal laws were dispensable but did not regard them as the most important dimension of religion," says John Collins, "so the Jews who wrote the Sibyllines and Testaments probably observed the distinctive commandments, but did not regard them as the

---

[43] I have quoted the translation of Louis H. Feldman, *Josephus*, with an English Translation by H. St. J. Thackeray, Ralph Marcus, Allen Wickgren, and Louis Feldman, 9 vols. (Cambridge: Harvard University Press, 1926-1965), 9:409-411.

[44] See especially Räisänen, *Law*, pp. 33-41.

[45] In *Mig*. 1.450 Philo scolds those who have abandoned literal observance of the Sabbath laws, the festal calendar, and circumcision in favor of keeping these laws in a strictly "spiritual sense." While this does show that Philo disagreed with such a stance, it also witnesses to the existence of some Jews who did not observe these distinctively Jewish parts of the Torah. In another passage, *Quaes. Ex.* 2.2, Philo seems to argue, in a way similar to Ananias, that literal circumcision was not necessary for proselytes, but only circumcision of the soul's passions. See the intriguing article by M. Friedländer, "The 'Pauline' Emancipation from the Law a Product of the Pre-Christian Diaspora," *JQR* 14 (1902): pp. 268-69 as well as Peder Borgen, *Philo, John, and Paul: New Perspectives on Judaism and Early Christianity*, Brown Judaic Studies no. 131 (Atlanta, Georgia: 1987), pp. 61-71, 233-54 and Alan F. Segal, *The Other Judaisms of Late Antiquity*, Brown Judaic Studies no. 127 (Atlanta, Georgia: Scholars Press, 1987), pp. 156-58.

heart of their religion."[46] There did exist in Paul's day, therefore, a precedent at least for expressing verbally the heart of biblical religion without reference to the peculiarly Jewish ideas of circumcision, food laws, and Sabbath observance.[47] Paul undoubtedly went further than his Jewish contemporaries in Galatians by forbidding circumcision and by arguing so stridently against those who insisted on the rite (5:4, 5:12, 6:12-13); but his claim that those who love actually fulfill the law would have received a welcome reception from many Hellenistic Jews, especially since the objects of this admonition were Gentiles.

Paul's opponents in Galatia, of course, took a different stance. To them there could be no division of the law into dispensible aspects (which, they pointed out, coincided conveniently with those parts of the law that proved most objectionable to Gentiles, 1:10) and indispensible aspects. Circumcision, food laws, the observance of the Sabbath, and keeping special Jewish festivals were part of the law, they argued, and must be undertaken to ensure membership in the people of God and aquittal on the day of judgment. There was much in the way of tradition which stood behind this position and their anger toward Paul's "man-pleasing" gospel. Under the Hellenistic reforms of Syrian rule, Jews had suffered bitterly rather than give up precisely the ritual observances at issue in Galatia.[48] Some Jews of the second temple period considered the breech of these commandments to be worthy of death.[49] And during Paul's day there was a resurgence of Jewish nationalism which probably called for the strict observance of these aspects of Torah.[50] Thus, we can imagine Paul's opponents replying to his argument in Galatians with words similar to those of Trypho a century later:

...You, saying you worship God, and thinking yourselves superior to other people, separate from them in no respect, and do not make your life different from the heathen, in that you keep neither the feasts nor the Sabbaths, nor have circumcision, and, moreover, though you set your hopes on a man that was crucified, you

---

[46] *Between*, p. 180.

[47] See Charles H. Cosgrove, "The Law and the Spirit: An Investigation into the Theology of Galatians," Ph.D. dissertation, Princeton Theological Seminary, 1985, p. 337.

[48] See 1 Macc. 1:44-48, where it is said that Antiochus commanded Jerusalem and the cities of Judah "to follow customs strange to the land, to forbid burnt offerings and sacrifices and drink offerings in the sanctuary, to profane sabbaths and feasts, to defile the sanctuary and the priests, to build altars and sacred precincts and shrines for idols, to sacrifice swine and unclean animals, and to leave their sons uncircumcised" (cf. 1 Macc. 1:11-15, 60-64 and Dan. 1:5-16.)

[49] See Jub 50:7-8, *OTP* 1:142: "Six days you will work, but the seventh day is the sabbath of the LORD your God. You shall not do any work in it, you, or your stranger who is with you. And let the man who does anything on it die."

[50] See Robert Jewett, "The Agitators and the Galatian Congregation," *NTS* 17 (1970-71):205-206 and James D. G. Dunn, "Incident," pp. 7-11.

yet hope to attain some good from God, though you do not do his commandments (*DialTrypho*, 10.3, cf. 8.4).[51]

Paul and his competitors in Galatia, therefore, were working with different ideas of the content of the law. Paul considered circumcision neither here nor there (5:6, 6:15); his opponents considered it so important that for a Gentile not to obey the command to be circumcised meant that he would not be justified (2:16).

Despite this wide divergence in outlook, however, the situation presupposed in Galatians is not one of a renegade Paul arguing against normative Judaism. The verbal precedent for Paul's position, especially in the effort to make Jewish ideas palatable to Gentiles, was in fact almost as good as that of his opponents. Thus, when Paul implies that those who belong to the eschatological age of the Spirit fulfill the law better than those who do not belong to it (5:14; cf. 3:10-13) and at the same time says circumcision for Gentiles is of no value (5:6, 6:15), he does not make a quantum leap out of Judaism into another religious system. He argues within the conceptual world of Hellenistic Judaism that the eschatological age predicted by the scriptures has arrived.

The Law and the Human Plight in Galatians

Most of what Paul says about the law in Galatians, however, is not an appeal to the Galatians to fulfill it by obeying its command to love but an attempt to remind them that since the eschatological age has arrived, there is no need to accept circumcision in order to be aquitted before God in the day of judgment. Paul argues further that to observe the Jewish customs of circumcision, food restriction, and Sabbath keeping in hope of attaining salvation is to step back into the age of the law's curse. "The crucial issue of the entire letter," as J. L. Martyn has said, is "What time is it?"[52] Paul's purpose is to persuade the Galatians that the change of the aeons makes any attempt to become righteous by accepting circumcision absurd. Thus, Paul begins the letter with a reference to our deliverance from "the present evil age" (1:4);[53] he later refers to the life which he "now" lives as a life lived "by faith in the Son of God who

---

[51] I have used the translation of A. Lukyn Williams, *The Dialogue with Trypho*, Translations of Christian Literature, Series I, Greek texts (London: Society for Promoting Christian Knowledge, 1930), p. 21.

[52] "Apocalyptic Antinomies in Paul's Epistle to the Galatians," *NTS* 31 (1985):418.

[53] The opening phrases of a Pauline letter often anticipate the *topoi* which Paul will cover in the body. It is significant for the understanding of Paul's argument in Galatians, therefore, that he begins the letter with a reference to the change of the ages. On the importance of the opening of Paul's letters to their remaining content see William G. Doty, *Letters in Primitive Christianity* (Philadelphia: Fortress, 1973), p. 32 and, with special reference to Galatians, George Kennedy, *New Testament Interpretation through Rhetorical Criticism* (Chapel Hill: University of North Carolina Press, 1984), pp. 147-48.

loved me and gave himself for me" (2:20); he speaks of the coming of the eschatological Spirit (3:1-5, 14; 4:29, 5:16-25); he reminds his readers that they no longer live "under law" or under the "elements of the world" but in the era in which faith has come (3:15-4:11); and, finally, recalling typical themes of Jewish eschatological expectation, he asserts that the Galatians are children of "the Jerusalem above" (5:26) and participants in a "new creation" (6:15). Paul claims that by succumbing to the advances of the "agitators" in their midst, the Galatians have effectively stepped back into the old aeon. "Now that you have come to know God," he says, "... how can you turn back again to the weak and beggarly elemental spirits, whose slaves you want to be once more?" (4:8-9). They have become subject once again to the plight of disobedience and, consequently, to the curse of the law.

Three passages in particular correlate the Galatians' desire to accept circumcision with the plight of Israel under the law in the old aeon: 2:15-16, 3:10-14, and 3:19-5:12. In the first Paul says that the reason even Jews have believed in Jesus Christ is that "by works of the law will no flesh be justified." In the second Paul claims that those who rely on the law for justification are under a curse because the law itself curses those who do not keep its precepts. And in the third passage Paul claims both that the purpose of the law was to enclose all things under sin and that those who receive circumcision will become enclosed under sin again.

In the following pages I hope to demonstrate by examining each of these passages, both in their immediate context in Galatians and within their wider religious context in the ancient Jewish literary world, that where Paul speaks negatively about the law he is viewing it from the standpoint of one of its purposes which is now obsolete: the purpose of "enclosing" humanity under sin. Thus, I hope to show that Paul does not propose the abrogation of the law in its every aspect in Galatians, but only the cancellation of its ability to enclose and curse the transgressor "under sin." If this idea can be sustained, then it will become clear that Paul's thinking remains within the common eschatological scheme identified in chapter two: humanity is in the plight of sin; but in the eschaton God will deliver it from that plight and will enable it to keep his law from a renewed heart. It will be evident, therefore, that Paul, like the Jewish writers covered in chapter two believed not only that the law could not be kept in the "present evil age," but that in the eschaton it *would* be kept with the aid of the Spirit.

A) Galatians 2:15-16

"Law" is mentioned for the first time in the epistle in this programmatic passage. Paul has just concluded his defense of his character (1:11-2:14) and in 2:15 broaches the subject which will occupy him until 5:13: to what extent does righteousness before God depend upon keeping the law?[54] Paul's answer is that faith in Jesus Christ, not works of the law, justify Jew and Gentile alike:

> We who are Jews by birth and not Gentile sinners, because we know that a man is not justified by works of the law but through faith in Jesus Christ, even we have believed in Christ Jesus in order that we might be justified by faith in Christ and not by works of the law, because "by works of the law" no flesh will be justified.

All are not agreed, however, on what Paul's answer, especially the phrase "works of the law," means. At least four suggestions have been proposed.

1. A number of scholars from Luther to the present have said Paul means that "believing" in Jesus Christ rather than "doing" the law in order to make a claim upon God is the only path to justification.[55]

2. Ernst Lohmeyer and Joseph B. Tyson have said that he means existence as a Jew is inauthentic existence because it is based on "doing."[56]

3. James D. G. Dunn has suggested that Paul is arguing against requiring Gentiles to accept the identity symbols of Judaism ("works of the law") since that would deny the unity of Christians in their common faith in Jesus Christ.[57]

4. A final idea, made famous by Adolf Schlatter and adopted by Ulrich Wilckens, is that Paul simply means doing the law is impossible and therefore the only hope of salvation is faith in Jesus Christ.[58] In the following paragraphs, I hope to show that, although the first three views have some value, the final one

---

[54] Betz, who regards Galatians as an "apologetic letter" and thus as an example of juridical rhetoric, claims that 2:15-21 is the "propositio" of Paul's argument; see *Galatians*, pp. 18-19 and p. 114. Kennedy, *Interpretation*, pp. 144-52 offers a convincing critique of Betz' idea that Galatians is judicial and proposes instead that it is an example of deliberative rhetoric: its purpose is not primarily to defend Paul and his gospel but to persuade the Galatians not to accept circumcision. On Kennedy's analysis, 2:15-21 is not the letter's propositio but provides a conclusion to Paul's defense of his ethos and a transition to "the specific issue which Paul must examine, the question of Law" (p. 148). Whether Galatians is juridical or deliberative, however, 2:15-16 introduces the most important subject in Paul's argument.

[55] Martin Luther, *Commentary on Galatians*, trans., Erasmus Middleton, ed. John Prince Fallowes (Grand Rapids: Kregel, 1979), pp. 64-69 (Anything done outside of faith is sin, but especially attempts to procure God's favor by works); Bultmann, *Theology*, 1:263-64 (Humanity cannot be justified by works of the law both because no one can keep the law and because keeping the law to assert one's self before God is already sin); Schlier, *Galater*, p. 56 (Both Paul and Jewish Christianity now know that righteousness is not achieved before God by works done in search of a reward but by faith alone); Bring, *Galatians*, pp. 89-90; Cranfield, "St. Paul and the Law," pp. 43-68; Daniel P. Fuller, "Paul and the 'Works of the Law'," *WTJ* 38 (1975-76):28-42 (Works of the law are done to make a claim upon God in violation of the true meaning of the law.)

[56] Ernst Lohmeyer, "Gesetz und Werk" in *Grundlagen paulinscher Theologie* (Tübingen: H. Kaupp, n.d.), pp. 33-74; Joseph B. Tyson, "'Works of the Law' in Galatians," *JBL* 92 (1973):423-31.

[57] Dunn, "Perspective" and "Works of the Law and the Curse of the Law (Galatians 3:10-14)," *NTS* 31 (1985):523-42.

[58] Adolf Schlatter, *Der Glaube im Neuen Testament*, 6th ed. (Stuttgart: Calwer Verlag, 1927), pp. 323-33; Wilckens, "Was heißt bei Paulus," and *Römer*, 1:131-37 and 142-46.

is the most probable. Paul's chief concern in these verses is to argue that, for those who participate in the old aeon, keeping the law is impossible.

The traditional Lutheran position (view 1), at least for this passage, is partially correct. Paul does assert the primacy of believing in Christ over doing the law as the means of attaining salvation. The chief problem with the Lutheran position is that its advocates frequently identify Paul's opponent in the passage as Judaism. Paul is not accusing Judaism, or even Jewish Christianity, of denying God's grace by thinking that "works of the law" will justify. Actually, he is doing the opposite. He is reminding certain Jewish-Christian missionaries of what every Jew should know—that no one can be justified before God by keeping the law. "We who are by nature Jews and not Gentile sinners," Paul says, "*because we know* that a person is not justified by works of the law but by faith in Jesus Christ, even we have believed in Christ Jesus...." Paul's point is simply that to deny justification to Gentiles unless they *do* something other than put their faith in God is to deny the commonly accepted Jewish teaching that God justifies the sinner because God is gracious, not because the sinner somehow deserves justification.[59] Thus, far from claiming that Judaism is a religion of works-righteousness, Paul says that the action of a particular group of Jewish-Christian missionaries does not agree with what Judaism believes.

Another problem with the Lutheran view is that it goes too far when it states that Paul opposes "making a claim upon God." Although it may be a legitimate inference from Paul's statement in 2:16 that he would oppose "making a claim upon God" by means of "works of the law," he does not say that explicitly.[60] The most natural way to take Paul's words, as we shall see below, is simply as a reminder to the Galatians and their "agitators" that no one can do the law, and therefore that no one can be justified by it.

The idea that Paul is denying the authenticity of existence as a Jew (view 2) seems implausible since Paul identifies himself with Judaism in 2:15. Moreover, it is incorrect to say that Paul opposed "doing" in itself at some philosophical level. He certainly opposes it as an entrance requirement; but Paul, no less than Judaism, considered "deeds" to be important on the day of judgment. Gal. 5:14 and 5:21 demonstrate how important they are to him even in Galatians, and Rom. 2:6-16, 14:10-12, and 1 Cor. 3:10-15 (cf. 6:9-10) show that "doing" held no small place in Paul's thinking generally.[61]

---

[59] Thomas R. Schreiner, "Paul and Perfect Obedience to the Law: An Evaluation of the View of E. P. Sanders," *WTJ* 47 (1985):254-55 takes a similar position, although he says that there is a sense in which first century Judaism generally believed in salvation by works since it taught that circumcision was necessary for salvation. It is debatable, however, whether most Jews did hold this view. The story of Izates' conversion to Judaism, cited above, shows that some Jews felt circumcision absolutely necessary for the salvation of a Gentile while some did not.

[60] He does say it in 1 Cor. 1:29, 31, 3:21, and 4:7.

[61] For the importance of "doing" in Paul see Adolf Schlatter, *Der Glaube*, pp. 323-418; Karl Paul Donfried, "Justification and Last Judgment in Paul," *ZNW* 67 (1976):90-110; Ulrich Wilckens, *Römer*, 1:144; and Klyne R. Snodgrass, "Justification by Grace—to the Doers: An Analysis of Romans 2 in the Theology of Paul," *NTS* 32 (1986):72-93.

James D. G. Dunn's idea that Paul means by "works of the law" Judaism's "nationalistic badges" of circumcision, Sabbath keeping, and dietary restrictions (view 3) certainly identifies Paul's chief concern in Galatians. Circumcision is especially prominent in the epistle (5:6, 5:11, 6:15), and Sabbath keeping (4:10) and food laws (2:11-15) also have a place. We have already seen in chapter one, however, that in Romans Paul's statements about "works of the law" cannot be limited to these three features of the law, and the same is true of Galatians. The curse of the law, according to 3:10a, for example, falls upon those who do not "remain in *all the things written* in the book of the law to do them." Yet it is the attempt to remain "in all the things written in the book of the law" which Paul defines in 3:10a as living "by works of the law." "Works of the law," therefore, on Paul's own definition, include more than circumcision, food laws, and Sabbath keeping.[62]

This becomes even clearer when we consider Paul's use of the word σάρξ both here and in the rest of the epistle. Paul gives the word special emphasis here, as commentators frequently note, by quoting from Psa. 142:2 (LXX) and changing the quotation to read "*no flesh* will be justified" instead of "*nothing living* will be justified." This makes it especially important to discover the meaning of the word "flesh" for Paul.[63] If we use Paul's handling of the term in the rest of the epistle as a clue to its meaning here, we find, significantly, that σάρξ has a decidedly ethical meaning in 4:17-26 where "fruits of the spirit" are contrasted with "works of the flesh." Unless there are strong indications to the contrary, therefore, the most reasonable conclusion would be that it carries this ethical nuance in 2:16, 3:1-5 and 4:21-31, and that in 2:16 Paul takes pains to change the wording of the Septuagint in order to say that humanity, because of its weakness and susceptibility to sin, cannot keep the law.

Dunn believes, however, that the word means *not only* human weakness and corruptibility but also carries the connotation "of a merely human relationship, of a heritage determined by physical descent as in the allegory of chapter 4 (4.23, 29)."[64] The point of the allegory in chapter 4, however, is not so much that

---

[62] Similarly, Hans Hübner, "Was heißt bei Paulus 'Werke des Gesetzes'?" in Erich Gräßer and Otto Merk, eds., *Glaube und Eschatologie: Festschrift für Georg Kümmel zum 80. Geburtstag* (Tübingen: J. C. B. Mohr [Paul Siebeck], 1985), pp. 130-31.

[63] There is some controversy over whether Paul actually quotes Psalm 142 (LXX) at all. Schlier, *Galaterbrief*, p. 58 claimed against F. Sieffert, *Der Brief an die Galater*, Dirtisch-exegetischer Kommentar über das Neuen Testament, vol. 7 (Göttingen: Vandenhoeck & Ruprecht, 1899) that the phrase must be a quotation since otherwise it would be superfluous. Mußner, *Galaterbrief*, pp. 174-75 has argued against Schlier that Paul's sentence, in its denial of righteousness *by works of the law*, differs so radically from the meaning of the phrase in the psalm, that it cannot be considered a citation. I hope to show below that Paul has the thought of the entire Psalm in mind in this section of his letter.

[64] Dunn, "Perspective," p. 116. Dunn's argument is close to that of Robert Jewett, *Paul's Anthropological Terms: A Study of Their Use in Conflict Settings*, AGJU, vol. 10 (Leiden: E. J. Brill, 1971), pp. 95-98. Jewett, like Dunn, claims that "...Paul substituted "flesh" for "living thing" because he wished to counter the Judaizers' claim that circumcised *flesh* was acceptable as righteous by God." This argument, however, neglects the sense of Paul's statement in 2:16. Paul

physical descent is irrelevant to justification before God, but that in the eschatological era both Jewish and Gentile believers are released from "bondage" to sin—from being "under law." Thus in 4:23 and 29 σάρξ still carries the ethical connotation of "humanity viewed from its inclination to sin." It is much more likely that Paul modified the neutral ζῶν of the LXX to the ethically "loaded" word σάρξ because he meant to say that when humanity is viewed from the perspective of its weakness and corruptibility, it is evident that no one can do the law.

A close look at the wider context of Psa. 142:2 (LXX) shows, moreover, that Paul is not simply proof-texting his statement but that he is echoing a part of scripture which moves, as his own thinking does, from plight to solution.[65] Psalm 142 (LXX) is a petition to God for deliverance from ὁ ἐχθρός (v. 3) and a statement of confidence that God will answer this request (vv. 11-12). The request and the confidence of the supplicant are made on the basis of God's δικαιοσύνη (vv. 1 and 11) and ἔλεος (v. 12). Most interesting for the interpretation of Galatians, however, is that the petition for deliverance from "the enemy" is accompanied by a statement of the supplicant's own lack of righteousness (v. 2), of his confidence that God will teach him to do his will, and of his hope that God's spirit (τὸ πνεῦμά σου) will guide (ὁδηγήσει) him ἐν τῇ εὐθείᾳ (v. 10). Thus, although the principle purpose of the psalm is to request deliverance from an enemy, an important subsidiary purpose is to request guidance

---

does not say "by works of the flesh shall no one be justified" but "by works of the law shall no flesh be justified." On the similarity between Paul and Qumran in their concept of "flesh" as humanity in its propensity toward weakness and sin, see A. Sand, *Der Begriff "Fleisch" in den paulinischen Hauptbriefen*, BU no. 2 (Regensburg: Pustet, 1967), p. 303.

[65] The usual view of Paul's use of scripture, especially in Galatians, is that he plucks quotations out of scripture willy-nilly to support his pre-determined conclusions; see Carl Clemen, "Die Auffassung des Alten Testaments bei Paulus," *Theologische Studien und Kritiken* 75 (1902):176-80; Rudolf Bultmann, "Prophecy and Fulfillment," pp. 72-75; Günther Klein, "Römer 4" and "Individualgeschichte," P. Vielhauer, "Paulus und das Alte Testament" in Günther Klein, ed., *Oikodome: Aufsätze zum Neuen Testament*, 2 vols., TBNT no. 65 (Munich: Chr. Kaiser Verlag, 1979), 2:196-228; Josef Blank, "Erwägungen zum Schriftverständnis des Paulus" in Johannes Friedrich, Wolfgang Pühlmann and Peter Stuhlmacher, eds., *Rechtfertigung, Festschrift für Ernst Käsemann zum 70. Geburtstag* (Tübingen: J. C. B. Mohr [Paul Siebeck], 1976), pp. 36-56; Nils Alstrup Dahl, "Promise and Fulfillment" in Studies in Paul, p. 124; and Hans Jürgen van der Minde, *Schrift und Tradition bei Paulus: Ihre Bedeutung und Funktion im Römerbrief*, Paderborner Theologische Studien vol. 3 (Munich: Verlag Ferdinand Schöningh, 1976). There has, however, been a recent resurgence of interest in viewing many of Paul's quotations from the Old Testament less as proof-texts and more as echoes of the themes contained in the sections of the Old Testament from which Paul quarried them. See C. H. Dodd, *According to the Scriptures: The Substructure of New Testament Theology* (London: Nisbet & Co., Ltd., 1952); Richard B. Hays, "Effects of Intertextual Echo in Romans: Preliminary Soundings," paper given at the 1985 meeting of the Society of Biblical Literature, Pauline Epistles Section; and James D. G. Dunn, "'Righteousness from the Law' and 'Righteousness from Faith': Paul's Interpretation of Scripture in Romans 10:1-10," in *Tradition and Interpretation in the New Testament: Essays in Honor of E. Earle Ellis*, ed. Gerald F. Hawthorne with Otto Betz (Grand Rapids: Eerdmans, 1987), pp. 216-28. I am grateful to Professor Dunn for making his article available to me prior to its publication and to Professor Hawthorne for making the Ellis *Festschrift* available to me shortly after its publication.

by God's Spirit and deliverance from unrighteousness. In both cases the supplicant states confidently that God, because of his righteousness (vv. 2 and 11) and
mercy (v. 12), will do (future) what the psalmist asks. Paul, in Gal. 2:16-21,
likewise says that since no one is righteous before God, the only hope for any-
one, whether Jew or Gentile, is trust ($\pi\iota\sigma\tau\iota\varsigma$) in God's deliverance, a deliverance
in which not only Christ (2:16) but the Spirit (3:1-5) play an important part.

The view articulated by Wilckens and Schlatter, therefore, emerges as the
correct one. In 2:16 Paul says simply that no one can do the law and claims—
correctly, as we saw in chapter two—that this is a common Jewish idea. Paul's
purpose in 2:15-16 is not to accuse Judaism of "legalism," nor to denigrate the
law as something oriented around "doing" rather than "believing," nor merely to
maintain that "nationalistic badges" are inappropriate within the newly constituted
people of God, but to say that with the coming of Christ the era of disobedience
to the law is drawing to a close, for those who believe in Christ have been deliv-
ered from "the present evil age" (1:4) in which the flesh and disobedience dominate existence.[66]

B) Galatians 3:10-14

Paul next addresses the antithesis between works of the law and justification
in 3:10-14. In 3:6-9 he has spoken positively of the connection between faith
and justification and this leads him in 3:10-14 to speak negatively once again of
the agitators' attempt to connect justification with works of the law.[67] Paul's
basic argument is relatively simple: he in some way associates the law with the
curse, claims that Christ has redeemed believers from the curse, and draws the dual
conclusion that 1) the Gentiles receive the blessing God promised Abraham

---

[66] Paul's references to the law in the difficult passage 2:17-21 have sometimes been used as
evidence that he argued from his pre-determined convictions about salvation in Christ to a
rejection of his Jewish heritage. Räisänen, for example, believes that 2:21 states Paul's
"aprioristic starting point" that "law and faith exclude each other as opposed principles," *Law*, p.
109, cf. "Galatians 2.16 and Paul's Break with Judaism," p. 548. Sanders's position in *Law*, pp.
27, 152, and 208 is not so sweeping, but frequently uses 2:21 as clear evidence that Paul's
thinking ran from solution to plight. Gal. 2:18-21, however, must be understood within the
larger context of 2:11-21. As Jan Lambrecht, "The Line of Thought in Gal. 2.14b-21," *NTS* 24
(1977-78):493, argues, the withdrawal of Peter and Barnabas from table-fellowship with Gentiles
in Antioch (2:11-14) is probably behind Paul's reference to "tearing down" and "building up" in
2:18. Paul refuses to build again the dividing wall between Jews and Gentiles which has been torn
down in Christ. To do this is to elevate the law above faith in Christ in importance, to claim that
righteousness is a matter of legal observance *rather than* faith in Christ, and thus to set aside God's
gracious and eschatological act in Christ (2:21, cf. 5:4). Paul knows that this way of viewing the
law is wrong because the law pronounces a curse upon all who disobey it (3:10-14, see below). He
has therefore died to the law as something which separates Jew from Gentile and God from
humankind. Now, in the eschatological age which began with Christ's death "for me" (cf. "for our
sins in" in 1:4), Paul "lives to God"—a life which presumably includes fulfilling the law in the
way described in 5:14.

[67] Betz, *Galatians*, p. 19.

through faith rather than through "works of the law" (3:14a) and 2) Christ's death
has effected the eschatological age of the Spirit (3:14b). The nuances of the
passage, however, have traditionally posed a number of problems.

There are, to my knowledge, five explanations of the passage, none of which
has gained a consensus.

1. The most popular interpretation is that Paul reminds his readers of the
curse which lies upon every Jew who trusts in the law for salvation and does not
perform all of its 613 commandments.[68]

2. A second view of the passage, often combined with the first, is that Paul
means doing the law is wrong. It is the way of faith (3:11) which leads to salvation not the way of doing and treasuring good works as a means of compelling
God to save.[69]

3. A third explanation is that Paul criticizes those who attempt to keep the
law legalistically. It is not keeping the law in itself which is cursed in Paul's
view but keeping it in such a way that one attempts to make a claim upon God
by doing so. Only through faith in Christ can the law be kept in the way it was
meant to be kept (Gal. 5:14, 6:2).[70]

4. E. P. Sanders believes that Paul's purpose in 3:6-14 is not to criticize the
way in which Jews keep the law or their purpose for doing so, but simply to deny
that convenantal nomism is a correct religious option and to assert that faith in
Christ is the way of salvation for everyone, Jew as well as Gentile. To this end
Paul "cites the only two passages in the Septuagint in which the *dik-* root is
connected with *pistis*" and "the only passage in the LXX in which *nomos* is connected with 'curse.'" He is simply interested in proof-texting his idea that
covenantal nomism is wrong and faith in Christ is right, not in providing rational
reasons why this is true such as "no one can do all the law."[71]

---

[68] Martin Noth, "'For all who rely on works of the law are under a curse'," in *The Laws of the
Pentateuch and Other Studies*, trans. D. R. Ap-Thomas (Edinburgh and London: Oliver & Boyd,
1966), pp. 108-117; John Bligh, *Galatians: A Discussion of St. Paul's Epistle* (London: St. Paul,
1969), pp. 256-60. Hübner, Law, p. 41. This view has come under attack from two directions.
First, critics point out that it takes as Paul's principle point a conclusion which he does not
actually state: that no one can possibly do all of the commandments (Fuller, "Works," p. 32;
Betz, *Galatians*, p. 145.) Second, some opponents of this view claim that if Paul used Deut. 27:26
to pronounce a curse on those who fail to do even one of the 613 commandments, his statement
was unintelligible to Jewish Christians, for Judaism never taught that perfect performance of the
law was necessary to salvation (Fuller, "Works," pp. 34-35; Sanders, *Law*, p. 20.)

[69] Schlier, *Galaterbrief*, pp. 89-91; Bultmann, *Theology*, 1:263; Mußner, *Galaterbrief*, pp. 225-
26; Bruce, *Galatians*, pp. 159-161 and "The Curse of the Law" in Morna D. Hooker and S. G.
Wilson, eds. *Paul and Paulinism: Essays in honour of C. K. Barrett* (London: SPCK, 1982), pp. 27-
36. One obvious objection to this view is that in 3:10 Paul speaks of a curse upon those who do
not do the law, not upon those who do it.

[70] Bring, *Galatians*, pp. 115-142; Fuller, "Works," pp. 32-33; Cranfield, "Paul," p. 48. Critics
of this view have pointed out that if Paul meant to criticize legalism rather than the law, he would
have expressed his meaning more explicitly. Paul never delineates two ways of keeping the law,
one acceptable and one misguided. See Räisänen's trenchant comments in *Law*, pp. 43-44.

[71] *Law*, p. 21. But as Hans Hübner has noted in *Law*, p. 153, Sanders's claim that Paul has quoted
the only passage in the Septuagint in which "law" is connected with "curse" does not prove that
Paul invested no significance in the idea that a curse lies on those who do not do *all* the law. Paul

5. A final explanation comes from James D. G. Dunn. He focuses on 3:14 and claims that Paul's point in the passage is to assert the unity of Jews and Gentiles in one people of God. He argues that the "curse of the law" is more specific than Sanders allows. It is not simply the curse on those who continue in "covenantal nomism," but the curse of the division which the law created between Jews and Gentiles. It is this curse from which Christ's crucifixion redeemed humanity.[72]

Common to all of these interpretations is the conviction that Paul's quotations from the Old Testament, especially in 3:10-12, have been molded so thoroughly to Paul's own argument that their original context is irrelevant to Paul's meaning. The last scholar to take the Old Testament context of Paul's quotations in this passage seriously was Martin Noth, and his essay was so widely criticized that most who have written on the passage since Noth have understandably avoided his methodology. Noth focused on Paul's quotation of Deut. 27:26 and claimed that Paul accurately preserved the meaning of the verse in its original context when he used it to support his dictum that "all who rely on works of the law are under a curse."[73] Deuteronomy 28, said Noth, expends far more effort detailing the curses which befall those who disobey the covenant than announcing the blessings which accompany obedience to it. This, he said, was an indication that the curses and the blessings in the chapter were qualitatively different from one another. Whereas obedience with its consequent blessing is *assumed* in Deuteronomy 28, as it was in other ancient near eastern treaties, said Noth, the curses are earned by disobedience. The curses, therefore, are a consequence of disobedience in a way that the blessings are not a consequence of obedience:

> On the basis of this law, which can and does demand fulfillment, there is no place for the idea of good, meritorious works and a reward which may be earned thereby; the blessing is not earned, but freely promised. On the basis of this law there is only one possibility for man of having his own independent activity: that is transgression, defection, followed by curse and judgment.[74]

---

may have been concerned to emphasize both the "all" and the "curse" as he seems to do in 5:3-4. Sanders also does not consider the possibility that the wider context of the passages which Paul quotes may be significant to his argument. He asserts against such a procedure that "what Paul says in his own words is the clue to what he took the proof-texts to mean," *Law*, p. 22. What Paul says in his own words, however, may demonstrate that his quotation is more than a prooftext, as we have seen above with respect to 2:16 and will again see below.

[72] "Works," pp. 532-539. Dunn's view of 3:10-14, like his exposition of "works of the law" in 2:16, however, does not adequately account for the "all" in 3:10. It is not simply the "nationalistic badges" of first century Judaism that Paul has in mind in this passage, but the whole law (cf. 5:3).

[73] Noth's essay "Die mit des Gesetzes Werken umgehen, die sind unter dem Fluch" originally appeared in *In piam memoriam Alexander von Bulmerincq*, Abhandlungen der Herder-Gesellschaft und des Herder-Instituts zu Riga, 6.3 (Riga: Ernst Plates, 1938), pp. 127-45.

[74] Ibid., p. 131.

Noth claimed moreover that from the perspective of the Deuteronomist, the curses had already occurred and are placed in Moses' mouth *ex eventu*. 2 Kings 22:11-20, he says, shows that at the time when Deuteronomy was found, it was generally thought not only that the curse was already operative but that there was no way to escape from it. This passage records how Josiah, after hearing his attendant read the newly found book of the law, tears his garments and directs the attendant to "inquire of the Lord" since "our fathers have not obeyed the words of this book, to do according to all that is written concerning us." The attendant goes to the prophetess Huldah who replies to his inquiries

> Tell the man who sent you to me, Thus says the Lord, Behold, I will bring upon this place and upon its inhabitants, all the words of the book which the king of Judah has read. Because they have forsaken me and have burned incense to other gods, that they might provoke me to anger with all the work of their hands, therefore my wrath will be kindled against this place, and it will not be quenched (2 Kings 22:15b-17).

Noth's conclusion is that in Gal. 3:12 Paul has accurately preserved the Deuteronomist's meaning. Because the only "possibility for man of having his own independent activity" according to the Deuteronomist is transgression of the covenant followed by the promised curses, and because transgression and curses have actually occurred with no hope for escape from them, Paul is correct in saying that "all who rely on works of the law are under a curse; for it is written, 'Cursed be every one who does not abide by all things written in the book of the law, and do them.'"[75]

Noth's essay has been justly criticized on a number of points. For example, his thesis that the Deuteronomist held out no hope for cursed Israel in his work simply cannot be sustained. Deuteronomy itself says that after the curses come upon Israel, her children will return to the Lord, obey him, and her fortunes will be restored (30:2-3), and it is now commonly recognized that the Deuteronomic history held out the possibility of repentance from sin and future blessing.[76]

Noth's mistakes, however, should not blind us to the usefulness of exploring the Old Testament context of Paul's quotation for insight into his meaning. One of Noth's points which is surely pertinent to an understanding of Gal. 3:10 was that from Paul's perspective, and indeed from the perspective of centuries of readers of Deuteronomy, the curses of Deuteronomy 28 had already occurred.[77] The context of Deut. 27:26, viewed from Paul's vantage, would have provided ample evidence that the covenant could not be kept and that those ὑπὸ νόμον (v. 23) were under a curse. Thus, after the verse which Paul quotes, a brief section of "blessings" appears and then a detailed "curse section" which is, in effect, a his-

---

[75] Ibid.
[76] Räisänen, *Law*, p. 125.
[77] Ibid., p. 126.

tory of Israel from the entrance into Canaan to the Babylonian exile (28:15-68). Everyone knew that the disobedience and subsequent curses spoken of here had indeed occurred.

If Paul is playing upon this common knowledge[78] in Gal. 3:10, then his meaning in the verse becomes intelligible. He is again reminding the Galatian "agitators" of something which they, of all people, should know: the attempt to keep the law—to do its "works"—in Israel's history had only led to failure and to the curse which the law pronounces on those who fail to do it.

Paul does not, however, leave the subject on this note. He goes on to state the solution to this plight, and does so by means of a contrast between two texts of scripture: Hab. 2:4 and Lev. 18:5. Three explanations of the contrast which Paul draws in these two verses have been offered.

1. The most popular explanation is that Paul uses Hab. 2:4 to refer to faith in Christ as the way of life and denies that the Torah's way of life, as expressed in Lev. 18:5, is valid.[79] Paul quotes Lev. 18:5 as a short-hand for the religious principle of Judaism—doing the Torah—and opposes faith in Christ to this principle. In the words of Hans Dieter Betz, he opposes the "way of life...structured by doing" with the way of life governed by "believing."[80]

2. Ragnar Bring has offered the less popular explanation that in v. 11 Paul enunciates the principle of justification by faith and in v. 12 claims that this principle is itself the fulfillment of the law which leads to life. The reason that the law does not rest on faith is that it is not the complete revelation: it was awaiting completion in Christ who "did" the law in the way it was meant to be done. Those who believe join Christ in this fulfillment of the law and therefore live.[81]

3. Finally, Daniel Fuller claims that Paul's seeming quotation of Lev. 18:5 is actually not a reference to scripture at all (it is introduced by no quotation formula) but a quotation of the slogan used by those who observed the law legalistically.[82]

The views of Bring and Fuller (views 2 and 3) are problematic for several reasons. Bring's idea that "doing" is used in Lev. 18:5 in a way roughly equivalent to "fulfilling" cannot be adequately supported either from the context of Lev. 18:5 or from Paul's use of the passage here. In Lev. 18:5 the point is clearly that Israel should distinguish itself from Egypt and Canaan by observing the "judgments" and "precepts" of Yahweh. Galatians 3:11 and 3:12 follow an identical pattern: Paul makes a statement and then follows it with scriptural support. Thus in 3:11 he states that no one is justified by the law and supports

---

[78] On this see possibility below.

[79] Betz, *Galatians*, pp. 147-48; Schlier, *Galaterbrief*, p. 91; Mußner, *Galaterbrief*, pp. 226-31.

[80] *Galatians*, p. 147.

[81] *Galatians*, pp. 128-32; see also Cranfield, *Romans*, 2:522, n. 2.

[82] "Paul and the 'Works of the Law'," *WTJ* 38 (1975-76): 28-42. For a lucid critique of attempts to deny that an antithesis between two texts from the Torah exists in Rom. 10:5-8 which is also pertinent here see Dunn, "'Righteousness from the Law'," pp. 217-219.

his statement with the quotation from Hab. 2:4, and similarly in 3:12 he states that the law is not from faith and supports this statement from Lev. 18:5. Furthermore, Christ is nowhere mentioned or implied as the one who fulfills the law. Bring's argument, therefore, is not persuasive. Fuller's idea that 3:12 does not actually quote Leviticus is likewise unpersuasive because in Rom. 10:5-6, where Paul again opposes life by doing the law to justification by faith, he explicitly says that Lev. 18:5 is a quotation from "Moses" (10:5).[83]

Some form of the explanation offered by Betz and the majority of commentators (view 1) must stand as the correct one: Paul opposes life by the law to life by faith and uses Lev. 18:5 as a description of life under the law. This does not mean, however, that Paul simply denies the validity of the law. He denies rather that life under the curse which the law pronounces on those who do not keep it is to be preferred to life lived by faith in God's eschatological deliverance. Once again, the Old Testament contexts of Paul's quotations help to clarify Paul's meaning.

In 3:11 Paul refers to Hab. 2:4, and if we examine the original context of this quotation we find that, like Paul, the prophet was concerned with God's eschatological deliverance. Habakkuk begins with a complaint about Israel's sinfulness, moves next to speak of how God will punish Israel's sinfulness at the hands of the Babylonians, then questions the Lord's justice in punishing Israel at the hands of a nation even more wicked than she, and finally God answers this second complaint by saying that one day he will deliver his people: the righteous person will live by trusting in God's deliverance.[84] If Paul is aware of this context when he quotes Hab. 2:4, then he is reminding his readers that they belong to the era of God's eschatological deliverance. The statement from Habakkuk that "the righteous shall live by faith," he says, gives the correct means for attaining righteousness. In Habakuk, of course, πίστις refers to the *faithfulness* of God, not to the *faith* of the righteous one. But the idea of trust in God's eschatological deliverance is present both in the original text and in Paul's quotation of it. Just as in Habakkuk the righteous person receives comfort from placing faith in God's faithfulness to rescue him or her from future destruction, so in Galatians righteousness comes to those who trust that in Jesus Christ God has initiated

---

[83] Bruce, *Galatians*, p. 163.

[84] I have assumed with most editors of the LXX that the B reading of Hab. 2:4 is correct: ὁ δὲ δίκαιος ἐκ πίστεώς μου ζήσεται. C witnesses and Heb. 10:37 have ὁ δὲ δίκαιος μου ἐκ πίστεως ζήσεται. 1QpHab 8:1-3 interprets the verse, in a way similar to Paul, to refer not to God's *faithfulness* but to *faith* in the Teacher of Righteousness; on this see Bruce, *Galatians*, pp. 161-62 and Betz, *Galatians*, p. 147, notes 82-83. I have also assumed that in Paul's quotation, as in the LXX, "by faith" modifies the verb "shall live" rather than the noun "the just one." Persuasive arguments for this way of reading the sentence appear in D. Moody Smith, Jr., "Ο ΔΕ ΔΙΚΑΙΟΣ ΕΚ ΠΙΣΤΕΩΣ ΖΗΣΕΤΑΙ" in Boyd L. Daniels and M. Jack Suggs, eds., *Studies in the History and Text of the New Testament in Honor of Kenneth Willis Clark*, Ph.D., SD, no. 29 (Salt Lake City Utah: University of Utah Press, 1967), pp. 13-35; H. C. C. Cavallin, "'The Righteous Shall Live by Faith': A Decisive Argument for the Traditional Interpretation," ST 32 (1978):33-43; and Richard B. Hays, *The Faith of Jesus Christ: An Investigation of the Narrative Substructure of Galatians 3:1-4:11.* SDLDS, no. 56 (Chico, Calif.: Scholars Press, 1983), pp. 150-51.

eschatological deliverance from sin (3:13-14). As Paul says elsewhere, "By the Spirit, through faith, we are waiting for the hope of righteousness" (5:5). The solution to the plight of continual disobedience to and curse by the law comes by means of God's eschatological provision in Christ. Those who have faith in that provision, says Paul, are made righteous.[85]

For a proper understanding of Paul's next statement, that the law is not ἐκ πίστεως it is crucial to grasp the eschatological nature of "faith" in the rest of chapter three. In 3:7-8 πίστις bears a specifically eschatological significance. There Paul uses it three times to say that those who believe are sons of Abraham because, like Abraham, they are reckoned righteous on the basis of faith. Abraham's faith was, in Paul's view, faith in a specific, future action of God, as 3:15-18 makes clear.[86] In a similar way the one who believes in Christ directs his or her faith toward specific, eschatological actions of God—the gift of the Spirit (3:14) and the death and resurrection of Jesus Christ (3:22).

It is this eschatologically oriented faith, partially fulfilled in the present, which Paul compares with life governed by the law in 3:12. Paul describes life governed by the law and lived outside of the eschatological era with a quotation from a section of Leviticus that reiterates the responsibility of Israel to shun the practices of the Gentiles, whether Egyptian or Canaanite:

> You shall not act according to the way of life of Egypt in which you lived. And you shall not act according to the way of life of Canaan, into which I will cause you to go, and you shall not live by their laws. You shall do my judgments and keep my statutes and live by them. I am the Lord your God. And you shall keep all my statutes and all my judgments and do them, which if a man does he will live by them. I am the Lord your God (Lev. 18:3-5, LXX).

The reason why this separation between Israel and the nations is necessary is given in 18:24-28: the land will eject any—whether Canaanite or Israelite—who pollute it. The gist of the passage is that the Canaanites polluted the land and are being expelled by the Israelites; if the Israelites pollute the land they too will be

---

[85] At least two recent studies of the term πίστις in the New Testament and in Paul have emphasized its eschatological character: Dieter Lührmann, *Glaube im frühen Christentum* (Gütersloh: Gütersloh Verlagshaus, 1976), cf. "Glaube" in *Reallexikon für Antike und Christentum: Sachwörterbuch zur Auseinandersetzung des Christentums mit der antiken Welt*, ed. Theodor Klauser, Carsten Colpe, Ernst Dassmann, Albrecht Dihle, Bernhard Kötting, Wolfgang Speyer, and Jan Hendrik Waszink, Lieferung 81 (Stuttgart: Anton Hiersemann, 1979):47-122 and Beker, *Paul*, pp. 267-69. Lührmann claims that in much of first century Judaism, including Paul, faith was that which made sense out of the contradiction between an unjust world and a just God, and thus was trust in the appearance of a future world where wrongs would be put right. See especially *Glaube im frühen Christentum*, p. 43.

[86] A. T. Hanson, "Abraham the Justified Sinner" in *Studies in Paul's Technique and Theology* (Grand Rapids: Eerdmans, 1974), pp. 52-66 argues that according to Paul Abraham did not simply believe in God but in God's future provision in Christ ("the seed.") Hanson's argument seems to take Paul's language too woodenly; but it does emphasize the legitimate point that, in Paul's view, Abraham believed God's promise to him would be fulfilled concretely and eschatologically.

expelled from it. This theme is repeated in 20:22-25 and reaches its culmination as the final and most terrible of the curses which will fall upon Israel for breaking the covenant in 26:14-43.

As we saw in chapter two, those who knew the history of Israel in Paul's day knew that the list of curses in Deuteronomy 28 had indeed fallen upon Israel for its disobedience, and that the curse of ejection from the land in Leviticus 18, 20, and 26 had come to pass. And many of them also looked forward to an eschato-logical day when God would intervene to set matters between himself and Israel right again. Jubilees, the Testaments of the Twelve Patriarchs, the Assumption of Moses, the Psalms of Solomon, and the Palestinian Targums of Deuteronomy and Leviticus, as we saw above, all attest to the importance within second temple Judaism of both Israel's historical plight and God's eschatological solution *as it is recounted in Deuteronomy and Leviticus.*

Thus when Paul claims that relying on works of the law leads to disobedi-ence and curse (3:10) and that the life lived by faith in God's eschatological deliverance is superior to life which persists in trying to do the law without the aid of the eschatological spirit (3:11-14) he was certainly going beyond his "former life in Judaism;" but he was doing so within the conceptual world of Judaism. Like the witnesses to ancient Judaism listed above, he proposes not the abrogation of the law but a time in which the curse of disobedience to the law is removed, sin is forgiven, and the eschatological spirit enables people to do God's will. For Paul the beginning of that eschatological period had come with the death of Christ (3:13), the extension of God's promises to the Gentiles (3:14a), and the advent of the Holy Spirit (3:14b).

In summary, Paul's argument in 3:10-14 runs, in a way familiar to the Judaism of his day, from plight to solution. The plight is one of being under the curse which accompanies disobedience to the law. The solution to this plight is experienced by those who have faith in God's eschatological provision. That provision is both the vicarious death of Jesus Christ, which removed the curse of the Law (3:13), and the gift of the Spirit, who enables believers to do the law (3:14, cf. 5:13-25).

C) Galatians 3:19-5:1

This section of Galatians, more than any other in the letter, and indeed in Paul's epistles, is regarded as proof positive of his radically unjewish approach to the law.[87] It is here that we find angels rather than God ordaining the law, the law

---

[87] C. E. B. Cranfield, *A Critical and Exegetical Commentary on Paul's Epistle to the Romans*, 2 vols., ICC, (Edinburgh: T & T Clark, 1975-79), 2:857 says that Gal. 3:15-25, probably more than any other passage in the pauline corpus, has lead interpreters to believe that Paul abrogated the Old Testament law.

assuming the role of "taskmaster,"[88] and the law apparently being indiscriminately interchanged with "the elemental spirits of the universe" to which the Gentile Galatian Christians were formerly "enslaved." The meaning of this section of the letter, however, is far from self-evident, and the history of its exegesis reveals more than a little confusion and contradiction. Much of the confusion stems from the compact way in which Paul expresses himself. Phrases which probably communicated paragraphs of information to the Galatians remain for us, nearly twenty centuries later, epigrammatic and obscure. Thus in order to understand this section, it is necessary to unpack it in considerable detail. When we do this with the conclusions from sections A) and B) above in mind, the object of Paul's wrath which emerges is not the law itself but the Galatians' desire to step back into the "present evil age" in which the curse of the law on those who disobey it is still operative. It is life "under law"—under the curse which the law pronounces on the transgressor—which Paul abrogates in this section, not the law as the codified will of God.

Interpreters of Galatians have traditionally pointed to four parts of this section as evidence that Paul overthrows the law and replaces it with the principle of faith. First is Paul's statement of the purpose of the law in 3:19-22 which associates it closely with sin and seems to distance it from God by assigning its origin to angels. Second, is Paul's polemic against life "under law" and his comparison of the law and to a "pedagogue" in 3:23-4:2 which, according to some, mean that the law was a temporary institution happily cast aside in the present eschatological age. Third is Paul's statement of the relationship between "elemental spirits of the universe" and the Law in 4:3-10. And finally, is the comparison between present Jerusalem, which is in bondage, and the Jerusalem above in 4:21-31. We will look at each of these passages below in an attempt to demonstrate that Paul's purpose in this section is not to abrogate the law as the expression of God's will, but to abrogate the law's curse.

1. The Purpose of the Law in Galatians 3:19-22

Paul, prompted by his statement that the law came after the promise to Abraham and therefore could not nullify that promise, asks in 3:19 "Why then the law?" His answer is made up of a series of enigmatic statements in vv. 19 and 20. Discussion of the passage has centered largely around 3:19 in which Paul says a) that the law was "added because of transgressions," b) that it was added "till the offspring should come," and c) that it was "ordained by angels through an intermediary." We shall look at each of these statements in turn.

---

[88] See Ernst Käsemann, *Commentary on Romans*, trans. by Geoffrey W. Bromiley (Grand Rapids: Eerdmans, 1980), p. 282.

There has been surprisingly little controversy in recent scholarship over how Paul's claim that τῶν παραβάσεων χάριν προστέθη should be understood. The meaning of the phrase depends upon whether χάριν is given a telic or a causal force.[89] If it is given a telic force, it is said, then the phrase states that the law was given for the purpose of transgressions—to produce them or to bring them to light; if a causal force, then it was given because of transgressions—to prevent them. Most commentators have chosen to give χάριν a telic force, and, although some of the older commentaries interpreted the law's purpose in this passage to be the revelation of sin as transgression (cf. Rom. 3:20), most modern interpreters agree that Paul here says that the law actually increases transgressions (cf. Rom. 5:20).[90]

It is, however, difficult to see why the meaning of χάριν should be so strictly delineated. It is especially puzzling why the word, if given a causal force, must mean "because of" in the sense of "preventing" transgressions. It could mean with at least equal probability that the law was given "because" sin was already present and needed to be reckoned and punished, in the sense of Rom. 5:13.[91]

This reading becomes more than merely possible when we consider Paul's restatement of the purpose of the law in 3:21-23. In v. 22 he says that the law was not able to "make alive" those who were under it but served only to "enclose all things under sin."[92] The word συγκλείω means "to enclose" "to besiege," "to shut up," or "to consign." It is used in Luke 5:6 to refer to enclosing a large number of fish in a net. In *1Clem* 55:4-5 it refers to the siege of Jerusalem by the Assyrians from which, according to the story, Judith rescued its citizens (Jdt. 7:20). Psa. 30:9 uses the word to describe being "shut up" in the hands of enemies and Psa. 77:50 says that God "consigned to death" the cattle of the Egyptians. The word then frequently refers to the action of surrounding and preventing the escape of something from its present location or state of existence.[93]

---

[89] Ernest De Witt Burton, *A Critical and Exegetical Commentary on the Epistle to the Galatians*, ICC, (Edinburgh: T & T Clark, 1921), p. 188 lays out the exegetical options clearly.

[90] Burton, *Galatians*, p. 188 views the purpose of the law as it appears in this passage to be the unmasking of sin as transgression. Mußner, *Galaterbrief*, pp. 245-46 comes close to this view. Betz, *Galatians*, p. 165; Bruce, *Galatians*, p. 176; and Räisänen, *Law*, p. 153 are representative of the majority of expositors who take 3:19b to mean that the law *increased* sin.

[91] See Walter Bauer, *A Greek-English Lexicon of the New Testament and Other Early Christian Literature*, trans. and adapted by William F. Arndt and F. Wilbur Gingrich, 2nd ed. revised and augmented by F. Wilbur Gingrich and Fredrick W. Danker (Chicago: University of Chicago Press, 1979), hereafter, BAGD, p. 877.

[92] Betz, *Galatians*, p. 175 and Mußner, *Galaterbrief*, p. 253 distinguish between "scripture" in 3:22 and "law." Two considerations, however, weigh against their views. First, Paul has just demonstrated that the part of scripture commonly called "the law" encloses all things under sin (Deut. 27:26 in Gal. 3:10 and Lev. 18:5 in Gal. 3:12). On this see Burton, *Galatians*, pp. 195-96 and Bruce, *Galatians*, p. 180. Second, in v. 22 Paul is still answering the question of v. 21, "Is the law then against the promises of God?" If he meant by "scripture" something different from "law" in v. 21, this part of his answer would be curiously irrelevant to the question.

[93] H. G. Liddell and Robert Scott, *A Greek-English Lexicon*, 9th ed., rev. H. S. Jones with R. McKenzie (Oxford: Clarendon Press, 1940), hereafter, LSJ, p. 1665.

Used to describe the action of the law upon "all things" it means that the law surrounded and prevented the escape of those under it from sin. It "besieged" them in their sinful state by defining and punishing sin. If we read 3:19b in this light the phrase "because of transgressions" probably means "because transgression needed to be defined, tabulated, and punished."[94]

The Exodus narrative of the giving of the law (Exodus 19-34) sheds further light on 3:19b. When Paul says that the law "was ordained through angels by the hands of a mediator" he is probably thinking of this story. In it Moses acts as mediator between God and "the people" (Exod. 20:20), and according to a tradition preserved in other parts of the New Testament (Acts 7:38, 53; Heb. 2:2) and in Josephus (*Ant.* 15.5.3), angels participated in giving the law to Israel.[95] These points of contact between Gal. 3:19 and Exodus 19-34 are generally recognized. Less frequently noticed, but also relevant to the understanding of this passage, is that according to Exodus 32-34, the law was "added" while the Israelites were engaged in the notorious sin of worshipping the golden calf, and thus it is easy to see how the law could be viewed as in some sense "enclosing" them in sin by defining it and making them more culpable for it. This at least seems to be the perspective of Pseudo-Philo's *Liber Antiquitatum Biblicarum.*[96] When the author reaches the point in his story where Israel begins worshipping the golden calf God tells Moses

> Hurry away from here, because the people have been corrupted and have turned aside from my ways that I commanded them. Are the promises that I promised to your fathers when I said to them, 'To your seed I will give the land in which you dwell'—are they at an end? For behold the people have not even entered the land yet *and now even have the Law with them,* and they have forsaken me (12:4).[97]

The author apparently views the apostasy of Israel as even worse because it was committed at the time the law was given. Paul's point, likewise, is that when

---

[94] The meaning of συνέκλεισεν in 3:22, and thus the meaning of 3:19b, is also clarified by Paul's combination of ἐφρουρούμεθα with συγκλειόμενοι in 3:23. Paul clearly uses the two words as synonyms and BAGD, p. 867, define φρουρέω as 1) "guard" and 2) "hold in custody, confine." BAGD illustrate the first meaning with 2 Cor. 11:32 where Paul uses it to refer to the guarding of the gates of Damascus by those who sought to kill him. Thus in 3:23 once again the law is seen as something which sealed those under it in sin, as in a besieged city, and prevented their escape.

[95] Deut. 33:2 and Psa. 67:18 seem to know this tradition as well. See Mußner, *Galaterbrief,* p. 247.

[96] According to D. J. Harrington, *OTP,* 2:299 Pseudo-Philo's *Biblical Antiquities* could not have been composed after A. D. 100 when the Palestinian text type on which it was apparently based was suppressed, and, because it seems to assume that sacrifices are still taking place within the temple (32:3), it was probably written before A. D. 70. "A date around the time of Jesus," he says, "seems most likely." Harrington also offers (p. 300) a convincing case that the *Biblical Antiquities* is of Palestinian origin. If he is correct on these two points, this document is an invaluable source for attitudes toward the law among Jews of Paul's day.

[97] Ibid., 2:320; cf. Exod. 32:7-8.

the law came it "besieged" those to whom it was given "under sin." In short, it made clear their plight.

It is in this light that Paul's statement that the law was added "till the offspring should come to whom the promise had been made" should be considered. Paul does not, as is frequently said, limit the law to a particular time and therefore deny the Jewish doctrine of the eternality of the law.[98] As we saw in section two above, he affirms the existence of the law in the eschatological age. The temporal limitation in this passage is placed not upon the law as a whole but upon the law's ability to "besiege" humanity "under sin." *This function* of the law began at Horeb and ended with the coming of Christ.[99]

Paul elaborates on this connection between the giving of the law and sin with the puzzling statement[100] that "the law was ordained by angels through an intermediary. Now an intermediary implies more than one; but God is one." Here the Exodus narrative of the giving of the law is clearly in view, and Paul says that the law was *in some sense* an intermediate step in God's purposes.[101] Whatever else 3:20 may mean, it is clear that mediation (3:20) implies disunity, disunity implies imperfection, and that the law is tied up with the state of disunity.[102] Thus the law, at least considered from one angle, cannot be the ultimate purpose of God. Considered from the angle of its purpose for enclosing and defining sin, it has ended. Paul's point, then, is that when the angels ordained and Moses mediated the law, it functioned to "enclose" Israel under sin; but now that the eschatological era has arrived in which God's unity has been made clear by the extension of his lordship over the Gentiles (4:28 cf. Isa. 45:23, 48:8-13),[103] the

---

[98] Mußner, *Galaterbrief*, pp. 246-47; Betz, *Galatians*, p. 168; cf. Räisänen, *Law*, pp. 56-57.

[99] Cranfield, *Romans*, 2:857-60, takes a similar position.

[100] It is frequently said that 3:20 has been explained in hundreds of different ways. See Bruce, *Galatians*, p. 178 and Cosgrove, "Spirit," pp. 161-62.

[101] Cosgrove's exhaustive effort, "Spirit," pp. 155-180, to show that the sin of the people rather than the imperfection of the law is in view here cannot be sustained. Cosgrove argues that the law had to be mediated by Moses and the angels at Sinai because the people were sinful and were therefore afraid to approach God. It was for this reason that they asked for a mediator. There is indeed evidence in the Exodus narrative that the people were afraid of the smoke, fire, trumpet, and thunder on the mountain; but it is extremely difficult to connect this fear with sin. Moreover, none of the evidence which Cosgrove adduces for the understanding of Exodus 32-34 in Paul's time explicitly connects the need for a mediator with the sin of the people.

[102] See the still valuable comments of Luther, *Galatians*, pp. 202-203. See also Cosgrove, "Spirit," pp. 161-80, Terrence Callan, "Pauline Midrash: The Exegetical Background of Gal 3:19b," *JBL* 99 (1980):549-67, and especially Westerholm, *Israel's Law*, pp. 176-79. Westerholm argues that Gal. 3:19 does not mean that the law came from angels rather than from God, although it does show that God gave the law in order to promote transgression. Westerholm goes on to argue, pp. 179-97, that the law in Paul's view had played out its purpose in salvation history and was no longer in any sense part of the new age of the Spirit. I find much of Westerholm's analysis persuasive; but would modify his argument to say that in 3:19, as elsewhere, Paul is concerned with only one purpose of the law, a purpose which has ended. Gal. 5:14 shows that Paul's statement in 3:19 does not exhaust the law's purpose. Viewed as an account of God's will, all but those portions which distinguish Jews from Gentiles continue to have validity in the age of the Spirit.

[103] Cosgrove, "Spirit," p. 177, called the Isaiah passages to my attention.

law, considered from the angle of its purpose at Horeb, is cancelled. Paul expresses himself boldly; but, as we shall see more clearly below, there is no reason to think that the purpose which he assigns the law in 3:19 exhausts the role of the law in salvation history.

In summary, the point of 3:19-22 is not that the law did not originate with God or was in every respect temporary, but that its purpose when "added" at Horeb was to define and curse transgression until the coming of the eschatological age. That age has already begun with the removal of the curse of the law (3:13) upon those who could not keep it, and with the the coming of the Spirit (3:14) who enables believers to keep the law (5:14). This, however, is not an "unjewish" idea. As we saw in chapter two, in parts of the Old Testament, the Dead Sea Scrolls, and the pseudepigraphical literature of the second temple period, sin was frequently defined in ancient Judaism as the breaking of the law. And as we saw in Pseudo-Philo above, the giving of the law served not only to define sin but to make it more culpable. Paul certainly goes further than this literature in the way in which he expresses the purpose of the law in Galatians; but he does not differ qualitatively from it on this point.

2. Life "under Law" and the Law as Pedagogue in Galatians 3:23-4:7

Paul's argument from 3:23 to 4:11 is an attempt to explain the meaning of the idea that the scripture συνέκλεισεν...τὰ πάντα ὑπὸ ἁμαρτίαν in terms of existence ὑπὸ νόμον. In 3:23 Paul claims that we were held guard and enclosed ὑπὸ νόμον. In 3:24-25 he says that the law was our pedagogue and then claims that after the coming of faith we are no longer "under a pedagogue." Paul apparently extends the pedagogue metaphor in 4:2 where he says that we were "under guardians and stewards," and changes it in 4:3 to enslavement "under the elements of the world." Finally, in 4:4-5, Jesus, who was born "under law" redeemed those "under law so that we might receive adoption as sons." If we can discover the meaning of the phrase "under law," therefore, we will enhance considerably our understanding of the purpose which Paul assigns to the law both in this passage and in Galatians generally.

Fortunately, it is relatively simple to determine the meaning of the phrase because in two places Paul clearly ties the words ὑπὸ νόμον to previous sections of his argument where he is more explicit. First, in 3:23, he says, "And (δέ) before faith came we were guarded by and enclosed under law (ὑπὸ νόμον ἐφρουρούμεθα συγκλειόμενοι) until faith was revealed." This is simply a restatement in different terms of what he has already said in 3:22: "But scripture enclosed (συνέκλεισεν) all things under sin (ὑπὸ ἁμαρτίαν) in order that the promise might be given to those who, by faith in Jesus Christ, believe." He connects 3:23 with 3:22 by δέ, repeats the important word συγκλείω and moves, as he did in 3:22, from plight to solution: in 3:22 scripture encloses all things under sin in order that the promise might be given to those who believe in

Jesus Christ, and in 3:23 we were guarded by and enclosed under law until faith was revealed. The significant change in Paul's restatement in 3:23 is that instead of describing the plight as being ὑπὸ ἁμαρτίαν, he describes it as being ὑπὸ νόμον: to be "under law," therefore, is to be "under sin."

Secondly, the concept of existence ὑπὸ νόμον is clarified by Paul's reference in 4:5 to the purpose of Christ's coming. He came "that those under law (ὑπὸ νόμον) should be redeemed (ἐξαγοράσῃ)." Aside from one reference in Eph. 5:16 and another in Col. 4:5, the only places that the verb ἐξαγοράζω appears in the New Testament are in Gal. 3:13 and here in Gal. 4:5. Thus it is likely that in Gal. 4:5 Paul is thinking in terms of the ideas expressed in Gal. 3:10-13, and especially the idea in 3:13 that "Christ redeemed (ἐξαγόρασεν) us from the curse of the law by becoming a curse for us...." If so, then Christ's work of redeeming those ὑπὸ νόμον is the work of redeeming those who are under the curse (ὑπὸ κατάραν, 3:10) of not being able to do the law. To be under law, therefore, is not only to be under sin, but to be under the curse which the law pronounces on sin.

It is this concept of a law which curses sin that informs Paul's comparison of the law to a pedagogue. The pedagogue in the ancient world was a slave entrusted most basically with the safe conduct of a child, or of several children, to and from school and other social institutions such as the theatre or gymnasium. He was usually given, in addition, the responsibility of teaching the children in his care necessary social skills and, on occasion, of helping them with their school work. He made certain that they conducted themselves with decorum at table, and kept them out of trouble when out of doors.[104] Frequently in the course of his duties he had to administer corporeal punishment or scoldings. Thus the *Ad Herennium*, in an illustration of the "simple style" of speaking "which is brought down to the most ordinary speech of every day" chooses to tell an anecdote about what is apparently an every-day occurrence: the severe scolding of a young man by his *pedagogus* (4.10.14).[105] Similarly, terracottas sometimes

---

[104] On the function of the pedagogue in Greek and Roman antiquity see E. Shuppe, "Paidagogos" in *Paulys Real-Encyclopädie der klassischen Altertumswissenschaft*, 24 vols., re-edited by Georg Wissowa (Stuttgart: J. B. Metzler, 1894-1963):18:2:24; Kenneth J. Freeman, *Schools of Hellas: An Essay on the Practice and Theory of Ancient Greek Education from 600 B.C. to 300 B.C.*, ed. M. J. Rendall (London: Macmillan and Co., Limited, 1922), pp. 65-69; A. S. Wilkins, *Roman Education* (Cambridge: Cambridge University Press, 1914), pp. 40-42; Paul Girard, *L'éducation athénienne au Ve et au IVe siècle avant J.-C.* (Paris: Librairie Hachette et Cie, 1889), pp. 114-26; Henri Irenee Marrou, *Histoire de l'éducation dans l'antiquité* (Paris: Éditions du Seuil, 1948), pp. 202-203; Fredrick A. G. Beck, *Greek Education, 450-350 B. C.* (London: Methuen & Co Ltd, 1964), pp. 105-109; Stanley F. Bonner, *Education in Ancient Rome from the Elder Cato to the Younger Pliny* (Berkeley: University of California Press, 1977), pp. 40-46; and David J. Lull, "'The Law Was Our Pedagogue': A Study of Galatians 3:19-25," *JBL* 105 (1986):481-98.

[105] *Cicero in Twenty Eight Volumes*, vol. 1, *(Cicero), Ad C. Herennium, De Ratione Dicendi (Rhetorica Ad Herennium)*, trans. Harry Caplan (Cambridge: Harvard University Press, 1954), pp. 260-63. See also Bonner, p. 340, n. 77.

show him tweaking the ear of his charge,[106] and vases depict him sitting behind the boy, eyes fixed and alert, ready to correct the first sign of misbehavior.[107] Comedy frequently viewed him as an over-restrictive figure whose watchful eye many young men longed to escape.[108] Thus his role was primarily one of correcting and guiding the child so that, in the words of the *Ad Herennium*, he or she might be safely brought to adulthood.[109] The point of comparison between the pedagogue and the law, therefore, is that they are both authorities who correct those under their care. Just as the pedagogue must constantly correct his wards in order to keep them out of trouble and in order to teach them necessary social skills, so the law points out and punishes sin.[110]

Thus Paul explains to the Galatians that, far from being able to make them inheritors of the promise and righteous, the law can only point out and punish their mistakes. To submit to it is to step backward from maturity to childhood, from the ability to live according to God's will to the period of constant mistakes and punishment. Again, it is not the law in its every aspect which is spoken of here, but the law as something which points out and punishes sin.

In 3:23-4:7, then, Paul amplifies what he has said about the purpose of the law in 3:19-22. The law came to define and punish sin. Viewed from this angle it is no more needed than the emperor needs his boyhood pedagogue to rap his knuckles.[111]

---

[106] Bonner, pp. 38-39. The photographs of terracottas on pp. 24-26 illustrate the close watch which the παιδαγωγός kept on the children in his care. In these pictures the child leans on the pedagogue, is carried by him, or is under his arm.

[107] See the illustrations in Freeman, *Schools of Hellas*, plates Ia and Ib, and Girard, *L'éducation Athenienne*, p. 111, fig. 8.

[108] See, for example, Plautus, *Bacchides*, 422-23 and Terence, *Andria*, 1.24. See also Marrou, *Histoire*, p. 202.

[109] 4.52.65. See also the informative discussion in Aristotle's *Politics*, 1336a and in Plutarch's *On the Education of Children*, 6-7, 16.

[110] The ἐπίτροποι and the οἰκονόμοι of 4:2 functioned in a way similar to the παιδαγωγός. The ἐπίτροπος was often the guardian of a king who was too young to govern his country. 2 Macc. 11:1, 13:2, and 14:2 provide readily accessible examples of his function. In these references Lysias acts as "guardian" for Antiochus V Eupator after the death of his father, Antiochus IV Epiphanes. See also Diodorus Siculus 11.79.6 where the Lacedaemonian Nicomedes is described as the ἐπίτροπος of Pleistonax the King during the King's minority. The οἰκονόμος was likewise an administrator, often a treasurer (see Rom. 16:23; Luke 12:42, 16:1, 3, 8), who looked after a large estate. Both of these figures, then, would be entrusted with making sure that the rightful heirs of the estate did not mismanage it during childhood.

[111] Again, Westerholm's comments on this passage in *Israel's Law*, pp. 195-96 are a model of clarity and good sense. I would only modify them by saying that it is not the law in its every function which Paul describes as temporal, but the law's role in pronouncing a curse upon the disobedient.

3. Galatians 4:3-11 and the "Elements of the World"

Paul continues this theme in 4:3-11 by comparing the Galatians' attempt to live under the law to life under the "the elements of the world" (τὰ στοιχεῖα τοῦ κόσμου, 4:3, cf. 4:9). This phrase has been the subject of extensive investigation, and scholarship has come to a wide variety of conclusions about its meaning. Not infrequently it has been taken to mean that Paul categorizes Jewish religion with Gentile religion as equally wrong-headed. Hans Lietzmann, for example, interprets both "the elements of the world" in 4:3 and "the weak and beggarly elements" in 4:9 as references to what Jewish and pagan religion had in common: observances of special days and festivals. The most important aspects of Jewish religious observance, he says, are the keeping of the Sabbath, the new moon festival, passover, new year, and other similar occasions whose dates were calculated by the movement of the heavenly bodies. Since the term στοιχεῖα was used to refer to these astral entities, Paul in 4:3 and 4:9 is claiming that there is no difference in this regard between Gentile and Jewish religion.[112] Gerhard Delling, in contrast to Lietzmann, says that the observance to which Paul refers in 4:3 and 4:8 can "by no means" be limited "to the cultic provisions alone" because the broad context of the phrase has the principle of the law in mind rather than particular aspects of the law. The phrase rather draws attention to the fact that under both Judaism and paganism people live in bondage; under both people are subject to "that whereon the existence of this world rests, that which constitutes man's being."[113] Mußner prefers to appeal to passages in 1 Enoch and in the Dead Sea Scrolls as evidence that in some sectors of Judaism there was a connection between Jewish calendrical observance and the stars. He then claims that in 4:3 and 4:8 Paul is connecting pagan worship of the "world elements" (which sometimes involved astral worship and a concern with calendrical observance) with observance of the Jewish calendar (4:10).[114] Bruce believes the "elements of the world" refer to "legalism as a principle of life;"[115] George Howard sees the phrase as a reference to "local deities" whether Jewish or Gentile;[116] and Betz, in a way similar to Lietzmann, claims that Paul's opponents viewed the ritual observances of Judaism as protection against the evil spiritual forces in the universe.[117]

Out of the wealth of exegetical study which lies behind these widely divergent opinions, however, one unshakeable conclusion emerges: "a man of NT days would take στοιχεῖα to refer to the 'basic materials' of which everything in

---

[112] *An Die Galater*, 3d ed., *HNT*, no. 10 (Tübingen: J. C. B. Mohr [Paul Siebeck], 1932), p. 26.
[113] "στοιχεῖα," in *TDNT*, 7:670-87.
[114] *Galaterbrief*, pp. 293-304.
[115] *Galatians*, p. 203.
[116] *Crisis*, p. 78.
[117] Betz, *Galatians*, pp. 205 and 217.

the cosmos, including man, is composed."[118] The word στοιχεῖα frequently appears in Greek and Hellenistic literature with reference to the basic material constituents which make up the world. Aristotle, in the course of an argument which seeks to answer the question of whether a single science can properly account for all substances, refers to the view of Empedocles

> that fire and water and the other things associated with them are the elements (στοιχεῖα) which are present in things and of which things are composed... (*Metaph.*, 3.2.2).[119]

Similarly, Philo, in an argument against those who think the world will be destroyed in a great conflagration and then reborn asks rhetorically

> As there are four elements (στοιχείων), earth, water, air and fire, of which the world is composed, why out of all these do they pick out fire and assert that it will be resolved into that alone? (*De Aeternitate Mundi*, 107)[120]

A few sentences later he refers to the physical composition of the world using the precise phrase which Paul uses in Galatians:

> For just as the annual seasons circle round and round, each making room for its successor as the years ceaselessly revolve, so, too, the elements of the world (τὰ στοιχεῖα τοῦ κόσμου) in their mutual interchanges seem to die, yet, strangest of contradictions, are made immortal as they ever run their race backwards and forwards and continually pass along the same road up and down (108).[121]

Stoic philosophy frequently had recourse in arguments against fearing death to the idea that humans are composed, like the rest of the world, of four elements. Thus Epictetus tells his pupils that he fears no calamity, even death, because death is simply a return to the physical elements of which both the body and the world are composed:

> Another, whose care it is, supplies food; Another supplies raiment; Another has given senses; Another preconceptions. Now whenever He does not provide the necessities for existence, He sounds the recall; He has thrown open the door and says to you, "Go." Where? To nothing you need fear, but back to that from which

---

[118] Delling, p. 684. I have relied upon the references in Delling's exhaustive article and in LSJ to guide my research in the following paragraphs.

[119] *Aristotle, The Metaphysics, Books I-IX*, trans. Hugh Tredennick, Loeb Classical Library (London: William Heinemann Ltd, 1933), pp. 116-117.

[120] Colson translation, p. 261.

[121] Ibid.

you came, to what is friendly and akin to you, to the physical elements (εἰς τὰ στοιχεῖα, 3.13.14).[122]

Similarly Marcus Aurelius says that

Death is like birth, a mystery of Nature; a coming together out of identical elements and a dissolution into the same (σύγκρισις ἐκ τῶν αὐτῶν στοιχείων, εἰς ταὐτὰ [λύσις]). Looked at generally this is not a thing of which man should be ashamed, for it is contrary neither to what is conformable to a reasonable creature nor to the principle of his constitution (4.5).[123]

There can be little doubt, then, that the average Greek reader of Paul's day would have understood the phrase "elements of the world" as a reference simply to the physical world.

In light of this information, we should be wary of reading too much into the phrase. The attested meaning of στοιχεῖα as the stuff of which the world is composed suggests that the most probable meaning of its occurrence in Galatians is simply "the world." Since the στοιχεῖα were sometimes used metaphorically to refer to "the basics" of education, Paul's educational metaphors in 3:24-4:2 may have suggested this round about way of stating his meaning.[124]

This correlation of τὰ στοιχεῖα τοῦ κόσμου with the simple word "world" provides an important indication of the phrase's meaning, for out of 36 occurrences of κόσμος in the undisputed pauline letters, 22 refer to the world in its state of rebellion against God. The "world" to Paul is God's fallen creation (Rom. 5:12-13) whose "wisdom" did not know God (1 Cor. 1:21) and whose standards of power and nobility God passed by in order to accomplish his saving purposes through other means (1 Cor. 1:26-28). It is the arena where those who preach the gospel appear as "spectacles" (1 Cor. 4:9). It is nothing but "refuse" (1 Cor. 4:13) against which the saints will eventually pronounce judgment (1Cor. 6:2), and to which God will eventually deliver a sentence of condemnation (1 Cor. 11:32). When Paul speaks of bondage to "the elements of the world" in Gal. 4:3, therefore, he is probably using a common phrase for the stuff which makes up the material world to say that the believer, whether Jewish or Gentile, at one time was under bondage to the world in its state of rebellion against God. To be sub-

---

[122] *Epictetus, The Discourses as Reported by Arrian, the Manual, and Fragments*, 2 vols., trans, W. A. Oldfather, Loeb Classical Library (London: William Heinemann Ltd, 1928), pp. 92-93.

[123] *The Meditations of the Emperor Marcus Antoninus*, 2 vols., ed. and trans. A. S. L. Farquharson (Oxford: Clarendon Press, 1944), pp. 54-55.

[124] See Heb. 5:12 and the comment of Heliodorus in *Grammatici Graeci* 1.3 (recorded in Delling, p. 683), who says that the letters of the alphabet are called στοιχεῖα by some people ἐκ μεταφορᾶς τῶν κοσμικῶν στοιχείων.

ject to the "elements" is to be subject to sin. It is to be "under law" (v. 5) and therefore under the curse which the law pronounces on those who transgress.[125]

Thus Paul reminds the Galatians that they are no longer babes who need to have their ears tweaked by an ever-present pedagogue, but are mature inheritors who possess the Spirit. In short, they are not "under bondage" to sin. Viewed from this angle, the purpose of the law was to point out and curse sin. Once again, his desire is not to exclude the law at all costs on the basis of his pre-determined solution of faith in Jesus Christ, but simply to state that the "solution" part of a well known eschatological pattern has arrived: bondage to sin is over and the era of keeping God's will by means of the Spirit has come.

4. Freedom from Bondage to the Plight of the Present Jerusalem in 4:21-5:1

After a personal appeal in 4:11-20, Paul picks up the idea of being ὑπὸ νόμον (4:21) once again, and expands upon it with the help of what he calls an "allegory" (4:21- 31):[126]

> Tell me, you who want to be under law, do you not hear the law? For it is written that Abraham had two sons, one by the enslaved woman and one by the free woman. But the one by the enslaved woman was born according to the flesh, and the one by the free woman was born through a promise.
> These matters are an allegory, for these women are two covenants, one from Mount Sinai—Hagar—bearing children for slavery. Hagar is Mount Sinai in Arabia, and she, with her children, corresponds to the present Jerusalem which is enslaved. But the Jerusalem above, which is our mother, is free. For it is written, "Rejoice O Barren One who does not bear. Break forth and cry aloud O One who has no pains of labor; because the children of the barren one are more than those of the one who has a husband."
> And you, brothers, are children of promise like Isaac. But just as then the one born according to the flesh persecuted the one born according to the Spirit, so it is now. Scripture says, however, "Cast out the enslaved woman and her son; for the son of the enslaved woman shall not become an heir with the son" of the free woman. Therefore, brothers, we are not children of the enslaved woman but of the free woman.

---

[125] Significantly, this corresponds well with the use of the phrase "the elements of the the world" in Col. 2:8 where it stands parallel to "philosophy," "empty deceit," and "human traditions." Eduard Schweizer, "Slaves of the Elements and Worshippers of Angels: Gal 4:3, 9 and Col 2:8, 18, 20," *JBL* 107 (1988): 455-68 argues similarly that the phrase "elements of the world" in Galatians and Colossians refers not to spiritual beings but to the power of the cosmos.

[126] Bruce and Betz represent the two positions which scholars have tended to take on the significance of the word "allegory" in 4:24. Bruce, *Galatians*, p. 217, claims that Paul "is not thinking of allegory in the Philonic sense...; he has in mind that form of allegory which is commonly called typology: a narrative from Old Testament history is interpreted in terms of the new covenant.... Typology presupposes that salvation-history displays a recurring pattern of divine action...." Betz, *Galatians*, p. 243, however, claims that the elements in Paul's "allegory" have no historical importance and are the servants of Paul's own, pre-determined idea.

The basic point of the allegory is that those who rely upon the law for justification are the children of a slave and are therefore in slavery (4:22, 23, 24, 25, 31),
and most commentators explain the passage as a comparison between slavery to
the law on one hand and the end of the law on the other.[127] Betz's comment on v.
25 is representative. He says that Paul's claim that Hagar, Mt. Sinai, and the
present Jerusalem are parallel and that the present Jerusalem is "in slavery with
her children"

> is one of Paul's sharpest attacks upon the Jews. He uses the self-understanding of
> the Jews in order to reject it. This self-understanding is well expressed by R.
> Jehoshua ben Levi (c. A. D. 280) in his interpretation of Exod 32:16 ("and the
> tables were the work of God, and the writing of God graven on the tables"): "read
> not *haruth* (graven) but *heruth* (freedom), for none is your freeman but he who is
> occupied in the study of Torah."[128]

Two pieces of evidence, however, militate against this understanding of
Paul's "allegory" and soften his statement in v. 25. First, Paul frequently speaks
of slavery to sin (Rom. 6:6, 6:19, 6:17, 6:20, 8:21) but only once, in Rom.
7:25, does he speak of slavery to the law, and there the reference is positive in
nature: Paul "serves" ($\delta o u \lambda \epsilon \acute{u} \omega$) the law of God in his mind but the law of sin in
his flesh. Although such evidence is not definitive for Galatians, it at least
weighs in favor of taking Paul's comment about Mount Sinai bearing children for
slavery (4:24, 25) as a reference to slavery to the sin under which the law has
besieged humanity rather than as a reference to slavery to the law itself. Here
again, it is not the law in its every aspect which Paul claims is annulled, but the
law in its ability to perpetuate slavery to sin. Secondly, Paul is not the only first
century Jew who correlated the present Jerusalem with a mother and who, in the
same context, both lamented the sinfulness of the city and hoped for its
eschatological renewal. These same elements are found in Psalms of Solomon 1
and in 4 Ezra 9-10. In Psalms of Solomon 1 the psalmist borrows the
comparison between the once prosperous Jerusalem and a mother with many
children from Isa. 54:1, just as Paul does in Gal. 4:27, and describes how these
children fell into the plight of disobedience to God:

> I cried out to the Lord when I was severely troubled, to God when sinners set upon
> [me]. Suddenly, the clamor of war was heard before me; "He will hear me, for I am
> full of righteousness." I considered in my heart that I was full of righteousness,
> *for I had prospered and had many children*. Their wealth was extended to the whole
> earth, and their glory to the end of the earth. They exalted themselves to the
> stars, they said they would never fall. They were arrogant in their possessions,

---

[127] Luther, *Galatians*, pp. 281-82; Mußner; *Galaterbrief*, pp. 324-25; Betz, *Galatians*, pp. 242,
246; Bruce, *Galatians*, pp. 220, 226.
[128] *Galatians*, p. 246.

and they did not acknowledge [God]. Their sins were in secret, and even I did not know. Their lawless actions surpassed the gentiles before them.[129]

It is clear in other psalms that only God's eschatological intervention will remedy this plight of sin in which Jerusalem, the mother of Israel, lies (17, 18:5-9).

The similarity between Gal. 4:21-31 and 4 Ezra 9:38-10:59 is even more striking. In this passage the seer meets a woman who is mourning the loss of her only son, a son born to her as a gift from God after many years of barrenness (cf. Sarah). The seer chides the woman because her loss is insignificant in comparison with the destruction of Jerusalem:

> You most foolish of women, do you not see our mourning, and what has happened to us? For Zion, *the mother of us all*, is in deep grief and great humiliation. It is most appropriate to mourn now, because we are all mourning, and to be sorrowful, because we are all sorrowing; you are sorrowing for one son, but we, the whole world, *for our mother* (10:6-9).[130]

Some further discussion follows, and then, suddenly

> While I was talking to her, behold, her face...shone exceedingly, and her countenance flashed like lightning, so that I was too frightened to approach her, and my heart was terrified. While I was wondering what this meant, behold, she suddenly uttered a loud and fearful cry, so that the earth shook at the sound. And I looked, and behold, the woman was no longer visible to me, but there was an established city, and a place of huge foundations showed itself (10:25-27).[131]

The author of 4 Ezra, like Paul in Gal. 4:21-31, moves from an allusion to Sarah's barrenness to a comparison between the desolation of a sinful Jerusalem and a mother's loss of her children to God's eschatological solution in the establishment of a new, heavenly Jerusalem.

Thus Gal. 4:21-31 does not deny Jewish self-understanding but affirms the well known Jewish idea that Israel, identified by synecdoche with Jerusalem, has broken God's law and finds its only hope in God's eschatological renewal. Paul certainly goes further than Judaism, especially his Jewish Christian opponents, in speaking more explicitly than they of the present Jerusalem's bondage to sin and existence under the curse of the law, but the fundamental pattern of moving from plight to solution is there. Israel's plight is sinful disobedience to the law; the solution to the plight comes when God cleanses his people of sin and they keep his law.

---

[129] *OTP*, 2:651, my emphasis.
[130] Ibid., 1:546, my emphasis.
[131] Ibid., 1:547.

Gal. 2:15-16, 3:10-14, and 3:19-5:1, therefore, do not propose the cancellation of the law, the *sine qua non* of Judaism. They are instead statements about the law motivated from the conviction that the time of God's redemption of Israel, and of all humanity, from sin has arrived. These passages serve as reminders to the Galatians of the time in which they should be living as those who believe in Jesus Christ, and thus they serve as arguments to persuade the Galatians not to submit again to the yoke of bondage to sin (5:1) by undertaking circumcision, food laws, and Sabbath keeping as if they had some value for justification before God (5:3).

Summary and Conclusion

My goal in this chapter has been to show that Paul's concept of the law in Galatians corresponds in significant ways to the role of the law in many first century expressions of Jewish eschatology. Like those Jewish texts, Paul presupposes that the "present evil age" is a period of disobedience to the law and of laboring under the curse of the law, but that in the eschatological age the law will be kept with the aid of the Spirit. In order to show this it was necessary to explain 1) that Paul, at least in some sense, preserved the idea that the law would be an important part of the eschatological age; 2) that Paul could remain within the plight-solution pattern and deny the necessity of circumcision, food laws, and Sabbath keeping in the new age; and 3) that Paul's statements about the law in Gal. 2:15-5:1 were not intended as an abrogation of the law in every respect.

In section one, therefore, I sought to demonstrate that Paul's reference to the necessity of fulfilling the law through the "love command" could only be explained as a positive reference to the fulfillment of the law by means of the Spirit in the eschatological age. In section two, I tried to show that although Paul's attitude toward the commands regarding circumcision, dietary restrictions, and Sabbath keeping has no exact parallel in the apologetic and ethical literature of Hellenistic Judaism, there is a large measure of agreement between Paul and this literature on the superiority of the ethical commands of the law to the law's so-called ceremonial requirements. Section three attempted to show that where Paul speaks negatively of the law he is thinking of one of the law's purposes: to "enclose" people under sin and to execute upon them the punishment required for disobedience.

If these ideas are correct, then the argument of Galatians flows not so much from a pre-determined notion that Christ is the savior of the world to the assertion that the world must need the salvation which Christ offers, but is based on the largely Jewish categories of universal sin and eschatological hope for freedom from sin. In Galatians at least Paul is fundamentally a Hellenistic Jew who believes that the long awaited period of freedom from sin has broken into "the present evil age."

CHAPTER FOUR

FROM PLIGHT TO SOLUTION
IN ROMANS

Introduction

Paul's attitude toward the law in Romans is frequently considered less harsh than that in Galatians. It is said that Paul's thinking has matured,[1] is presented in a more systematic way,[2] or has become more moderate under the disapproval of his Jewish-Christian peers.[3] Nonetheless, Paul's thinking about the law in Romans continues to be considered something almost entirely new, something constructed not on Jewish presuppositions but on the basis of Paul's christology. Either Paul's thinking about the law and sin is so profound[4] or, in the view of a few, it is so inconsistent and banal,[5] that it could only have been developed on the basis of his pre-determined notion that Jesus was messiah and the way to salvation. Thus, it is only because Paul thinks backwards, from his conviction that Christ brings salvation to the idea that the law can no longer save, that he can make such statements as Jews no more than Gentiles can keep the law (1:18-3:20), the law effects wrath (4:15), multiplies sin (5:20), is used by sin (7:5, 1-13), cannot be obeyed (3:1-20; 7:14-25), and is the wrong way to righteousness (9:30-10:8).

In this chapter I hope to show that, with a few exceptions, Paul's comments about the law in Romans are not motivated solely by his christology but are built upon the plight-solution framework which we examined in chapter two and found

---

[1] Drane, *Paul*, pp. 135-36. Drane believes that in Romans Paul achieves a sensible synthesis of his teaching in Galatians and 1 Corinthians, a synthesis which brings him close to the ethical teaching of Jesus. See also C. H. Dodd, "The Mind of Paul: I" and "The Mind of Paul: II," pp. 80-81 and 122-24.

[2] Günther Bornkamm, "The Letter to the Romans as Paul's Last Will and Testament," in Karl P. Donfried, ed., *The Romans Debate* (Minneapolis, Minnesota: Augsburg Publishing House, 1977), pp. 25, 29; Anders Nygren, *Commentary on Romans*, trans. Carl C. Rasmussen (Philadelphia: Muhlenberg Press, 1949), p. 4.

[3] Hübner, *Law*, pp. 60-65.

[4] See for example Rudolf Bultmann, "Paul," in *Existence and Faith*, pp. 113-16; Käsemann, *Romans*, p. 196; Werner Georg Kümmel, "Römer 7 und das Bekehrung des Paulus" in *Römer 7 und das Bild des Menschen im Neuen Testament*, 2d ed. (Munich: Chr. Kaiser Verlag, 1974), p. 117; C.K. Barrett, *The Epistle to the Romans*, HNTC (New York: Harper & Row,1957), pp. 142, 144, 147-53; Hübner, *Law*, pp. 113-124; Cranfield, *Romans*, 1:341, and Weder, "Gesetz und Sünde."

[5] Sanders, *Law*, passim, but for his position *in nuce* see pp. 144-148; Räisänen, *Law*, again passim, but see especially pp. 199-202 and 264-69.

in Galatians in chapter three. My method will be similar to that followed in
chapter three. I will attempt to show first that Paul reserves an important place
for the law within the eschatological situation which the gospel has introduced,
and second that his negative statements about the law are largely claims that outside of Christ the law is impossible to obey and brings upon the sinner the curse
of disobedience.

Paul's Positive References to the Law (8:4 and 13:8-10)

Rom. 8:4 and 13:8-10 have typically posed a problem for interpreters
because they seem to stand in tension with the negative statements which Paul
makes about the law elsewhere in the letter. On a simple reading of the text, the
meaning of these passages is clear: those who walk in the Spirit rather than in the
flesh fulfill the law (8:4), and believers should fulfill the decalogue (quotations
from Exod. 20:13-17) by loving their neighbors (quotation from Lev. 19:18).
Despite these lucid statements of the positive place of the law in the believer's
existence, scholars have been quick to explain them away. Hans Hübner reads
them as directives to fulfill the law in a different way from Judaism, to fulfull it,
that is, without making it into an opportunity of boasting before God in one's
achievements.[6] C. E. B. Cranfield believes that Rom. 13:8-10, in view of its
statement that the debt of love is never repaid, means that even the believer never
fulfills the law.[7] And Reimer Grönemeyer argues the curious position that 8:4
refers to Christ's fulfillment of the just requirement of the law while 13:8 should
read "he who loves has ended the law."[8]
It should be observed, however, that the subject under discussion when 8:4
appears in the text is not legalism or Christ's fulfillment of the law, but ethics.
Thus, beginning with 6:1, Paul has been defending himself against charges of
antinomianism and insisting on righteous behavior within the believing community. "Are we to continue in sin that grace may abound?" he asks (6:1). "Are
we to sin because we are not under law but under grace?" (6:15). His answer up
to 8:4 is that by dying with Christ in baptism we have also died to sin (6:1-14),
that as slaves of righteousness we are obedient to a certain "standard of teaching"
(6:15-23, esp. v. 17),[9] and that as those who have "died," we have been

---

[6] *Law*, pp. 113-124, 135.
[7] *Romans*, 2:676. Rom. 8:4, according to Cranfield, 1:384, echoes Jer. 31:31-34 and Ezek.
11:19-20 and thus has in view the eschatological situation in which believers will fulfill the law.
[8] "Zur Frage nach dem paulinischen Antinomismus: Exegetisch-systematische Überlegungen
mit besonderer Berücksichtigung der Forschungsgeschichte im 19. Jahrhundert," Dokotorwürde
Diss., University of Hamburg, 1970, pp. 134-40.
[9] Many scholars have questioned the authenticity of this verse. For a full bibliography see
Käsemann, *Romans*, pp. 180-181. The classical statement of the case against the verse in German
is found in Bultmann, "Glossen im Römerbrief" in *Exegetica: Aufsätze fur Erforschung des Neuen
Testaments,* ed. Erich Dinkler (Tübingen: J. C. B. Mohr [Paul Siebeck], 1967), p. 283. The phrase

"discharged from the law" (7:1-6) *insofar as* it arouses sin in us (7:5, 7-25). Thus Paul's concern in the larger passage of which 8:4 is a part is to address the role of ethics in the believer's life. 8:4 fits snugly into this context as a statement that those who have the eschatological spirit are empowered to do the holy, righteous, and good law (7:12) which, before the dawning of the eschaton, could only arouse sin (5:20, 7:5, 8:3).[10] This reading is further confirmed by the immediate context of 8:4 (8:1-11) in which those who cannot submit to God's law (τῷ γὰρ νόμῳ τοῦ θεοῦ οὐχ ὑποτάσσεται, 8:7) are contrasted with those who can (ὑμεῖς δὲ οὐκ ἐστὲ ἐν σαρκὶ ἀλλὰ ἐν πνεύματι, εἴπερ πνεῦμα θεοῦ οἰκεῖ ἐν ὑμῖν, 8:9). There is no contrast of boasting in achievements with boasting in suffering and no polemic against "legalism." There is certainly no hint that somehow Christ fulfilled the law's requirement, for 8:4 says clearly that it is fulfilled ἐν ἡμῖν. The verse, then, is a simple statement that whereas before Christ's death and the coming of the Spirit humanity was enslaved to sin and death, after those eschatological events, believers can fulfill the law.[11]

If this is the correct reading of 8:4, however, there is no reason to assign any other interpretation to 13:8-10.[12] The ethical concerns of Paul in chapters 12-15 hardly need demonstration, and Paul's claim that believers should love their neighbors and thereby fulfill the second half of the decalogue could not be more lucid. These considerations militate against giving πλήρωμα the nuance of "termination"[13] or seeing here any subtle difference between Paul and Judaism.[14] Again, there is no polemic against legalism, but an uncomplicated admonition, reminiscent of the Testaments of the Twelve Patriarchs,[15] to fulfill the commands of the law by loving one's neighbor.

"But...you...have become obedient from the heart to the standard of teaching" Bultmann calls a "stupiden Zwischensatz" interpolated by a later exegete who used the unpauline phrases "from the heart" and "type of teaching," who clearly meant by "type of teaching" the teaching of Paul himself, and who destroyed the balance between "freedom" on one side and "obedience" on the other. In English see Victor Paul Furnish, *Theology and Ethics in Paul* (Nashville: Abingdon, 1968), pp. 197-98. Käsemann, *Romans*, p. 181, correctly points out against this thesis that "formal expressions from the tradition are not surprising in baptismal exhortation" and that "without the intervening expression the solemn statement would simply repeat v. 16b and rhetorically overlap the thanksgiving."

[10] τὰ δικαίωμα τοῦ θεοῦ refers simply to the "requirement" or "ordinance" of God's law; see BAGD, p. 198 and LSJ, p. 429. It is possible that Paul is referring to the command "you shall not covet" in 7:7.

[11] For a similar understanding of this verse see Eckart Reinmuth, *Geist und Gesetz: Studien zu Voraussetzungen und Inhalt der paulinischen Paränese*, Theologische Arbeiten, no. 44 (Berlin: Evangelische Verlagsanstalt, 1985), pp. 69-70 and Peter Stuhlmacher, "Paul's Understanding of the Law in the Letter to the Romans," *SEÅ* 50 (1985):98-100.

[12] Sanders, *Law*, pp. 96-97, correctly observes, *pace* Hübner, *Law*, that since Rom. 13:8-10 was probably written in close chronological proximity to Gal. 5:14 and uses the same Old Testament text (Lev. 19:18), it is unlikely that Paul meant anything different in Rom. 13:8-10 than what he says in Gal. 5:14.

[13] Grönemeyer, "Frage," pp. 134-40.

[14] See especially Hübner, *Law*, pp. 83-85 and Käsemann, *Romans*, pp. 360-64.

[15] TSim 4:7, "And you, my children, each of you love his brothers with a good heart, and the spirit of envy will depart from you" (*OTP*, 1:786); TIss 5:2, "Love the Lord and your neighbor; be

In summary, the most likely reading of 8:4 and 13:8-10 reveals that in Romans as in Galatians Paul did leave a place in his thinking for obedience to the law in the eschatological age. There is no indication in these texts that he counselled believers to fulfill the law in some non-legalistic sense, and no thought of Christ somehow fulfilling the law's requirement. Rather, he says straightforwardly that believers should keep the law.[16]

Do these statements, then, stand in direct contradiction to Paul's negative assessment of the law in the rest of the letter? Has Paul been incautious or his thinking tortured in 8:4 and 13:8-10? Some have thought so. Hans Lietzmann claims that Paul simply forgot what he said in chapter 7 and 10:4 when he penned 8:4 and 13:8-10. Commenting on the latter passage Lietzmann says:

> Daß hier wie 8:4 unbefangen von "Erfüllung des Gesetzes" als etwas erstrebenswerten spricht und Kap. 7 und 10.4 vergessen zu haben, ist charakteristisch für seine unschematische Art zu reden.[17]

Heikki Räisänen believes that the two passages give evidence of Paul's psychological struggle with the law. Paul's inability to accept rationally his own break with the law, says Räisänen, has driven him to self-contradiction. Paul's view, therefore, cannot be reduced to a system which will accommodate all of his various statements.[18] Similarly, E. P. Sanders says that Paul wanted to exclude the law on soteriological grounds (Christ, not Torah, saves) and because it divided Jew from Gentile (by commanding circumcision, certain dietary observances, and Sabbath keeping); but he also wanted to preserve certain ethical norms which the law advocated. He never solved this logical dilemma, but simply excluded the law in some circumstances and appealed to its authority in others.[19]

Sanders and Räisänen use these arguments as evidence that Paul's thinking about the law was controlled by his christology. Paul's view of the law is

---

compassionate toward poverty and sickness" (*OTP*, 1:802); TDan 5:1-3, "Observe the Lord's commandments, then, my children, and keep his Law. Avoid wrath, and hate lying, in order that the Lord may dwell among you, and Beliar may flee from you. Each of you speak truth clearly to his neighbor, and do not fall into pleasure and troublemaking, but be at peace, holding to the God of peace. Thus no conflict will overwhelm you. Throughout all your life love the Lord, and one another with a true heart" (*OTP*, 1:809).

[16] Paul has, of course, defined obedience to the law in a way different from his Judaizing opponents. They took a strict attitude toward observing such particularly Jewish commands as circumcision whereas Paul took a more liberal attitude toward these requirements (1 Cor. 7:19, Gal. 6:15). Nonetheless, as we have seen in chapter three, the argument between Paul and his opponents is not between a renegade Paul who has redefined the law at will and normative Judaism but, to a large measure, between two Jewish ways of looking at the law.

[17] Hans Lietzmann, *Einführung in die Textgeschichte der Paulusbriefe: An die Römer*, 4th ed., HNT, no. 8 (Tübingen: Verlag von J. C. B. Mohr (Paul Siebeck), 1933), p. 113. Käsemann, *Romans*, pp. 217-18, 361-62, believes, similarly, that Paul has taken over Jewish catechetical traditions with which he is not in full agreement.

[18] Räisänen, *Law*, pp. 199-202.

[19] Sanders, *Law*, pp. 93-104. See also Räisänen, *Law*, p. 69.

inconsistent, they say, because his chief concern was to show that salvation was found through Christ, not to promote a particular attitude toward the law.

In the paragraphs that follow I hope to show that this assessment of Paul's view of the law is largely mistaken. Paul's negative statements about the law do not stand in tension with his positive statements but describe the law from the perspective of the unbeliever. From his or her perspective, says Paul, the law cannot be kept (1:18-3:20; 9:30-10:8), brings wrath (4:15), and multiplies sin (5:20, 7:1-13). Paul's comments about the law in Romans, therefore, run not simply from solution to plight but are clearly intelligible on Jewish theological terms as running from plight to solution. Paul claims that whereas the unbeliever lives under the curse of disobedience to the law, the believer has escaped that curse through the death of Christ and the coming of the Spirit.

Paul's Negative Statements about the Law
(1:18-3:20, 4:1-25, 5:20, 7:1-25, and 9:30-10:8)

Two schools of thought dominate the discussion of Paul's negative statements about the law in Romans. One school claims that they are theologically profound. Paul says that the law cannot be fulfilled and is therefore abrogated,[20] or he says that the law can be fulfilled but that the Jewish fulfillment of it is already sin,[21] or he criticizes the Jews for fulfilling the law in the wrong way—with a view to making a claim upon God rather than by faith in God's messiah.[22] In any case his statements are carefully formulated and theologically astute. The second school believes that Paul's statements about the law are haphazard and inconsistent, an indication of his *ad hoc* method of argumentation and of his rejection of Judaism's central religious principle. His attitude toward the law is far from profound and says more about Paul's psyche than about his theological acumen.[23] Both schools believe that Paul's christology controls his statements about the law in Romans, and that what he says, whether profound or not, would have been largely incomprehensible to Judaism. His critique of the law is made on presuppositions which no Jew could accept. Paul's dialogue with

---

[20] Van Dülmen, *Gesetzes*, pp. 125-127. See also Wilckens, *Römer*, 2:210. Unlike van Dülmen, Wilckens believes that for Paul Christ was in some sense the "Ziel" of the law, although he was also its "Ende."

[21] See, for example, Bultmann, "Romans 7," pp. 148-49; *Theology*, 1:266-67; Franz J. Leenhardt, *The Epistle to the Romans: A Commentary*, trans. Harold Knight (London: Lutterworth Press, 1961), p. 262; Käsemann, *Romans*, pp. 277-78.

[22] Barrett, *Romans*, p. 193; Cranfield, *Romans*, 2:509-510; Nygren, *Romans*, pp. 376-78; Robert Badenas, *Christ the End of the Law: Romans 10.4 in Pauline Perspective*, JSNTS no. 10 (Sheffield, Eng.: JSOT Press, 1985), pp. 101-105.

[23] See, for example, Räisänen, *Law*, pp. 231 and 258.

the unbelieving Jew throughout the epistle, therefore, is one-sided, produced on Paul's own terms, and has an air of artificiality about it.[24]

I hope to show below that this assessment of Paul's argument in Romans is, to a large extent, faulty. As in Galatians, so in Romans, Paul argues chiefly from a presupposition common in several strands of Judaism that the present age is an age dominated by disobedience to the covenant but that the coming age will be an age of observance of the law and freedom from sin. In only three places, Rom. 2:17, 5:20 and 7:5-13, does Paul step out of this pattern and view the plight from the perspective of his christological convictions; but even in these passages he does not assign to the law a temporary place. Thus Paul does not carry on a conversation with a straw man throughout the epistle, and the fundamentals of his argument were intelligible on the presuppositions of at least some sectors of Judaism.

A) Romans 1:18-3:20

Two aspects of Paul's argument in this passage have prompted interpreters to claim that Paul has constructed it principally on the basis of his christology. One is Paul's conclusion that "no human being (σάρξ) will be justified in his sight by works of the law, since through the law comes knowledge of sin" (3:20). In chapters two and three we saw that this statement is not an impossible one within the Judaism of Paul's day: the law did, in fact, define sin according to much Jewish literature. In this statement in particular Paul alludes to humanity in its weakness and inability to do God's will by modifying the ζῶν of Ps. 142:2 (LXX) to σάρξ.[25] The other reason for considering this section to be determined purely by Paul's christological convictions must occupy us at greater length. It is that in 2:12-16 and 26-29 Paul speaks of Gentiles who obey the law. According to Sanders, Paul claims that some Gentiles are justified by works in order to prove that the Jew has no prior claim upon God for salvation. In an effort to say that the Jew is just as sinful as the Gentile, the momentum of Paul's argument has driven him to make a statement that he did not believe himself: some Gentiles will be saved because of the good works that they do whereas some Jews will not be saved because they have not produced good works. What Paul meant to say was that both Gentile *and Jew* are hopelessly mired in sin and therefore need a universal savior; what he actually says is that some Gentiles will

---

[24] Charles H. Cosgrove, "'What If Some Have Not Believed?' The Occasion and Thrust of Romans 3:1-8," *ZNW* 78 (1987):90-105.

[25] Leander A. Keck, "The Function of Rom 3:10-18: Observations and Suggestions" in *God's Christ and his People: Studies in Honour of Nils Alstrup Dahl*, ed. Jacob Jervell and Wayne A. Meeks (Oslo: Universitetsforlaget, 1977), pp. 151-54 argues persuasively that Paul's argument in 1:18-3:22 is based on the premises of the catena of quotations in 3:10-18. Paul's argument thus parallels both in theme and in method 2 Esd. 7:21ff., AssMos 5:2-6, and CD 5.13-17, all of which speak of a creation overcome by sin and in need of eschatological salvation.

be saved by their works and some Jews will not be saved because of their wickedness. All of this demonstrates, we are told, that Paul thought backwards from solution to plight. He was less concerned with the form that the plight took than that it corresponded to the solution which he was convinced was correct: salvation is found in Christ.[26]

Sanders catalogues the usual explanations of the passage and formulates his theory against them. He lists four common ways of understanding 2:12-16 and 25-29:

> (1) The Gentiles of 2:14 are Gentile Christians not Gentiles who obey the Jewish law. (2) Paul is speaking hypothetically: if anyone could obey the law he would be righteoused; but no one can.... (3) The doers of the law in 2:13 are those who do the law in the right way, not according to the mode of a supposed Jewish legalism, but on the basis of faith.... (4) V. 2:13 only means that Christians will be judged in the future, which is in accord with such passages as 2 Cor. 5:10 and Rom. 14:10.[27]

Sanders himself proposes a fifth explanation—that Paul has incorporated a Hellenistic synagogue sermon into his argument, and that much of what this sermon says stands in irreconcilable tension with Paul's conviction that salvation does not come according to works.[28]

A sixth explanation, that of Klyne R. Snodgrass, offers a refreshing alternative both to previous interpretations and to Sanders's radical approach. Snodgrass believes, like Sanders, that we should take Paul's language at face value. The claim that Paul is referring to Christians in the passage, or is expressing dissatisfaction with legalism, or that he is speaking hypothetically all have the great disadvantage of simply not taking Paul's words literally when he says that those who do good, whether Jew or Greek, will be justified. Snodgrass proposes, therefore, that Paul *does* believe all people will be judged according to their obedience to the revelation God has given them. Snodgrass goes on to argue, however, that this idea does not stand in tension with Paul's belief that salvation comes through God's grace, for like the Old Testament and Judaism

---

[26] Sanders, *Law*, pp. 123-32; see also Räisänen, *Law*, pp. 101-109, esp. p. 108.

[27] *Law*, pp. 125-26. See also Räisänen, *Law*, pp. 103- 106. For position (1) see Augustine, *De Spiritu et Littera* 43-49; Cranfield, *Romans*, 1:152; A. König, "Gentiles or Gentile Christians: On the Meaning of Rom. 2:12-16," *Journal of Theology for South Africa* 15 (1976):53-60; and F. Flückiger, "Die Werke des Gesetzes bei den Heiden," *TZ* 8 (1952): 17-42. For position (2) see van Dülmen, *Gesetzes*, pp. 74-78 and Lietzmann, *Römer*, p. 44 (with reference to 2:26). For position (3) see J. Cambier, "Le jugement de tous les hommes," *ZNW* 67 (1976-77): 187-213. For position (4) see Günther Bornkamm, "Gesetz und Natur: Röm 2:14-16" in *Studien zu Antike und Urchristentum: Gesammelte Aufsätze*, 3d ed., 3 vols., BEvT, no. 28 (Munich: Kaiser Verlag, 1970), 2:93-118

[28] Ibid., pp. 129-32.

before him, Paul held that it was only by God's grace that even the obedient were saved.[29]

Snodgrass's theory is a model of prudent exegesis and common sense; but despite its attractiveness it is haunted by Paul's conclusion to this section of his argument. Paul's concluding summary which, as so often in his epistles, reveals his position in a nutshell, contains a catena of quotations on universal sinfulness and the claim that

> ...whatever the law says, it says to those who live by the law in order that every mouth might be stopped and the whole world be held accountable to God, because no flesh will be justified before him by works of the law, for through the law comes the knowledge of sin (3:19).[30]

Although Paul certainly would not deny that those who were faithful to the revelation given them were saved by God's mercy without perfect obedience to the law,[31] his point in this section of Romans is that no one, whether Jew or Gentile, has kept God's commands.

If Snodgrass's reading is wrong, then the most plausible approach is what Sanders lists as theory (2), the approach which says that Paul is speaking hypothetically. This interpretation believes Paul to be saying that if Gentiles kept the law they would be saved, but they do not keep it. It is exegetically satisfying for two reasons: a) with one modification, it fits the view of the Gentile's place on the day of judgment which we find in Hellenistic Jewish literature of Paul's day, and b) Paul nowhere in Romans 2 says unequivocally that there are Gentiles who will be saved by keeping the law. Both of these claims require further discussion.

Beginning with a), it is clear that in at least some strands of first century Judaism Gentiles were considered as equally likely candidates for keeping the law as Jews and would be judged on the same basis as Jews. Philo claims that not hearing but doing the law is what counts (*Praem.*, 82, 79) and that the proselyte will be honored above "the nobly born" who allows himself to fall into unrighteousness (*Praem.*, 152). One need not be a proselyte to act righteously, however, for among the "truly wise" and "truly good" Philo numbers the sages of Greece, the Magi of Persia, and the Gymnosophists of India (*Probus* 71-88).[32]

---

[29] "Justification by Grace—to the Doers," *NTS* 32 (1986):72-93.

[30] This observation also militates against the interpretations of this passage which claim that Paul is speaking of Christians who keep the law from their hearts (Flückiger, Cranfield, and König).

[31] Snodgrass, "Justification," p. 81 mentions Abraham and David in Romans 4 as examples of sinners who, in Paul's mind, God justified by his grace because of their faithfulness to God and despite their sinfulness.

[32] Philo believed that the rational law which governed the universe and the law revealed to Moses were one (*Opif.* 3; *Moses* 2.48; *Somn.* 274). Thus there could be those among the gentiles who, on the basis of their skillful apprehension of the laws observable in nature, could obey the law. Afterall, this was how such worthies as Abraham, Isaac, Jacob, Enoch, and Noah, who existed before the giving of the law by Moses, lived in accordance with it (*Abr.* 5, 46, 275; *Moses*

Similarly in the Testament of Abraham, Abraham inquires of his heavenly tour-guide Michael how the fearful figure whom he has just seen judging souls decides who will be punished and who will go free. Michael answers:

> This is a son of Adam the protoplast—the one called Abel, whom Cain the evil one killed. And he is sitting here to judge all creation (κρῖναι πᾶσαν τὴν κτίσιν) and to expose both the righteous and sinners (recension A, 13:5-10, my translation.)

Clearly all creation is judged alike. TZeb 8:1-6 likewise claims that in the last days God will have compassion on everyone on earth who has shown compassion to others. Paul's statement that "circumcision indeed is of value if you obey the law; but if you break the law, your circumcision becomes uncircumcision" (2:25) fits comfortably within this tradition. He says what many Hellenistic Jews also knew to be true—that God is an impartial judge who puts more weight on deeds than on "outward" symbols such as circumcision and national affiliation.[33]

Paul's view differs from that of Philo and the Testament of Zebulon, however, in one significant way, and this brings us to point b) above. Whereas they are optimistic about the possibility of some Gentiles doing what was "truly wise" and "truly good," Paul nowhere says that the Gentiles of whom he speaks will be good enough to receive aquittal on the final day. The point of this section is that all peoples, both Jew and Gentile, are "under sin" (ὑφ᾽ ἁμαρτίαν, 3:9) and will not be justified before God by works of the law (ἐξ ἔργων νόμου οὐ δικαιωθήσεται πᾶσα σάρξ ἐνώπιον αὐτοῦ, 3:20). Condemnation, not salvation, is Paul's concern.[34] Thus in his effort to indict Jews who feel that they are not subject to the same standards of judgment as Gentiles, Paul reminds his readers that God will judge Gentiles by the law written on their hearts and Jews by the "oracles" which he has given them. No special privilege will be given to

---

2.48.) Philo's ideas probably have their source in Aristotle's theory of "natural law" (*Eth. Nic.* 5.7; *Rh.*, 1.13.2, cf. 1.10.3), Stoicism, and Judaism; see Harry Austin Wolfson, *Philo: Foundations of Religious Philosophy in Judaism, Christianity, and Islam*, 2d printing, revised, 2 vols. (Cambridge, Mass.: Harvard University Press, 1948), 2:165-82. On Paul's affinities in this passage with Philo see Jouette M. Bassler, *Divine Impartiality: Paul and a Theological Axiom*, SBLDS no. 59 (Chico, Calif.: Scholars Press, 1982), pp. 143 and 259, nn. 74-75. On Paul's affinities with Aristotle, the Stoics, and other ancient philosophers, including Philo, see Friedrich Kuhr, "Römer 2:14f. und die Verheissung bei Jeremia 31:31ff.," *ZNW* 55 (1964):255-60 and Günther Bornkamm, "Gesetz und Natur," pp. 102-104. Some scholars deny that what Paul says in Rom. 2:12-16 has its basis in the philosophies of Greece and Hellenistic Judaism; see Felix Flückiger, "Die Werke des Gesetzes bei den Heiden (nach Röm. 2, 14ff.)," *TZ* 8 (1952):29-34; Käsemann, *Romans*, pp. 63-64; and Albrecht Dihle, *The Theory of Will in Classical Antiquity*, Sather Classical Lectures, vol. 48 (Berkeley: University of California Press, 1982), pp. 80 and 202-203, n. 61.

[33] The biblical idea that literally circumcised Israel could become "uncircumcised" through disobedience also coheres well with Paul's claim that those who are uncircumcised, yet obedient, would be blessed by God. See Lev. 26:41, Deut. 10:16, Jer. 4:4, 9:23-25, 11:6, and Amos 9:7.

[34] Similarly, Bornkamm, "Natur," p. 99, van Dülmen, *Das Gesetzes*, p. 78, and Lietzmann, pp. 41-42.

either party. Paul never says that either τὰ ἔθνη of 2:14 or ἡ ἀκροβυστία of 2:26 will be saved. In the former case they will eventually stand before God and will be accused or defended by their consciences, and in the latter case Paul uses a so-called third class condition to say that only if the uncircumcised person keeps the requirements of the law will he or she be reckoned as a member of God's chosen people. In neither case does Paul say that the Gentiles in view keep enough of the law to stand aquitted before God. It is entirely likely, in view of Paul's statement that "real circumcision is a matter of the heart, spiritual and not literal" that he has in the back of his mind the idea that those who participate in Christ's death and walk in the Spirit fulfill the law; but at this stage in his argument he is still speaking hypothetically in the service of his main theme that both Jew and Greek are in need of the righteousness of God.[35]

Thus neither Paul's statement that no one will be justified by doing the law (3:20) nor his contention that a Gentile who kept the law would be judged more favorably than a Jew who did not forces Paul out of the conceptual world of Hellenistic Judaism or into a stance which contradicts his conclusion in 3:9 and 3:20 that all are sinners. Both elements were common within his milieu and he only entertains the possibility that Gentiles outside of Christ will keep the law.[36]

It must be conceded, however, that Paul's use of the tradition that Gentiles can keep the law to set up a hypothetical argument against the claim that Jews are "better off" (3:9; cf. 2:27) is unusual. Here Paul's conviction that the gospel is the power of God for salvation to both Jew and Greek (1:16) has probably led him to construct his argument in a highly polemical way which a Jew would find startling. Nonetheless, it is not simply a matter of Paul taking up traditions which were ultimately inconsistent with his own argument nor of his making wholly unjewish statements. His thesis is still built upon the framework identified in chapter two as a common one within some sections of the Old Testament and Judaism: everyone sins and everyone stands in need of God's eschatological redemption.

---

[35] Bassler, *Divine Impartiality*, p. 145.

[36] Hypothetical arguments were a well known and thoroughly studied rhetorical device in the ancient world, and it is not insignificant that Epictetus, with whose diatribe style Paul's method of argumentation in precisely this section of Romans has many affinities, discusses them at length in *Discourses*, 1.7. See also Quintilian 5.10.95-99. Apparently hypothetical arguments concerning the status of the Gentiles at the last judgment were also entertained by the rabbis. Betz, in his essay "An Episode in the Last Judgment (Matt. 7:21-23)" in *Essays on the Sermon on the Mount*, trans. L. L. Welborn (Philadelphia: Fortress, 1985), pp. 138-39 cites a rabbinic tradition from the Babylonian Talmud in which the question of God's justice in condemning the Gentiles is raised. One issue in the discussion is *if there were Gentiles* who kept the law, would they be rewarded at the last judgment? The conclusion is that they would not be rewarded as greatly as those who had received specific commandments and had obeyed them.

B) Romans 4:1-25

Once again the majority of interpreters claim that in this passage Paul moves outside the boundaries of Jewish thinking on the law. Either he has denied the basic soteriological tenet of Judaism—that salvation is by works[37]—or he has misrepresented Judaism, in the interest of his polemics, as a religion of salvation by works.[38] Often his treatment of Abraham in the passage has been used as decisive evidence of his break with Judaism. In Judaism, it is said, Abraham "was found faithful when tested and it was reckoned to him as righteousness" (1 Macc. 2:52; see also James 2:23); he was thus justified by works (faith*fulness*) rather than by faith.[39] Moreover, Judaism considered Abraham to be the world's most pious man and thus one who earned his salvation by what he did. According to many, Paul tries to topple these convictions with the arguments that Abraham was justified by faith rather than by works and that Abraham was actually in need of such justification because he was "ungodly" (4:3 and 4:5). Paul's statement in 4:15 that "the law brings wrath" is viewed as corroborative evidence of this flight out of Jewish views of the law into a view determined by his christology.

These interpretations are informed, however, both by a misunderstanding of the situation which Paul seeks to address in Romans 4 and by a failure to take into account one Hellenistic Jewish tradition about Abraham that views him as a sinner in need of God's mercy. Paul's purpose in discussing Abraham is to demonstrate from scripture[40] that redemption from sin applies to uncircumcised Gentiles as well as to circumcised Jews. Paul seeks to draw this conclusion from his treatment of how and at what time Abraham was justified (4:9-18). Abraham, he says, was justified by faith rather than by circumcision and had faith before he was circumcised (4:9-11). Thus uncircumcised Gentiles are saved in the same way—by faith, not by circumcision (4:12) and keeping the law (4:13-15). Paul evidently has in view in this argument the problem which he encountered in Galatia—he wants to refute the idea that it is necessary for Gentiles not only to believe in Jesus as Christ but to become circumcised as well in order for them to

---

[37] Cranfield, *Romans*, 1:227; Käsemann, *Romans*, p. 107; Leenhardt, *Romans*, pp. 113-14; Otto Kuss, *Der Römerbrief, übersetzt und erklärt*, 3 vols. (Regensburg: Verlag Friedrich Pustet, 1963), pp. 180-81; Heinrich Schlier, *Der Römerbrief*, 2d ed. HTKNT, vol. 6 (Freiburg: Herder, 1979), p. 123; Wilckens, *Römer*, p. 263; Martin Dibelius, *A Commentary on James*, rev. Heinrich Greeven, trans., Michael A. Williams, Hermeneia (Philadelphia: Fortress, 1975), pp. 168-74.

[38] Räisänen, *Law*, pp. 171, 177-191.

[39] See Käsemann, *Romans*, p. 107 and Dibelius, *James*, pp. 168-74.

[40] C. Thomas Rhyne, *Faith Establishes the Law*, SBLDS, no. 55 (Chico, Calif.: Scholars Press, 1981), pp. 63-93 argues that 4:1-25 is Paul's proof of the statement in 3:31 that he establishes the law. Paul provides proof from the law for his thesis and therefore demonstrates that he upholds the law. Sanders, *Law*, p. 33, argues somewhat differently that Paul seeks to prove from scripture that all without exception are saved by faith (in Christ).

be reckoned righteous on the final day.[41] Paul attacks this idea in Galatians with the Jewish notion (Gal. 2:15) that salvation comes by trust in God's eschatological ability to provide for the justification of sinners rather than by performing particular rites like circumcision or festival keeping, and he attacks the same notion here in a similar way. Neither in Galatians nor here, therefore, does Paul attack *Judaism*, rather in both places he argues against *Jewish Christian missionaries* who teach that acceptance of circumcision is required before one can enter the eschatological community and experience God's forgiveness and empowering Spirit. Here, as in Galatians, Paul reminds his readers of what every Jew should know: that God justifies people by their trust in his eschatological provision not by performing some rite or other, and he uses Abraham as his key witness. Abraham, he says, did not earn God's favor by becoming circumcised but trusted in God's ability to forgive his ungodliness.

This portrait of Abraham is not, moreover, significantly different from the picture drawn of him in the Testament of Abraham. There Abraham is the "all pious" (πανόσιε, 13:2), and is frequently called "righteous." The angel Michael refers to him as "merciful, hospitable, righteous, truthful, God-fearing, refraining from every evil deed" (4:6), and God himself makes the forthright statement ἰδοὺ γάρ 'Αβραὰμ οὐχ ἥμαρτεν (10:20). Nonetheless it is evident that Abraham does sin and must rely on God's mercy and forgiveness for salvation. Thus in chapter 9 Abraham must repent of his refusal to obey God's messenger Michael when the latter came to lead him through death to God's presence. In his prayer of repentance Abraham confesses that he is a "sinful and unworthy servant" of God (9:3-5). Later, as he is being conducted on his tour of the earth prior to his death he harshly condemns a pair of thieves and a couple engaged in sexual indiscretions to painful deaths. God is displeased with Abraham's lack of compassion and quickly aborts his tour of the earth "lest he should see the entire inhabited world..." and "...destroy everything that exists. For behold Abraham has not sinned and he has no mercy on sinners" (10:12-13).[42] This quaint episode reveals the sense in which Abraham "has not sinned": he has not robbed or committed adultery. In another sense, however, Abraham has indeed sinned, for he has been unmerciful, and his lengthy prayer of repentance for his lack of compassion, followed by God's acknowledgement and forgiveness, demonstrates the awareness of those among whom this story circulated that even Abraham the πανόσιε was a sinner in need of God's forgiveness (ἀφίημί σοι τὴν ἁμαρτίαν, 14:14; see also 14:12).

In Paul's treatment of Abraham in chapter 4, therefore, he does not oppose a supposed Jewish doctrine of salvation by merit nor does he lash back at Judaism's picture of Abraham with his own profound analysis; but he reminds Jewish

---

[41] In this observation Sanders, *Law*, p. 33, is correct. Peter Stuhlmacher, "Paul's Understanding," pp. 87-104 has argued persuasively that Paul wrote Romans in order to refute rumors against him spread by Jewish-Christian opponents of his gospel.
[42] *OTP*, 1:887.

Christians of what they, as Jews, should already know—that even Abraham was forgiven not on the basis of his circumcision but on the basis of his trust in God's compassion.

It is with this in mind that we must read Paul's assessment of the law in 4:13-15. Paul has just said in 4:9-12 that it is faith not circumcision which is the crucial requirement of children of Abraham, and it is the law of circumcision which he continues to have in view in 4:13. It was not, he says, through the law of circumcision that Abraham and his seed received the promise but through faith. In 4:14-15 he widens his view to take in the whole law: "If it is the adherents of the law (οἱ ἐκ νόμου) who are to be heirs, faith is null and the promise void" (4:14). The least complicated reading of this verse is probably the best: if the promise is based on keeping the law (particularly the law of circumcision) then faith is of no avail and the promise is rendered ineffective, because the law cannot be kept.[43] The law, Paul explains (4:15), brings wrath. By this he probably means something similar to what he says in Gal. 3:19-22—the law was promulgated in a situation of sin, had the effect of making those who sinned more culpable, and confined those to whom it came "under sin." As we saw in our study of the law in Galatians, however, Paul does not step out of the conceptual world of Judaism with such statements. Many Jews recognized that disobedience to the law was sin and that as sin it had historically brought God's wrath upon Israel.

In summary, Romans 4 does not provide evidence that Paul had abandoned the Jewish understanding of Abraham. Instead Paul attempts to refute the idea, probably advanced by Jewish-Christian missionaries, that in order to belong to the people of God, Gentiles must become circumcised. Paul's argument involves reminding his opponents of what Jews believe about Abraham and about the law. Abraham, says Paul, was a sinner who relied on God's mercy, not upon his own works, for forgiveness (4:7), and the law, which Israel has violated, has not brought the eschatological inheritance, but wrath.

C) Romans 5:20

Rom. 5:20 goes further than 4:15 in both describing the law as something which insinuated itself onto the stage of the human plight and as something which increased sin. Two aspects of the verse seem to propel Paul out of the orb of contemporary Jewish eschatological expectation. First, according to many interpreters, the passage implies that the law is a temporal entity which appeared on the scene for a specific purpose and for a prescribed period of time, but which has been abolished with the coming of Christ. If this interpretation is correct, then this passage would stand in stark contrast to Paul's statements elsewhere

---

[43] Cranfield, *Romans*, 1:240.

(8:4, 13:8-10) and to the Jewish belief in the eternality of the law. Second, the passage claims that the law came in order to increase sin. This too seems to violate Jewish presuppositions that the law prevented rather than increased sin. Both of these aspects of the passage require comment.

The principle motivation for the claim that in 5:20 Paul regards the law as a temporary entity is Paul's use of the word παρεισῆλθεν to describe the appearance of the law on the scene of salvation-history. F. F. Bruce, for example, believes Paul's meaning here is that "the law of Moses is a parenthetic dispensation in the course of God's dealings with the human race"[44] and translates 5:20a "the law came in by a side road."[45] Egon Brandenburger similarly says that in this passage Paul sharply devalues the law by calling into question the Jewish teaching on its eternality and assigning it a negative and therefore outmoded place in salvation history.[46]

If we look closely at the use of the word παρεισέρχομαι in ancient Greek literature, however, it appears unlikely that in Rom. 5:20 it refers to the law's temporality. The word can be used of a thought occurring to someone, of medical instruments being inserted, or of one thing coming or going "in beside" another;[47] but its most common use is in military or political contexts where it refers to an army or an individual gaining entrance to a city by stealth.[48] Polybius offers three clear examples of this meaning. He uses it once with reference to how Hiero became king of Syracuse by first being elected outside the city by the army and then gaining entrance (παρεισελθών) to it by means of his relatives,[49] a second time to refer to Cleomenes' army gaining entrance (παρεισελθών) to Megapolis through the help of certain malcontents who lived there,[50] and a third time to tell how the Campanians took Messene by treachery "after being admitted" to the city "as friends" (παρεισελθόντες δ' ὡς φίλοι).[51]

The word, then, possesses negative overtones; but it does not connote temporality. In fact it can refer to the establishment of permanent situations such as the rule of a city by a new people or to the long and prosperous reign of a new king.[52] When Paul uses the word in 5:20 he is probably thinking, as he was in Gal. 3:19 and possibly in Rom. 4:15, of the law's entrance into the situation of

---

[44] *The Letter of Paul to the Romans: An Introduction and Commentary*, 2d ed. (Leicester, Eng.: Inter-Varsity Press, 1985), p. 126.

[45] *Galatians*, p. 176.

[46] *Adam*, pp. 249-50.

[47] LSJ, p. 1333; BAGD, pp. 624-25.

[48] Diod. Sic. 16.66-95; Polyb., 1.7.3, 1.8.4, 2.55.3; Plut. *Mar*. 23.1. Lucian uses the word in a non-military context to refer to entering a house by stealth at midnight in *Dial. Meret.*, 12.3 and Philo uses the word to describe how disease and evil insinuated themselves into human reasoning powers after the fall in *Opif.* 150. Most important, of course, is Paul's use of the word in Gal. 2:4 to refer to the invasion of "Judaizers" into the church at Antioch.

[49] 1.8.4.

[50] 2.55.3.

[51] 1.7.3.

[52] The rule of Hiero over Syracuse, despite its questionable beginnings, was long and exemplary according to Polybius.

sin at Horeb. If so παρεισῆλθεν probably describes the "surprise attack" which the law made on those engaged in sin at the foot of the mountain, and says nothing one way or the other about the law's permanence.

The purpose for which the law "came in" presents a different problem, however, for Paul claims that the law entered "to increase the trespass" (ἵνα πλεονάσῃ τὸ παράπτωμα). The word πλεονάζω carries clear connotations of a quantitative increase in transgressions,[53] and thus there is no escape from the unjewish sound of Paul's claim. Here he appears to be looking back at the situation of life under the law's curse from the perspective of one who is already participating in the eschatological situation and wants to explain in detail the effect of the law prior to the dawning of the eschaton. His meaning is probably similar to that of 7:5: outside of the eschatological situation, the law brings to mind the very actions it prohibits, leaving the recipient with the suggestion of the action but helpless to forestall the desire to do it. Here indeed Paul says something about the law with which few Jews of his day would agree,[54] and says it from the perspective of the solution which he has experienced. Nonetheless, as in Galatians, it is only this sin-increasing aspect of the Torah which ceases in the eschatological age, not the law in its every aspect.[55]

In summary, Rom. 5:20 does not call into question the status of the law but speaks of one of its purposes after its entrance into the human situation at Sinai: it increased sin. Paul probably means by this statement not only what he says in Gal. 3:19-22 and Rom. 4:15—that the law made sin worse by making it more culpable—but something new as well—that the law actually increased quantitatively the number of sins by suggesting the sin but being powerless to prevent it. This latter aspect of Paul's meaning does indeed place Paul outside the camp of first century Judaism which, as far as we know, viewed the law as something which defined and prevented sin, rather than as something which incited it. Rom. 5:20 does not, however, move Paul outside the expectations of Judaism that the law would have a place in the age to come.

D) Romans 7:1-25

This passage has traditionally formed a *crux interpretum* for the idea that Paul's view of the law in Romans has little to do with Jewish conceptions and that Paul argues from his christological solution to a plight which no

---

[53] It probably also carries the qualitative connotation present in Gal. 3:19 and Rom. 4:15; see Cranfield, *Romans*, 1:293.

[54] For numerous references to the idea that the law was a blessing and was intended to give people life, see Bonsirven, *Judaïsme*, 1:302-03 and Sanders, *Paul*, pp. 110-111.

[55] Eberhard Jüngel, "Das Gesetz zwischen Adam und Christus: Eine theologische Studie zu Röm 5, 12-21" in *Unterwegs zur Sache: Theologische Bemerkungen*, BEvT, vol. 61 (Munich: Chr. Kaiser Verlag, 1972), pp. 170-72 says correctly that even after the law has performed the function of increasing sin it is not abandoned by Paul.

unbelieving Jew could have understood. Here Paul says that the law no longer
reigns over the believer (7:1), that the believer has died to the law (7:4), and that
"we have been released from the law, dying to that by which we were being
suppressed in order that we might serve in the newness of the Spirit and not in
the oldness of the letter" (7:6). Can there be any doubt, after reading such clear
statements, that Paul has rejected the law? If the passage stood on its own
without its context, that could, of course, be the only conclusion. The context
demonstrates, however, that Paul did not intend for his words to be understood as
a simple rejection of the Torah.

Prior to 7:1-6 Paul assumes a connection between the law and sin (6:14-15).
Those controlled by sin are "under law," probably meaning that they are under the
law's curse. Paul reminds his readers in 6:14-15 that they are no longer under this
curse but "under grace"—they are recipients of a new relationship with God in
which the law no longer pronounces its curse. In 7:1-6 Paul elaborates on this
point and goes even further to say that the law was the instrument through which
sinful passions were aroused—passions which, as the law itself says, could only
result in death. Paul recognizes that such statements could be understood as an
unqualified attack upon the law and seeks to prevent such a misunderstanding by
his defense of the law in 7:7-25 Finally in Romans 8:1-4 he moves to a
thoroughly positive evaluation of the law in its new role in the eschatological age
of the Spirit. Paul can, from the standpoint of this new age, speak of "the law of
the Spirit of life in Christ Jesus" which has "set you free from the law of sin and
death" (8:2). Previously the law was on the side of flesh (8:3), but in the new
age its just requirements can be fulfilled by those who walk in the Spirit (8:4).

Not all, of course, have found this understanding of chapters 6-8 convincing,
and 7:7-25 in particular has led many to say that Paul has abandoned Jewish
presuppositions and argues from his prior conviction that Jesus is Lord. The
symbols Paul uses are Jewish; but he has invested them with a Christian
meaning entirely foreign to Judaism. Two such approaches to 7:7-25 presently
dominate the scholarship. One approach claims that Paul's Christian convictions
have given him a profound grasp of the problem of legalism and the other that
they have produced a bumbling account of the relationship between the law and
sin that is inconsistent with itself and with what Paul says elsewhere. Bultmann
offers an excellent example of the first position when he says in his article on
"Romans 7 and the Anthropology of Paul"

> [Paul's] fundamental reproach is not that the way of the law is wrong because, by
> reason of transgressions, it fails to reach its goal (that is the position, say, of IV
> Ezra), but rather that the *direction* of this way is perverse and, to be sure, because
> it intends to lead to "one's own righteousness" (Rom. 10:3; Phil. 3:9). It is not
> evil works or transgressions that first make the Jews objectionable to God; rather

the intention to become righteous before him by fulfilling the law is their real sin, which is merely manifested by transgressions.[56]

Sanders gives the best example of the second position. He says that the most important fact we learn from Romans 7 is that Paul

> did not begin his thinking about sin and redemption by analyzing the human condition, nor by analyzing the effect of the law on those who sought to obey it. Had he done so we should doubtless find more consistency. What is consistent in Paul's description of the human plight...is the assertion of its universality. Similarly, what is consistent in his treatment of the law is the assertion that it does not righteous and that God saves another way. Paul can say that that is the case because God always planned it that way—the majority statement—or because the fleshly nature of humanity makes obedience to the law impossible (Rom. 7:14-25), or because sin uses the law to provoke transgression, which leads to death (7:7-13). It is the conclusion which is consistent, not the treatment of the law: all are condemned; all can be saved by God through Christ.[57]

Again, I think both approaches are incorrect, although as with Rom. 5:20, there does seem to be a sense in which Paul argues backwards from solution to plight in 7:7-13. There, picking up the theme of 7:5, he says that the command not to covet actually produces coveting in the unbeliever by suggesting the sin but providing no means of resisting it. Thus sin uses the command for its own ends in the unbeliever (7:11).[58] In saying this Paul is once again going beyond what Judaism, as far as we know it, would have said. The law did not in Judaism actually produce transgressions; it prevented them by showing people what God required. Despite this, Paul does not argue against legalism nor does he apply to the law the simple dictum, well known in the ancient world, that the forbidden fruit is the sweetest.[59] He says something quite different which he will reiterate

---

[56] In *Existence and Faith*, p. 149.

[57] *Law*, p. 81.

[58] Paul may be dependent upon Jewish tradition about the fall of Adam when he chooses the commandment "You shall not covet" in his example of how the law itself can incite sin. See, among others, S. Lyonnet, "'Tu ne convoiteras pas' (Rom vii 7)" in W. C. van Unnik, ed. *Neotestamentica et Patristica: Eine Freundesgabe, Herrn Professor Dr. Oscar Cullmann zu seinem 60. Geburtstag überreicht* (Leiden: E. J. Brill, 1962), pp. 157-65 and "L'histoire du salut selon le ch. 7 de l'epitre aux Romains," *Bib* 43 (1962): 117-51; Gerd Theissen, *Psychological Aspects of Pauline Theology*, trans. John P. Galvin (Philadelphia: Fortress, 1987), pp. 202-211; Käsemann, *Romans*, pp. 196-97; Schlier, *Römer*, pp. 223-24; Cranfield (with reservations), *Romans*, 1:343-44, 352; Wilckens, *Römer*, 2:79; Bornkamm, "Sünde, Gesetz und Tod: Exegetische Studie zu Röm 7:1" in *Das Ende des Gesetzes: Paulusstudien*, BETh, no. 16 (Munich: Chr. Kaiser Verlag, 1958), p. 59. Robert H. Gundry, "The Moral Frustration of Paul Before His Conversion: Sexual Lust in Romans 7:7-25" in *Pauline Studies: Essays Presented to F. F. Bruce on his 70th Birthday*, ed. Donald A. Hagner and Murray J. Harris (Grand Rapids: Eerdmans, 1980), pp. 229-34, however, offers an extensive critique of this view.

[59] Ovid, *Ars Am.*, 3.4.17. See Räisänen, *Law*, p. 142.

in 8:3: the law raises the subject of sin, but does nothing to deal with sin after it has done so.

The primary fault with the approaches to Romans 7 represented by Bultmann and Sanders, however, is in their treatment of 7:7-14. Bultmann errs in failing to see the ordinariness of what Paul says and Sanders mistakenly reads into this section concerns which Paul did not intend to address.

As profound as Paul's insight into the connection between willing and doing in Rom. 7:14-25 may be, it is not unique in the literature of the ancient world. Hildebrecht Hommel[60] and, more recently, Gerd Theissen[61] have done pauline scholarship a great service by pointing out the importance to Romans 7 of the long debate in the ancient Greek and Roman worlds over willing and doing. The debate proper begins with the observation of Medea in Euripides' tragedy on the conflict which rages within her before she murders her own children:

> O my children, my children, there is a home and a country for you, where you must go and leave me behind and dwell for ever motherless! But I go into exile in strange lands. I shall never have any joy of you, never watch your happiness, never see you married, never grace your weddings or raise high the bridal torch for you. O my hard heart is the curse of me! ...O heart, no, do not do it! Unhappy woman, let them be. Spare their lives: their lives will give you joy, though you and they must part.
>
> No, by the avenging fiends of hell! It shall never be. Never will I deliver these children of mine to my enemies to be brought to scorn. Anyway the thing is done; there is no escape; even now the crown is on her head, I know, and the royal bride enfolded in the robe of death.
>
> And now I would bid these little ones farewell, for I have to travel over the cruellest of roads, and send them by a yet more cruel. Here, children, here, give mother your hands to kiss! O hands and mouths, O noble childish form and face I love so well, happiness be yours even in that far place! Of happiness here your father has robbed us. O the sweet touch of your soft childish faces, so fragrant breathing! Go, go! I cannot bear to see you any more. My fate sweeps over me.
>
> I see the full horror of what I am going to do. But anger is stronger than reflection with me (θυμὸς δὲ κρείσσων τῶν ἐμῶν βουλευμάτων); and anger is the root of the worst evils in the world (*Medea*, 1021-1036, 1056-1080).[62]

Similarly, in *Hyppolytus*, Phaedra ponders the source of evil in life and concludes:

---

[60] "Das 7. Kapitel des Römerbriefs im Licht antiker Überlieferung" in Fritz Maass, ed., *Theologia Viatorum: Jahrbuch der Kirchlichen Hochschule Berlin*, 1961/1962 (Berlin: Walter de Grutyer & Co., 1962), pp. 90-116.

[61] *Psychological Aspects*, pp. 211-21.

[62] *The Medea & Hippolytus with Introduction, Translations, and Notes*, trans. Sydney Waterlow (London: J. M. Dent & Co., 1906), pp. 169-71. My guides through this literary and philosophical tradition have been Hommel, "Das 7. Kapital des Römerbriefs," Theissen, *Psychological Aspects*, and Dihle, *Theory of Will*.

We know the good and recognize it; but we fail to attain it (τὰ χρήστ' ἐπιστάμεθα καὶ γιγνώσκομεν, οὐκ ἐκπανοῦμεν δ'); some from indolence, and others from rating some other pleasure higher than the truly good (380- 83).[63]

Euripides seems to be saying in both of these passages that evil occurs when people, despite their knowledge of the good, fail to do it, either through being overcome with anger, giving in to sloth, or putting some pleasure above the good.

In the ensuing years the problem which these two passages posed was debated by philosophers and tragedians. Plato,[64] Xenophon,[65] and the two Stoic philosophers Epictetus[66] and Chrysippus[67] disagreed with Euripedes' assessment and claimed instead that doing wrong is largely a matter of ignorance about what is truly good. The thief, says Epictetus, only steals because he thinks that by doing so he can advance his own pleasure, and this he considers to be good. Thus, wrong behavior can be corrected by convincing those who do it of what is truly good:

> He...who can show to each man the contradiction which causes him to err, and can clearly bring home to him how he is not doing what he wishes and is doing what he does not wish (πῶς ὃ θέλει οὐ ποιεῖ καὶ ὃ μὴ θέλει ποιεῖ), is strong in argument, and at the same time effective both in encouragement and refutation. For as soon as anyone shows a man this, he will of his own accord abandon what he is doing (2.26.4-5).[68]

On the other side were those who agreed with Euripides that frequently something within the person beyond his or her control leads to evil actions. Thus at about the same time that Epictetus sided with Plato, Xenophon, and Chrysippus, Plutarch quoted the famous passage in *Medea* to illustrate his conviction that even though we know what is right we often, and unreasonably, do not do it.[69] Ovid and Seneca agree with Plutarch. In *Metamorphoses* 7.16-20 Medea, who is engaged in a futile attempt to overcome her love for Jason, wonders

---

[63] Waterlow, pp. 122-23.

[64] *Prt.*, 352D-360E.

[65] *Mem.*, 3.9.4.

[66] Arrian, *Epic. Dis.*, 1.28.68.

[67] A summary of Chrysippus' teaching on the relationship between knowledge and error can be found in Galen's extensive attempt at a refutation of it in *On the Doctrines of Hippocrates and Plato*, book 4. Galen criticizes Chrysippus for his inconsistency on the subject, claiming that he alternately asserted and denied that wrong action was sometimes the result of irrational behavior.

[68] Oldfather, pp. 432-33. On the difference between Paul and Epictetus in this passage see Adolf Bonhöffer, *Epiktet und das Neue Testament*, Religionsgeschichtliche Versuche und Vorarbeiten, vol. 10 (Gießen: Verlag von Alfred Töpelmann, 1911), pp. 60-61.

[69] *Mor.*, 533D. Epictetus also appealed to Euripides' *Medea* but did so in the service of his theory that wrong doing originated in ignorance (*Epic. Dis.*, .1.28.7).

What is the cause of all this fear? Come, thrust from your maiden breast these flames that you feel, if you can, unhappy girl. Ah, if I could, I should be more myself. But some strange power holds me down against my will. Desire persuades me one way, reason another. I see the better and approve it, but follow the worse.[70]

In Seneca's *Medea* we find that at the moment of conflict over the slaying of her children Medea echoes the passage from Euripedes:

A double tide tosses me, uncertain of my course; as when rushing winds wage mad warfare, and from both sides conflicting floods lash the seas and the fluctuating waters boil, even so is my heart tossed. Anger puts love to flight, and love, anger. O wrath, yield thee to love (939-44).[71]

In the second century Galen refers to Euripides' *Medea* yet again in the course of an attempt to point out contradictions in Chrysippus' comments on the unity of the soul. Galen is a stauch advocate of the notion that sometimes people do evil even though they know it is unreasonable and harmful to do so:

Medea...was not persuaded by any reasoning to kill her children; quite the contrary, so far as reasoning goes, she says that she understands how evil the acts are that she is about to perfom, but her anger is stronger than her deliberations; that is, her affection has not been made to submit and does not obey and follow reason as it would a master, but throws off the reins and departs and disobeys the command, the implication being that it is the action or affection of some power other than the rational (*On the Doctrines of Hippocrates and Plato*, 4.2.27).[72]

Greek and Latin writers are not unique, however, in their contemplation of this problem. The Dead Sea Scrolls demonstrate a similar concern with the human inability to do what is right, as we have already seen to some extent in chapter 2. It will be helpful in the present context to highlight several of the most important passages. In 1 QS 4.22-26 the writer speaks of the glory of Adam which will at some future time belong to the community. In that time "there shall be no more lies and all the works of falsehood shall be put to shame." The present, however, is characterized by a struggle against evil:

Until now (עַד הֵפָּה) the spirits of truth and falsehood struggle in the hearts of men and they walk in both wisdom and folly. According to his portion of truth so does a man hate falsehood, and according to his inheritance in the realm of falsehood so is he wicked and so hates truth. For God has established the two spirits in

---

[70] Trans., Frank Justus Miller, 2 vols. (London: William Heinemann, 1925), 2:343.

[71] *Seneca's Tragedies,* trans. Frank Justus Miller, 2 vols. (London: William Heinemann, 1916), p. 307.

[72] Trans. and ed. Phillip De Lacy, 3 parts (Berlin: Akademi-Verlag, 1978), 1:245.

equal measure until the Renewal, and he knows the reward of their deeds from all eternity.[73]

Similarly, in 1QH 11.19-24 the hymn-writer grieves over the "(evil) inclinations of man, of his return to (dust, and of his leaning) towards sin and the sorrow of guilt" (11.19) but looks forward to a time of freedom from "iniquity and wickedness" in the eschaton (11.22-24). The Testaments of the Twelve Patriarchs likewise refer on occasion to a battle between good and evil within one's "conscience" (TJud 20:2) or "breast" (TAsh 1:5). "There are two ways, good and evil, concerning which there are two inclinations within our breasts which decide between them," says TAsh 1:5. The Testaments are more optimistic than Qumran, Paul, or even Galen about the individual's ability to choose the "good way" ; but the battle rages nonetheless.[74]

These examples from classical and Jewish texts demonstrate clearly the affinity between what Paul says and what those around him were saying about the origins of the common experience of doing wrong. Paul's concern, like that of this literature, is to say that although one may agree rationally with God's law, sin gains the upper hand through the flesh and prevents one from carrying out the law:

For I know not what I do, for what I want, this I do not perform, but I perform that which I hate. But if that which I do not want, this I perform, then I agree with the law that it is good (7:15-16).

---

[73] Vermes, p. 78. Dihle, *Theory of Will*, p. 73 distinguishes sharply between Greek and Hebrew thought on the source of good and evil action. In Greek thought, says Dihle, people make decisions about what they should do on the basis of knowledge, whereas in Hebrew thought they make such decisions on the basis of will: one either wills to go his or her own way or wills to do God's commands. Qumran and Paul follow the Hebrew rather than the Greek tradition. It is a serious thing to disagree with such a distinguished classisist on matters in which he is expert; but Dihle's scheme seems to take no account of the interplay between Greek and Hebrew thought which occurred in the Hellenistic Age. It is not at all impossible that Paul or even some of the Qumran covenanters had absorbed aspects of the debate on the motivation for human action that flourished during the second temple period and later. On the presence of Hellenistic philosophy and literature in Palestine during this period see Hengel, *Judaism and Hellenism*, pp. 83-102. Käsemann, *Romans*, p. 201 claims that Paul and Qumran are separated from the classical sources by their apocalyptic viewpoint. This is true; but the problem is essentially the same whether or not it is described in apocalyptic terms.

[74] Herbert Braun, "Römer 7,7-25 und das Selbstverständnis des Qumran-Frommen" in *Gesammelte Studien zum Neuen Testament und seiner Umwelt*, 2d ed. (J. C. B. Mohr [Paul Siebeck], 1967), pp. 100-119 is typical of many scholars when he argues that Paul and Qumran have a similar concept of the seriousness of sin and its inescapable presence but that Paul and Qumran diverge on the question of the place of the Torah in redemption. According to Braun, redemption at Qumran involves receiving the power to do the Torah whereas in Paul it involves freedom from the Torah. See also Wilckens, "Was heißt bei Paulus," pp. 90-92 and Römer, 1:221-22. As we have seen above, however, Paul and Qumran both reserve a place for obedience to the law in the eschaton.

Despite Bultmann's interesting interpretation of this passage as an argument against doing the law, it must be said that Paul nowhere says that doing the law is wrong. Assuming the role of the unbeliever, he simply says that, although he agrees with God's law, his fleshly nature prevents him from doing it.[75] Thus he reminds his readers in rather common terms of the plight under which those who do not walk in the eschatological Spirit stand. Generally speaking, they are fated to struggle and fail to do the good.[76]

Sanders's position is no more convincing than that of Bultmann. Sanders claims that Paul's argument in 7:1-13 is inconsistent with his argument in 7:14-15 (which in any case, says Sanders, unrealistically proposes that no one does anything good) and that both positions are inconsistent with what Paul says elsewhere about the connection between the law and sin. Paul's "majority statement" on the law according to Sanders is found in Gal. 3:22-24 and Rom. 5:20, and "is echoed in Rom. 3:20, 4:15." It is that God gave the law in order to reveal sin and make it worse so that he could save all who are under sin through Christ. In Rom. 7:7-13, however, sin uses the law "to produce transgressions against God's will," and in Rom. 7:14-25 law and God are placed on one side, sin and transgression on the other, and the two fight against one another in a remarkably dualistic manner.[77] In addition to this inconsistency with his other statements about the law and sin, says Sanders, Paul's pessimistic view of human nature in 7:15-23, where he opines that "the fleshly human is incapable of doing anything which the law commands," runs counter to what he says in Phil. 3:6 about his own ability to keep the law as an unbeliever.[78]

Sanders's charges of inconsistency, however, will not stick. It is difficult to see how Rom. 7:7-13 is inconsistent with the "majority statement" of Gal. 3:22-24, Rom. 3:20, 4:15, and 5:20. Sanders's claim that Paul is inconsistent is based on his idea that in 7:7-13 the law produces sin "against God's will" whereas in the other passages God uses the law to produce sin so that he can save the world through Christ. Nowhere, however, does 7:7-13 say that the law produced

---

[75] Käsemann, *Romans*, p. 201 thinks that to equate Paul's insight with Ovid's is to drain Paul's view of theological depth. This is only true if the depth of the struggle in *Metamorphoses* 7.16-20 and the tradition which stands behind it is underestimated.

[76] I have assumed with the majority of scholars that Paul is speaking in 7:14-25 of the situation of the unbeliever although there is a venerable tradition of interpretation to the contrary. See Martin Luther, *Luther's Works*, vol. 25: *Lectures on Romans: Glosses and Scholia*, ed. Hilton C. Oswald (Saint Louis: Concordia, 1975), pp. 327-43. That the "I" of 7:14-25 is "sold under sin" (7:14), that there is no mention of the Spirit, and that the general movement of the passage is from plight under the law and sin (7:1-6) to solution in Christ's death and the Spirit (8:1-4) seem to me to speak decisively against associating the "I" with the believer. See Augustine, *Confessions*, 8.5, 7, and 10; Kümmel, *Römer 7*, pp. 103-110; and Cranfield *Romans*, 1:340-71. I have not ventured to argue that this passage is autobiographical, although the argument presented here would equally be compatible with such a reading of this passage. Beker, *Paul*, p. 241 and Theissen, *Psychological Aspects*, pp. 177-221 are sympathetic with an autobiographical reading of the passage.

[77] *Law*, pp. 73-81; Räisänen, *Law*, p. 113.

[78] *Law*, p. 80; Räisänen, *Law*, pp. 101-113, 118-19, and 230.

transgressions independently of God's will; in fact, it does not mention God's will at all. Only in Paul's use of the passive in 7:13 do we find the slightest hint about who willed the connection between the law and sin. There Paul says that "sin, in order that it might be shown (φανῇ) to be sin, worked death in me through what was good...." With no indication to the contrary we should consider the author of the action behind the passive form φανῇ to be God. If so, then Paul's view in 7:7-13 is not inconsistent with his "majority statement;" here, as elsewhere, the connection between the law and sin was designed by God.

In 7:14-25 Sanders claims similarly that God's will and the law have now become allies against sin and transgression. Sin appears as a force separate from God and to some extent out of his control until he can launch a rescue operation apart from the law in the death of Christ (8:1-4). Again, however, Sanders has read the question of God's will into the text. God is only mentioned once—in the genitive case as a qualifier of νόμος. The purpose of this genitive is to distinguish "God's law" from that other law "which dwells in my members." In this context "God's law" means no more than "God's commands." At issue in the passage is not a battle between God's will and the law on one side and sin on the other, as Sanders claims, but the battle within the individual between the desire to do the law and the inability to fulfill that desire. Paul says nothing in 7:14-25 about whether or not God *wills* this interior conflict; but in light of his other statements about the connection between the law and sin, it is much safer to assume that God does will it than that he does not.

Finally, Sanders, followed closely by Räisänen, contends that in 7:7-14 Paul has allowed his argument to run amok. Paul seriously proposes that no one outside the community of those who believe in Christ can do good. "The human plight, without Christ, is so hopeless in this section," says Sanders, "that one wonders what happened to the doctrine that the creation was good."[79] Räisänen agrees:

> In his search...for grounds for his not uncritical attitude to the Torah, Paul made a tremendous generalization: the prohibitions of the law *always* incite to transgressions, and this is indeed the real *purpose* of the law as well.[80]

He does all this, furthermore, in violation of what he says in Phil. 3:6 about the possibility of being "blameless" with respect to the law outside of Christ.

Once again, however, Sanders and Räisänen have read something into Romans 7 which is not there. Paul does not intend to give a full account of the motivation for action in this chapter, but, in accord with an ancient debate, to speak briefly and theoretically of what happens within an individual when he or she does wrong. He speaks in sweeping terms, but that is not unusual when one

---

[79] *Law*, p. 75.
[80] *Law*, p. 149.

is speaking theoretically. It would be immaterial to his point to issue a caveat to the effect that of course everyone knows that sometimes people do what is right. That is assumed (2:12-16) and is not the issue.

Sanders and Räisänen[81] have a final court of appeal, however, which is usually considered to be the decisive proof for their argument. Phil. 3:6, it is said, clearly shows that when Paul sets aside his christology and speaks of his "former life in Judaism" he acknowledges that the law in its entirety can be kept perfectly. There he says that before his conversion he was blameless with respect to the law:

> If any other person thinks he has reason for confidence in the flesh, I have more: circumcised on the eighth day, of the people of Israel, of the tribe of Benjamin, a Hebrew born of Hebrews; as to the law a Pharisee, as to zeal a persecutor of the church, as to righteousness under the law blameless (κατὰ δικαιοσύνην τὴν ἐν νόμῳ γενόμενος ἄμεμπτος, Phil. 3:4-6).

Phil. 3:6 will not, however, bear the burden of proof which these scholars place upon it. Protests of blamelessness are a common phenomenon in ancient Judaism and do not infer that the law had been kept. Thus the biblical psalmists frequently speak of their righteousness when comparing themselves to the wicked—the flagrant violators of God's laws (Pss. 7:8-9, 17:3-5, 18:20-29, 26:9-12). It is likely therefore that the blamelessness of which they speak is a *comparative* blamelessness and is not meant absolutely. Similarly 2 Chron. 15:17 asserts that "the heart of Asa was blameless all his days"; but chapter 16 goes on to catalogue his sins. We have already seen that Abraham in the Testament of Abraham can be called "righteous," "sinless," and "all holy" in comparison with other people and still sin. Thus in Phil. 3:6 Paul compares himself to his enemies ("the dogs" of 3:2) and says that he was as righteous as they before his conversion. Such a statement does not imply that he thought of himself as sinless or able to keep the whole law.[82]

In Romans 7, then, Paul's purpose is to show that the law is not evil but "holy and righteous and good." In order to do this he shows how the law

---

[81] See also Bultmann, "Romans 7," p. 148; *Theology*, 1:266; Kümmel, *Römer 7*, p. 113; and Krister Stendahl, "Paul and the Introspective Conscience of the West" in *Paul among Jews and Gentiles*, pp. 80-81.

[82] John M. Espy, "Paul's 'Robust Conscience' Re-examined," *NTS* 31 (1985): 161-81, has produced a devastating critique of Krister Stendahl's widely accepted argument that Paul believed that he had kept the law perfectly prior his conversion. Espy, p. 164, points out that "the letter to the Philippians, practically alone among the Pauline writings, nowhere speaks of any Christian or group of Christians as having once been in sin; nor, for that matter, does it mention the 'dying' (to sin) and 'rising' of baptism. The theme is rather an attitude of sacrifice than a state of justification or an experience of conversion: not what Christians should cease to be, but how they should regard what they have, or believe themselves to have. Therefore it is an error to look to this letter for a balanced statement on Paul's pre-Christian condition; life in sin is simply not under discussion here."

multiplies sin by bringing certain sinful actions to mind but providing no possibility of overcoming them (7:7-13) and how the individual is so dominated by the flesh that on his or her own strength it is impossible to do the law (7:14-25). The first observation is indeed made from the standpoint of the solution rather than from the standpoint of the plight, for it views the law in a new perspective unknown in the Jewish world; but it neither argues against "legalism" nor implies the abrogation of the law. The second section, likewise, is not motivated by an attack on Jewish "legalism" but simply makes a familiar observation—that it is frequently difficult to do what one knows to be right—in order to show that it is the individual and sin, not the law, which are responsible for the human plight of disobedience to God. Nothing in Romans 7, moreover, shows that Paul's argument has run amok under the intoxicating influence of his desire to make Christ the savior of the world. Except for brief statements in 7:5 and 7:7-13 he says here what he and much of Judaism say elsewhere: humanity is "under sin," and people must trust God to provide an eschatological solution to this dilemma.

E) Romans 9:30-10:8

Paul's last extensive treatment of the law in Romans has, once again, been used as clear evidence that Paul thought backwards from solution to plight. Basically three positions on the meaning of this passage emerge from the wealth of literature written about it. One school believes that the passage accuses Israel of not keeping the law. Israel tried and failed to do what the law commanded with the result that it continues to exist under the curse of the law. The Gentiles, however, who ironically never even tried to live by the law have found righteousness apart from the law in Christ.[83] The second school says that the passage contrasts Gentile pursuit of righteousness by faith with Jewish pursuit of righteousness by means of the law. These scholars claim that the most important aspect of Paul's explanation of Israel's failure is his claim that Israel's fulfillment of the law is wrong. Some of these scholars believe that Paul charges Israel with fulfilling the law in order to flaunt her merits before God and thus compel him to save her.[84] Sanders, whose position otherwise belongs in this category, says that Paul does not charge Israel with legalism but simply with attaining the wrong sort of righteousness—Israel's fault is that her religion is centered around the law rather than around Christ.[85] The third school of interpretation claims that the passage does not contrast law and Christ but views them in a complementary relationship. Thus, it says, Paul's meaning is that both believing Gentiles and

---

[83] Van Dülmen, *Gesetzes*, pp. 125-27; Wilckens, *Römer*, 2:210-216.

[84] Bultmann, *Theology*, 1:266-67; Leenhardt, *Romans*, p. 262; Käsemann, *Romans*, pp. 277-78.

[85] Sanders, *Law*, pp. 36-38.

unbelieving Israel are seeking the same goals—righteousness and law—but the Gentiles have attained it through Christ while unbelieving Israel has failed to attain it. The reason for this failure according to this school is that Israel pursued the law in the wrong way—by works rather than by faith.[86] Members of the first school translate τέλος in 10:4 "Ende" or a combination of "Ende" and "Ziel."[87] Those who belong to the second school tend to interpret τέλος as "termination," and to see the "righteousness which is based on the law" in Rom. 10:5 as standing in contrast to the "righteousness based on faith" in Rom. 10:6.[88] Members of the third school generally translate τέλος as "fulfillment" or some near equivalent and see the two righteousnesses of 10:5 and 10:6 as complementary.[89]

The latter two schools have, I believe, made the passage more complicated than it is. Paul's problem with Israel in this section is, as advocates of the first school hold, simply that it has failed to keep the precepts of the law. Thus the guiding images of 9:30-10:4 are two groups of runners, one which pursues righteousness and attains it by faith and the other which pursues the goal of the righteousness of the law but fails to attain it:[90]

> What, then, shall we say? Gentiles who did not pursue righteousness have laid hold of righteousness—righteousness by faith. But Israel, although they pursued a law of righteousness, did not reach the law first.... They tripped on the stone.... For Christ is the goal of the law for the purpose of righteousness.

The images of pursuit (διώκοντα), laying hold (κατέλαβεν), reaching first (ἔφθασεν), and stumbling (προσέκοψαν), clearly point to a foot race in which two groups of competitors are trying to reach the finish, one attaining it and the other falling short. Paul does not condemn the pursuit of the goal, which is identified both with righteousness (9:30) and the law (9:31, 10:4); nor does he condemn the law, for Israel's failure is precisely that it "did not reach the law

---

[86] Barrett, *Romans*, p. 193; Cranfield, *Romans*, 2:509-510; Nygren, *Romans*, pp. 376-380; Badenas, *Christ*, pp. 101-105.

[87] Van Dülmen, *Gesetzes*, p. 126; Wilckens, *Römer*, 2:217.

[88] Bultmann, *Theology*, 1:263, 280; Leenhardt, *Romans*, pp. 265-66; Käsemann, *Romans*, pp. 281-83; Sanders, *Law*, p. 39.

[89] Cranfield, *Romans*, 2:515-22; Badenas, *Christ*, pp. 112-133. Barrett, *Romans*, pp. 197-99, uses the word "end" but associates it with the words "purpose" and "intention." According to Barrett, *Romans*, pp. 197-98, "Christ is the end of the law, with a view not to anarchy but righteousness." Nygren's position, pp. 379-381, is an exception: he takes 10:4 to mean that Christ is the "end" of the law and claims that 10:5-6 shows "that there is an absolute contrast between righteousness by law and righteousness through faith..." (p. 380).

[90] Badenas, *Christ*, 101-105.

first,"[91] and Christ is said to be the goal of the law.[92] Instead, Paul's complaint is that Israel pursued the law "not from faith but as if it could be obtained by works (ἐξ ἔργων)" and that she sought "to establish her own righteousness" (9:32). The meaning of the first phrase, if we allow 3:20 to control our understanding of ἐξ ἔργων, is that Israel refuses God's eschatological gift and power for righteousness, and instead continues to rely on its insufficient works for salvation. The second phrase probably echoes Deut. 9:4-10:10[93] where Moses reminds the people of Israel that it is not because of their own righteousness (οὐχὶ διὰ τὴν δικαιοσύνην σου, 9:5; see also 9:4, 6) that God is allowing them to enter the land but because of the wickedness of the land's present inhabitants. To speak of one's own righteousness in such contexts is to speak of insufficient obedience. Thus in Rom. 10:3 Paul claims that present-day unbelieving Israel is at fault because her own righteousness is insufficient and she has failed to submit to God's gracious eschatological provision for solving her plight.

This reading of 9:3-10:4 is confirmed by 10:5-8 where Paul contrasts two passages from the Torah, one, ascribed to Moses, which says that the one who does the law, shall live (Lev. 18:5), and one, ascribed to "the righteousness based on faith" which uses the words of Deut. 9:4 and 30:12-14 to describe the gospel.[94] As we saw in chapter three, a substantial portion of Leviticus is taken up with prophesying the failure of Israel to abide by Lev. 18:5 and the subsequent curse of ejection from the land. From the perspective of the first century reader, especially the diaspora Jew, the prophecy had clearly been fulfilled. The curse for disobedience had come. Deut. 30:12-14, however, is found within a context that points to a future period after the disobedience of Israel and the subsequent curse. In chapter 29 Moses speaks of the punishment which would come upon Israel if they should break the covenant:

---

[91] Sanders's argument, *Law*, p. 42 that when Paul used νόμος here he "did not say precisely what he meant" and that what he actually meant was "'righteousness by faith'" is not convincing. See Klyne Snodgrass, "Spheres of Influence: A Possible Solution to the Problem of Paul and the Law," *JSNT* 32 (1988):99-107.

[92] Badenas, *Christ*, pp. 38-80, has produced an exhaustive study τέλος in the Greek literature of the ancient world. He concludes that during the era in which the NT was written, the word most often meant "the sum, the final cause, the goal, the purpose, the decisive factor, or the *summum bonum*" (p. 80). Only rarely in the extant literature does it mean "termination."

[93] Paul's conflation of Deut. 9:4 with Deut. 30:12-14 in 10:6-8 shows that Deut 9-10 was in Paul's mind at this point in Romans.

[94] Badenas argues in *Christ*, pp. 118-33 that 10:6 is not set in contrast to 10:5. His arguments are not, however, convincing. Here, according to most interpreters, Paul attempts to support (γάρ, 10:5) his statement in 10:4 by pitting the personified "righteousness by faith" against Moses who poses as spokesman for "righteousness by law." Paul quotes Deut. 30:12-14 to represent the position of faith, and Lev 18:5 the position of law. Badenas argues, however, that the crucial δέ of 10:6 is not adversative but connective (cf. 7:8, 10:10, and 11:15), that the "righteousness by law" of 10:5 and the "righteousness by faith" of 10:6 are equivalent expressions, and he disparages all attempts to read Rom. 10:5-8 through the spectacles of Gal. 3:10-14. It is not clear, however, that in 10:6 δέ can be taken as anything but adversative, and, given the chronological proximity of Galatians to Romans, it is difficult to see why Paul's contrast of Lev. 18:5 with Hab. 2:4 in Gal. 3:10-12 should not be considered analogous to what Paul says here.

The generation to come, your children who rise up after you, and the foreigner who comes from a far land, would say, when they see the afflictions of that land and the sicknesses with which the Lord has made it sick—the whole land brimstone and salt, and a burnt-out waste, unsown, and growing nothing, where no grass can sprout, an overthrow like that of Sodom and Gomorrah, Adamah and Zeboiim, which the Lord overthrew in his anger and wrath—yea, all the nations would say, 'Why has the Lord done thus to this land? What means the heat of this great anger?' Then men would say, 'It is because they forsook the covenant of the Lord, the God of their fathers, which he made with them when he brought them out of the land of Egypt, and went and served other gods and worshiped them, gods whom they had not known and whom he had not allotted to them; therefore the anger of the Lord was kindled against this land, bringing upon it all the curses written in this book; and the Lord uprooted them from their land in anger and fury and great wrath, and cast them into another land, as at this day' (Deut. 29:22-27).

It was clear to first century Jews, especially those in the diaspora,[95] that the covenant had been broken in the manner described here, and, in fact, the predicted punishment had occurred. According to Deuteronomy 30, however, the story would not end on that bleak note. If disobedience occurred and the curses came, Israel could still repent, return to the Lord, and obey his commands. If they did so the Lord would

restore your fortunes, and have compassion upon you, and he will gather you again from all the peoples where the Lord your God has scattered you. If your outcasts are in the uttermost parts of heaven, from there the Lord your God will gather you, and from there he will fetch you; and the Lord your God will bring you into the land which your fathers possessed, that you may possess it; and he will make you more prosperous and numerous than your fathers. And the Lord your God will circumcise your heart and the heart of your offspring, so that you will love the Lord your God with all your heart and with all your soul, that you may live (Deut. 30:3-6).

The theme of obedience to God's commands in those days continues until 30:11 where the section from which Paul quotes begins.

Clearly Paul has chosen his quotation carefully. He has picked a passage which refers to the ease with which the law would be obeyed in the future to demonstrate that in Christ this long awaited period had arrived. Prior to the coming of Christ Israel lived under the curse pronounced upon those who had not lived by the law (10:5); but now the promised eschatological age in which God would circumcise the heart of his people had come. Now fulfillment of the law was available in the terms of which Deut. 30:11-14 spoke (10:6-8).

---

[95] J. D. G. Dunn, "'Righteousness from the Law'," pp. 219-221 comments on the popularity of Deut. 30:1-10 in the diaspora during the second temple period. He mentions Philo's allusion to Deut. 30 in *Praem.* 163-72 and the quotation of Deut. 30:7 on tomb inscriptions in Asia Minor to support his contention.

In summary, Rom. 9:30-10:8 says neither that Israel failed because she pursued the wrong thing (righteousness by the law) nor that she failed because she pursued the right thing (righteousness) in the wrong way (by works). Rather, the passage says that before the coming of Christ Israel failed to do the law, but that now the eschatological age, in which obedience to the law is possible, has arrived. The failure of present day Israel, says Paul, is that it persists in relying upon its own (insufficient) righteousness for acceptance before God. Thus once again Paul's thinking runs from plight to solution. The plight does not appear as an enigmatic shadow cast by the light of his christology but in a form that many Jews of his day could understand. Paul says simply that Judaism and all of humanity had broken God's law but that Christ had ushered in the promised era of obedience and blessing.

Summary and Conclusion

Throughout this chapter we have seen that scholars have typically taken one of two approaches to Paul's view of the law in Romans. Some have said that it represents a qualitatively different and considerably more profound view of the law than that of the Judaism of his day. Part of this group says that whereas Judaism saw the law as a means of working its way to God's acceptance, Paul saw that the very effort to do this was itself sin and so spoke of the keeping of the law as misguided. Thus it is the keeping of the law which brings wrath (4:15), increases sin (5:15, 7:7-13), and in itself is already sin (7:14-25). This, of course, was something which made little sense within a Jewish context. Another part of this group claims that Paul did not think of keeping the law as itself sin, but only the *legalistic* keeping of the law. There is a way of keeping the law that is acceptable before God, but the Jews did not know that way because it was discernable only from the standpoint of faith. For this school the law brings wrath (4:15) and increases sin (5:20; 7:7-13) when it is not sufficiently kept or when it is kept in a legalistic manner. A second group of scholars sees Paul's statements about the law in Romans as inconsistent and motivated by the conclusion that Christ is the universal savior[96] rather than by a desire to state a convincing case leading to that conclusion. The plight of unbelieving Israel is simply that she does not accept Christ and instead clings to the Torah. Thus Paul attacks the Torah in various ways: it cannot be kept (3:20); it was used by God to increase sin so that God could save all through Christ (4:15; 5:20); it is used by sin to stimulate sin (7:7-13); and it fought unsuccessfully against sin forcing God to send Christ (7:14-8:4).

---

[96] This is the phrase that Sanders uses to describe the presupposition from which Paul argues (see, for example, *Paul*, p. 443). Interestingly, it is not a pauline phrase. Paul never connects Christ with the terms "savior" or "salvation" although he can certainly describe the gospel in terms of salvation (Rom. 1:16, 10:10).

The common element between these two groups is that they claim that Paul argued his view of the law entirely in light of his christology. Paul's view, in other words, makes sense only on his presuppositions. In this chapter, as in chapter three, we have found reason to question this method of approaching Paul's view of the law. Although it is true that Paul can speak in ways that would have appeared startling and polemical to most Jews of his day (2:27; 5:20; 7:5; and 7:7-13), all that Paul says about the law is not motivated by his christology. The basic pattern underlying Paul's statements about the law in Romans, in fact, is that outside of Christ humanity is subject to the common human plight of disobedience to the law whereas "in Christ" believers walk by the Spirit and so fulfill the requirements of the law.

Thus in Romans, as in Galatians, Paul remains within the pattern described in chapter 2. Outside of Christ all are under sin with its consequence of disobedience to God's law. Believers, however, have received the eschatological gifts of atonement (3:21-26), forgiveness (4:7), participation in Christ's death (6:1-7:6), and the Spirit (8:1-17). Thus, with the exceptions of the distinctively Jewish requirements of circumcision, dietary regulation, and Sabbath observance, Paul expected his communities to keep the law in a way that was impossible for those outside.

CHAPTER FIVE

PAUL, TORAH, AND JUDAISM IN
GALATIANS AND ROMANS

This study began by posing the problem of Paul's intelligibility against the background of his Jewish heritage. How could the same Paul who considered Israel's gifts and call to be irrevocable say what he did about the Torah? The first chapter sought to impose some order on the various answers given to that question during the last century, and indicated the value of exploring another answer. Chapter two laid the ground work for that answer, and chapters three and four tested it on the proving ground of the two epistles in which Paul is most concerned with the relationship between the law and Judaism. It remains, however, to summarize the argument of these chapters and to draw some conclusions.

A Summary of the Argument

In chapter one we saw that basically four answers had been given to the question of how far Paul's Jewish background influenced his teaching about the Torah. Three of these answers gave Paul's Jewish background an important place in the origins and understanding of his view of the law. Some said that Paul's teaching had refuted the chief doctrine of Jewish soteriology: works-righteousness (Windisch, Grundmann, Bläser); others believed that Paul knew nothing of the gentle religion of the rabbis but formulated his doctrine against the forbidding religion of the Jewish diaspora (Montefiore, Parkes, Schoeps); still others claimed that Paul had applied to the coming of Christ the supposed Jewish teaching that the law would cease or would be radically modified in the messianic age (Schweitzer, Schoeps, Davies). In time, however, these views began to crumble and a fourth view gained the ascendency, reaching its climax in the work of E. P. Sanders. This view, presently in the majority, maintains that Paul's attitude toward the law cannot be explained within the context of Judaism. Instead, it can only be comprehended on the basis of Paul's experience with Christ. It was this unique experience rather than any rational critique or logical application of ideas from his Jewish heritage which led him to say what he did about the law.

Chapter one concluded, however, by noting signs of restlessness with the christological position. Its principal spokesman, E. P. Sanders, has been criticized from several directions. Heikki Räisänen disagreed with Sanders over whether Paul falsely attributed to Judaism the belief that salvation came by

works; Hans Weder claimed that the disparities between Paul and Judaism catalogued by Sanders were unimportant to an appreciation of Paul; and James D. G.
Dunn claimed that Sanders had left us with an enigmatic Paul who was divorced
from his historical and cultural environment.   In light of these criticisms it
seemed appropriate to attempt again to interpret Paul's view of the law against his
Jewish heritage, and to look especially at how the law figured in the eschatological expectations of both Judaism and Paul.

Chapter two, therefore, examined the Old Testament and certain writings of
the second temple period and discovered within them that eschatological hope was
frequently expressed in terms of God's intervention to rescue his people from sin.
We looked first at the law, the prophets, and the writings and found that humanity
was said to be caught in the plight of sin, that sin was defined in terms of
disobedience to the law, and that hope was extended that at some point in the
future God would rescue his people by providing them with the ability to obey
his law. We then turned to the literature of the second temple period and found
that there too, especially in the Dead Sea Scrolls, the human plight was defined in
terms of disobedience to God's word and that the eschaton would be a period of
obedience to the law by means of God's Spirit. Chapter two concluded that the
plight-solution pattern, articulated with reference to disobedience and obedience to
God's law, was current and even widespread within Judaism during the era in
which Paul wrote.

Chapter three explored Paul's view of the law in Galatians and found that,
although it has been considered his most "unjewish" and "antinomian" epistle, it
nonetheless operates within the plight-solution pattern so common in the Jewish
literature discussed in chapter two. Paul, we discovered, reserves a place for the
law among the eschatological community of believers and claims that the eschatological Spirit enables believers to fulfill the law of love. His negative attitude
toward those parts of the law which separate Jews from Gentiles (circumcision,
food laws, and Sabbath keeping) does not threaten the place which he gives to the
ethical commands of the law in the eschatological age, for in shifting the emphasis off those specifically Jewish commands he follows a common tendency within
the literature of Diaspora Judaism. Finally, his negative statements about the
place of the law in salvation history describe the law as something which cannot
be obeyed without the power of the Spirit, and therefore as something which pronounces a curse upon disobedience; but they do not imply that the law has been
abrogated *simpliciter*. Only the law's effect of defining sin and enclosing the sinner under sin along with the subsequent curse of the law has been abolished, not
the law itself. Thus despite Paul's negative attitude toward circumcision, food
laws, and Sabbath keeping, and despite his belief that the curse of the law upon
sin has ended with the eschatological age, his thinking about the law in Galatians
is best understood as a development of the plight-solution pattern described in
chapter two. Paul claimed that people are subject to the plight of the law's curse
upon sin in the present evil age unless they enter the eschatological community
where the power of the Spirit enables believers to keep the law.

Chapter four found that the plight-solution pattern also exists in Romans. Here too Paul reserves a place for the law in the eschatological age, expects believers to fulfill the law by walking in the Spirit, and describes the human plight in terms of disobedience to the law with its consequence of wrath. With several exceptions Paul formulates his statements about the law in ways not incompatible with contemporary thinking on its role and human inability to keep it. Here too, then, Paul's thinking about the law flows from plight (no one keeps the law and everyone stands under the wrath which this disobedience brings) to solution (in the eschatological age the Spirit provides the ability to keep the law).

Paul's understanding of the law in the two epistles where he speaks of it most extensively, therefore, can be explained on the basis of an eschatological pattern common in Judaism. Just as both canonical and non-canonical writings of Paul's day looked forward to a time in which God would rescue his people from disobedience to the law and the curse which that disobedience brought, so Paul claims that in Christ's death and in the presence of the Spirit within the believing community, the period of redemption from sin and the law's curse has dawned. Paul's view of the law in Romans and Galatians, then, is intelligible on the basis of Jewish presuppositions and does not derive solely from his christology.

Conclusions

If this description of the historical foundation underneath Paul's view of the law is correct, several conclusions follow. First, the standard description of Paul's conversion as the radical reorientation of a life centered around Torah to a life centered around Christ needs to be modified.[1] If the argument of the last two chapters is correct, Paul did not regard Christ and Torah as mutually exclusive but as complementary: Christ's death and the sending of the Spirit meant that the curse of the Torah had ceased, sin had been forgiven, and the law could now be kept. Paul's talk of his "former manner of life in Judaism" in Gal. 1:13-14 (cf. Phil. 3:4-11) should no longer be regarded as a statement about Paul's flight from Judaism to a new religion, but as an indication of a switch, in light of his experience with Christ, from one Jewish way of looking at the law to another. We know both from Acts (9:15; 22:15, 21; 26:17, 19-20) and Romans (1:5, 15:18) that Paul viewed his conversion as a call to preach Christ to the Gentiles. It is probably this call which led him to re-evaluate the content of the law and to exclude those portions of it which posed cultural stumbling blocks to the Gentiles. In doing this, however, he remained within a venerable tradition among Diaspora Jews of emphasizing the ethical and universal rather than the particularly

---

[1] Wilckens, "Die Bekehrung des Paulus," p. 23; Seyoon Kim, *The Origin of Paul's Gospel* (Grand Rapids: Eerdmans, 1982), pp. 274-75; Christian Dietzfelbinger, *Die Berufung des Paulus als Ursprung seiner Theologie*, WMANT, no. 58 (Neukirchen-Vluyn: Neukirchener Verlag, 1985), pp. 119-20.

Jewish aspects of the law. Thus his conversion did not involve the abolition of the Torah or a flight out of Judaism. Krister Stendahl is correct when he says that

> ...the usual conversion model of Paul the Jew who gives up his former faith to become a Christian is not the model of Paul but of ours. Rather, his call brings him to a new understanding of his mission, a new understanding of the law which is otherwise an obstacle to the Gentiles.[2]

This does not, of course, mean that Paul's conversion did not involve a radical change of outlook, nor does it mean that every aspect of his theology can be explained on Jewish presuppositions. Paul's concept of participation in Christ as it appears in such key passages as Gal. 2:19-20, 1 Cor. 6:12-20, 10:18-22, and Rom. 6:1-14 is one of the most important aspects of Paul's theology, and yet attempts to explain this concept on Jewish models have been unsuccessful.[3] And certainly Paul's christology goes far beyond Jewish expectations for the Messiah. If the basic contention of this study is correct, however, it is nevertheless difficult to speak of the pattern of Paul's religion as fundamentally different from that of at least some strands of Judaism in the second temple period. It is worth remembering that the Judaism of that period was, like Paul, deeply concerned with eschatological expectation, and it is precisely in Paul's eschatology that he remains fundamentally Jewish.

Second, the reconsideration of the Lutheran and Bultmannian interpretation of Paul which is presently under way is a hermeneutically healthy enterprise. This study has, I hope, contributed to that enterprise by questioning the idea that Paul "says that *man's effort to achieve his salvation* by keeping the *Law* only leads him into sin, indeed this effort itself in the end is *already sin*."[4] We have found

---

[2] "Paul among Jews and Gentiles" in *Paul among Jews and Gentiles*, p. 9.

[3] Albert Schweitzer's views on the subject in *Mysticism*, for example, are now widely regarded as eccentric. Klyne Snodgrass, "Spheres of Influence," pp. 93-113 offers the suggestion that Paul's language of participation in Christ may help us to understand his ability to speak both positively and negatively about the law. Outside the sphere of being in Christ the law has a negative function, but for those "in Christ" it assumes a positive role. This is a sensible thesis which I would clarify only by saying that Paul's Jewish eschatological convictions rather than his concept of participation in Christ is the source of Paul's ability to speak both positively and negatively about the law.

[4] *Theology* 1:263. See also Hübner, *Law*, p. 122. Bultmann's view on "boasting" in Paul for the most part is not excluded by our study. Bultmann points out that Paul argues against the attitude of "self-confidence which seeks glory before God and which relies upon itself" ("καύχησις" in *TDNT*, 3:649; see also *Theology*, 1:242-43), and this is surely a correct observation. 1 Cor. 1:18-31 demonstrates how vexed Paul became with those who thought that God could only work through the wise and rhetorically skillful "of the world," and says that "God chose what is low and despised in the world, even things that are not, to bring to nothing things that are, so that no human being might boast in the presence of God" (1 Cor. 1:28; cf. Gal. 2:16 and Rom. 3:20). Paul, moreover, clearly denounces those who boast of a special privilege before God because they possess the law but fail to see that they are sinners in need of God's forgiveness (Gal. 6:13; Rom. 2:17, 23; 3:27; 4:1-8). Nonetheless, contra Hübner, *Law*, pp. 101-124, Paul does not forbid

instead that Paul does not criticize "doing" the law, but only the failure to do it. Paul's concern is not so much that unbelieving Israel tries to do the law and thus make a claim upon God, but that she continues in her disobedience by not having faith in God's provision through Christ and the Spirit for obedience to the law. Thus, Paul has nothing against "doing" or against the concept of the human as "doer," but claims that outside the believing community it is impossible to keep the law.

This does not mean that Paul thought all who believed in Christ were able to keep the law flawlessly. "The flesh rises in protest against the Spirit, and the Spirit against the flesh," he says in Gal. 5:17 (cf. Rom. 8:18-27). Paul's conviction that although the new age of freedom from sin had begun, it had not fully come prevented him from assuming that believers would be sinless. Paul's attitude was similar to that of the Qumran covenanters who, as we saw in chapter two, viewed themselves as the eschatological community which would eventually be free from sin, but who also knew that the eschaton had not yet fully arrived. Like Paul's communities, the covenanters experienced the struggle between flesh and spirit in the period between the dawn of the eschaton and its consummation.[5]

Third, Paul's assessment of the human plight of disobedience is not inconsistent with Jewish ideas. It demonstrates neither that he had produced a series of *ad hoc* statements about the connection between the law and sin which show no coherence nor that he had penetrated to a unique insight into human sinfulness. On one hand Paul's statements about the law are fundamentally consistent, for they are based largely on a consistent pattern which he took over from Judaism. There can be no doubt that Paul's statements vary with the exigences of the particular situations which he seeks to address; but they have a common origin in the assumption that outside the eschatological community the law cannot be kept while within that community it can. On the other hand, Paul's statements about the inability of people to do the law outside of the believing community are not more profound than those in the Old Testament, in Judaism, or in the Greco-Roman world. What Paul says about the law in this regard is, in fact, quite ordinary. Many who pondered the question of evil reflected on the inability of people to choose the good consistently.

This does not mean that Paul's assessment of the human plight lacked acumen; nor should we lament that it is no more insightful than that of Ovid or 4

---

boasting in doing what is good. Gal. 6:4 clearly allows some form of boasting when it is based on a truthful assessment of one's self. Similarly in 2 Cor. 5:17 Paul allows the Corinthians to be proud of him as long as their boast is based on what he knows to be true in his heart rather than on mere appearances (cf. 1 Cor. 9:15), and Paul can boast in the exemplary behavior of his congregations in 1 Thess. 2:19; 2 Cor. 7:4, 14; 8:24-9:3; and Rom. 15:17-19. Thus while Paul does criticize relying on a false estimate of one's ability to do the law and relying on possession of the law for aquittal at the judgment, he does not criticize doing or even boasting in good works.

[5] See, for example, 1QH 16 where the hymn-writer says "...I know that man is not righteous except through Thee and therefore I implore Thee by the spirit which Thou has given [me] to perfect Thy [favours] to Thy servant [for ever], purifying me by Thy Holy Spirit, and drawing me near to Thee by Thy grace according to the abundance of Thy mercies."

Ezra. What Ovid and 4 Ezra say about the human inability to do good is by no means trite, and Paul's expression of the problem in familiar terms is a tribute to his grasp of a quandary which has vexed many from ancient times to the present.

Much scholarship in the last decade has served to isolate Paul—to make him a stranger both to his contemporaries and to the post-enlightenment world. He is frequently viewed as a solitary figure whose scruples over the conduct of the Gentile mission led him to strike out on his own,[6] whose views originated in personal obsessions,[7] whose writings were widely misunderstood in the early church,[8] and whose converts were quickly persuaded of other views.[9] This study has shown that, at least in one of the most important aspects of his theology, this picture of Paul is too stark. Paul's view of the law was neither a new break-through which few could understand or accept nor an idea developed *ad hoc* under the pressures of the moment, but was based on familiar ideas and echoed a familiar theme: the period of disobedience would end with the arrival of the eschatological age.

---

[6] Paul J. Achtemeier, "An Elusive Unity: Paul, Acts, and the Early Chruch," *CBQ* 48 (1986):23-26; James D. G. Dunn, *Unity and Diversity in the New Testament: An Inquiry into the Character of Earliest Christianity* (London: SCM Press, 1977), p. 254.

[7] Räisänen, *Law*, pp. 231-36; Theissen, *Psychological Aspects*, pp. 228-65.

[8] For two classic statements of this position see Adolf von Harnack, *Marcion: Das Evangelium vom fremden Gott: Eine Monographie zur Geschichte der Grundlegung der katholischen Kirche*, 2d ed. TU, vol. 45 (Leipzig: J. C. Hinrichs'sche Buchhandlung, 1924), pp. 195-215 and Ernst Käsemann, "Paul and Early Catholicism" in *New Testament Questions for Today*, pp. 236-51.

[9] Achtemeier, "Elusive Unity," pp. 25-26.

PAUL'S VIEW OF THE LAW ACCORDING TO
LLOYD GASTON AND JOHN G. GAGER

In recent years Paul's view of the Jewish law has become a central concern to those interested in the roots of "Christian anti-Semitism." A number of these scholars, taking the "traditional" view of Paul's attitude toward the law, have seen Paul as an apostate from Judaism who looked back on his "former manner of life" with scorn and who encouraged other Jews to imitate him in leaving the life of Torah for allegiance to Christ. Because Paul's attitude was so bitter toward Judaism, and because Paul felt that Jews had been replaced as the people of God by Christians, these scholars argue, Paul's attitudes planted the seeds of anti-Semitism which only needed the fertile soil of second and third century conflicts between church and synagogue to flourish.[1]

Although this study has by-passed discussion of Paul's supposed anti-Semitism, my conclusions have certainly been incompatible with the view that Paul repudiated Judaism and therefore with the view that he was anti-Semitic.[2] If Paul believed that with Christ the curse of sin had ceased and the means of keeping the law—the Spirit—had been given, as I have argued here, he believed what many Jews of his day believed. Where Paul differed from current expectation, of course, was in his attitude toward the inclusion of the Gentiles as Gentiles within God's eschatological kingdom, and this was enough to anger many of his fellow Jews. He also differed from many, although not all, of his "fellow countrymen" in believing that salvation, whether for Jew or Gentile, was contingent upon believing in the crucified Messiah Jesus, and it is here that this study takes issue with another set of scholars interested in the origins of anti-Semitism.

These scholars argue that Paul did not believe that faith in Christ was necessary for Jews. Jews could continue in their faithfulness to Torah with its prescriptions for conduct, atonement, and repentance and could by this means be saved. Faith in Jesus Christ as Paul saw it was merely a way of allowing the Gentiles to become part of God's elect people. Paul's disagreement with certain Jews was not that they refused to believe in Jesus Christ and so be saved, but that

---

[1] See, among others, Rosemary Radford Ruether, *Faith and Fratricide* (New York: Seabury, 1974).

[2] Even if Paul had turned his back on Judaism this would not, in my opinion, make him anti-Semitic or anti-Jewish unless those terms are so broadly defined as to make them practically meaningless. To believe that a religion, philosophy, or idea is not valid is not to question its right to exist.

they refused to believe Gentiles could share in the privileges of God's people by faith in Jesus Christ without taking the step of circumcision and without observing either food laws or the Sabbath.

This position, advocated most recently by Lloyd Gaston and John G. Gager,[3] comes close to the interpretation of Paul's view of the law advocated in this study on one key point: we agree that Paul nowhere teaches that the law has been abrogated by Christ. That, however, is where the similarity between our understandings of Paul ends. Gaston and Gager would disagree with my contention that Paul had adopted an eschatological scheme common in second temple Judaism. They would also disagree with my belief that Paul considered Israel's failing to be its inability in history past to keep the law as a people. They would disagree with me further that Paul saw the answer to the Jewish plight, and to the plight of all humankind, to be faith in God's future justification of all who have faith in Jesus Christ. Since the presuppositions of Gaston and Gager about Paul's relationship to Judaism diverge so widely from most scholarship on Paul, I have not burdened my argument with continuous references to their work. But their work represents a serious attempt to understand Paul and deserves a response, especially from those who write on Paul and the law.

Gager's work is divided into three parts, the first dealing with the modern debate on the origins of anti-Semitism, the second arguing (against "traditional" scholarship) that Judaism was, with a few exceptions, regarded with respect in ancient Rome and that anti-Semitism within Christianity does not derive from some current of anti-Semitism in the pagan world. That anti-Semitism is basically a pagan phenomenon, says Gager in this part of his work, is a myth carefully cultivated to exonerate Christianity of the charge that Christianity is anti-Semitic at its very roots. If not anti-Semitism at least anti-Judaism, pervades the New Testament.[4] It is present in Matthew and Luke-Acts and "reaches its peak in the gospel of John" (p. 151).

---

[3] Lloyd Gaston, *Paul and the Torah* (Vancouver: University of British Columbia Press, 1987); John G. Gager, *The Origins of Anti-Semitism: Attitudes toward Judaism in Pagan and Christian Antiquity* (New York: Oxford University Press, 1985). Gaston's work is essentially a collection of previously published essays presented in the order of their appearance in various scholarly publications. Gager's treatment is more systematic and therefore will dictate the order in which I discuss both works below.

[4] Gager reserves the term "anti-Semitism" for hostile statements about Jews which show little or no knowledge of Judaism. See his definition, *Origins*, p. 8. By "anti-Judaism" he appears to mean the idea that Christians have replaced Jews as the people of God. See *Origins*, p. 183. Gaston, however, uses the word "anti-Judaism" to refer to "a fundamental attack" on any of the three pillars on which Judaism stands: God, Torah, and Israel, and appears to accept Rosemary Ruether's charge that "theological anti-Judaism is the fundamental root of later cultural and political anti-Semitism," *Torah*, p. 17. Gaston's definition of anti-Judaism and Ruether's position on the origins of anti-Semitism are in my opinion incorrect for reasons too numerous to discuss here. If they are correct, however, and their solution to the problem is accepted, then it appears that any theological (and philosophical?) idea which denies the validity of any other theological idea must be abandoned because such exclusivism introduces the possiblity of another Holocaust. On the question of whether Paul's desire to see Jews converted to Christianity can be considered

But in the third and final part of his work Gager argues that neither anti-Semitism nor anti-Judaism is present in Paul's writings, for, says Gager, Paul nowhere repudiates the law or Judaism, nor does he anywhere claim that Jews need to believe in Jesus Christ in order to continue to participate in the covenant people of God. Paul kept Jews and Gentiles distinct from one another in his theological thinking. Gentiles certainly had to believe in Jesus Christ in order to participate in God's covenant, and they did not have to keep those requirements of the law which were required of proselytes. Paul, on the other hand, has very little to say to Jews. His letters are addressed to Gentiles, and, where they quarrel with Jews, do so on the basis that some Jews have opposed the idea that Gentiles can become members of God's people merely by believing in Jesus Christ. As Gager argues for these conclusions, he continuously acknowledges his debt to Gaston's work, and only in rare instances does Gager say anything substantively different from what Gaston has already said about Paul. [5]

Before beginning his analysis of the pertinent texts in Paul's epistles, Gager describes his position on several "hermeneutical issues" which, he claims, affect the outcome of any interpretation of Paul's view of the law. The texts with which one begins to interpret Paul's view of the law, says Gager, will determine the result of one's investigation: if the interpreter begins with such texts as Rom. 2:25 ("Then what advantage has the Jew? Or what is the value of circumcision? Much in every way.") and Rom. 3:31 ("Do we then overthrow the law by this faith? By no means!") then he or she is likely to conclude that Paul did not abrogate the Torah; but if the interpreter begins with those texts where Paul seems to speak negatively of the Jewish law, then a more negative decision about Paul's relationship to the law and Judaism is likely. Where one concludes depends upon where one begins.

We have seen this hermeneutical principle in action in chapters three and four above. In both cases we began our discussion of Paul's view of the law with texts in Galatians and Romans which took a positive posture toward it. And, at least on this aspect of Paul's thinking, our conclusion matched that of Gager and Gaston: Paul does not abrogate the Torah but continues to respect it as God's will.

Related to this hermeneutical principle are Gager's comments on "loose ends" in Paul's letters. Gager makes the familiar statement that Paul was writing occasional letters, not theological treatises and that we should not expect consistency from everything he says on a particular subject, especially on the Jewish law. Moreover, says Gager, Paul was probably the first Christian writer and therefore "lacked one of the essential prerequisites for any coherent system of thought, to wit, a body of literature and a sense of extended tradition" (p. 208). It is futile,

anti-Judaism or anti-Semitism, see W. D. Davies, "Paul and the People of Israel," in *Jewish and Pauline Studies* (Philadelphia: Fortress Press, 1984), pp. 134-35 and p. 143.

[5] Gager, *Origins*, pp. 209-212, describes three areas of disagreement with Gaston, but characterizes them as "minor quibbles," *Origin*, p. 212.

therefore, to look for complete consistency in Paul's letters and "when there appear to be loose ends in his thinking...we must not treat them as inimical to sound interpretation" (p. 209).

Although I would certainly quibble with the specific language of Gager's point,[6] his belief that in order to understand Paul's position on a certain topic we need not be able to fit every statement Paul makes into a system is well taken. Every interpretation of Paul's view of the law encounters difficult texts which are better labelled "more information needed for interpretation." But this should not prevent the interpreter from being able to decide Paul's basic attitude on various issues, including his attitude toward the Jewish law.

Perhaps the most important hermeneutical issue for both Gager and Gaston, however, is the idea that the historical context in which Paul writes presides over everything Paul says about the Jews and the law. Gager states that

> ...it is essential to recognize that Paul's letters were written to congregations overwhelmingly made up of Gentiles. Any interpretation that loses sight of this particular setting is bound to go astray." (p. 205).

Gaston concurs:

> A priori, one would not expect the Apostle to the Gentiles to be engaged in a dialogue with Judaism but rather with Gentile Christians, explaining how such central concepts as Torah relate to them (p. 4, cf. pp. 116-134).

This hermeneutical decision, as we shall see below, allows Gager and Gaston to interpret a number of texts in which Paul's language could include both Jews and Gentiles to refer to Gentiles alone. Since Paul is writing to Gentiles, the reasoning goes, nearly everything he says is meant exclusively for Gentiles, and non-Christian Jews are left out of the picture.

Here, however, Gager and Gaston have misused a valid hermeneutical rule. Taking into account the historical context of a text, especially an occasional letter, is clearly important for discerning the author's meaning; but Paul may have had occasion to discuss concepts of universal significance in order to address the specific situation of Gentiles in Galatia or Rome or Philippi. So in Phil. 2:11 when Paul says "every knee shall bow, whether heavenly, earthly, or subterranean, and every tongue shall confess that Jesus Christ is Lord to the glory of God the Father" we should not infer that he means every *Gentile* knee shall bow and tongue confess, even if he is addressing a predominantly Gentile church. The scene is the eschaton and the language is cosmic and all-encompassing, even

---

[6] For example, although Paul may have been the first "Christian" writer from our perspective, from his perspective he was writing within the "body of literature and extended tradition" of Judaism.

though the problem at hand is probably the mundane squabbles of the Philippian congregation (see 4:2). When Paul does not *say* "every Gentile" we should not understand him to *mean* "every Gentile" unless the context of the argument itself demands that meaning.

This is the nub of my argument with Gager and Gaston. In every text where the "traditional" interpretation understands Paul to say that salvation is possible only through Jesus Christ for both Jew and Gentile, Gager brings up the hermeneutical principle of the historical context and claims that because Paul is writing to Gentiles his words are valid only for Gentiles. In his discussion of Romans 2-3, for example, Gager says that

> ...the only radical element in (Paul's) preaching will be that Christ now offers to Gentiles what Israel always claimed to be possible only with the Torah, namely, righteousness and knowledge of God. Throughout Romans and Galatians this will be the burden of Paul's polemic. Not that the Torah ceases to be "useful" for Jews, but that its significance for Israel has now been replicated for Gentiles through Christ. From this it follows, of necessity, that boasting, as Paul understands it, must be the central, indeed the only point of disagreement between Paul and other Jews (p. 214).

The student of Romans immediately thinks of 3:21-23 where Paul says that

> A righteousness apart from the law has now been revealed, although it is attested in the law and the prophets, a righteousness through faith in (or through the faith of) Jesus Christ *for all who believe.* For there is no difference, *for all have sinned* and fall short of the glory of God, being justified freely by his grace through redemption in Christ Jesus.

But Gager believes that Paul's primary focus since 3:20 has been on the Gentiles. The *Gentiles* are those among whom there is no distinction, it is *Gentiles* who have all sinned, and the *Gentiles* alone are asked to "have faith in Jesus whom God now justifies." Gager claims that "it is not at all clear that Paul is thinking here of Jews" (p. 216). Gaston also believes that the passage is only relevant for Gentiles. The *all* of 3:22, he says, is meant to include the Gentiles, not to exclude the Jews (p. 122).

This reading is probably not correct, however, for several reasons. That Paul has both Jew and Greek in mind in 3:9-31 is clear from 3:9 where Paul explicitly mentions both groups and gathers them under one indictment with the word "all." He says, "For we have already charged that *all, both Jews and Greeks*, are under sin." That both groups are in view is also clear from Paul's statement in 3:22 that "there is no difference." The word διαστολή occurs only three times in the NT, and all three uses belong to Paul. It occurs once in 1 Corinthians where it refers to "different kinds of tongues" (14:7) and twice in Romans where it is used in nearly identical grammatical constructions and in similar contexts. Here in 3:22 Paul says, οὐ γάρ ἐστιν διαστολή and in 10:12, except for a significant variation, he uses identical language: οὐ γάρ ἐστιν διαστολὴ ᾿Ιουδαίου τε καὶ ῞Ελληνος. It seems clear from the parallels in these two sentences that when Paul speaks of there being "no difference" in Romans, whether in 3:22 or in 10:12, he means that there is no difference between Jew and Greek, not, as Gager says, that there is no difference between various groups of Gentiles.

In verses 23-24, furthermore, πάντες is the subject not only of the verbs ἥμαρτον and ὑστεροῦνται but of δικαιούμενοι as well, and "justification" for "all" says Paul comes through "redemption in Jesus Christ." Πάντες is not qualified by the word "Gentiles," and if διαστολή in 3:22 refers to the lack of difference between Jews and Gentiles, then it is virtually impossible to read the πάντες of 3:23 as anything but a reference to the whole world, both Jews and Gentiles, who without distinction need to be justified by "redemption in Christ Jesus." This is only what we would expect, however, since Paul began his epistle with about as clear a statement on this subject as one could hope for:

> For I am not ashamed of the gospel, for it is the power of God for salvation to all who believe, to the Jew first and also to the Greek (Rom. 1:16).

Curiously, Gager does not deal with this verse and Gaston does so only briefly. Gaston says that the interpreter's emphasis should be placed on the word "all" not on the word "believer," and that Paul's point is that through Jesus Christ Gentiles are included in the people of God previously made up only of Jews (p. 118). Thus Gaston translates the verse

> For I am not ashamed of the gospel, since it is the power of God for salvation for *every* believer, for the Jew of course, but *also* for the Greek" (p. 169, emphasis his).

Gaston believes that in this verse Paul defines his gospel (p. 118); but surely it is more appropriate to say that the verse tells what the gospel does—it is the channel of God's salvation for both Jew and Greek. For a definition of Paul's gospel we must look elsewhere, and one is handy a few verses earlier in 1:1 and 1:9. In v. 1 Paul says that he was

> set apart for the gospel of God, which was proclaimed through his prophets in the holy scriptures concerning his Son, who was born from the seed of David according to the flesh, and was set apart as Son of God in power, according to the Holy Spirit, by the resurrection from the dead, Jesus Christ our Lord....

In v. 9 Paul again refers to the gospel as "the gospel of his [God's] son." It is, therefore, the gospel of God's son which in v. 16 brings salvation to the Jew first and also to the Gentile. Paul will unpack this statement in 1:18-3:30 where he will describe the common plight of sin and the common solution of the gospel for both Jew and Gentile.

The treatment of Rom. 9:31-10:8 in the work of Gager and Gaston is also inadequate. They claim that Paul's argument with the Jews in 10:3 is not that they are trying to achieve righteousness without believing in Jesus Christ, but that they are ignorant of the righteousness which God has decided to give to the *Gentiles* through faith in Jesus Christ. Paul's statements in 10:4-12 likewise argue that Jew and Gentile are on equal footing now that Gentiles can participate in the people of God through faith in Christ (Gager, pp. 224-25; Gaston, pp. 126-134).

At least on Gaston's reading of 9:31-10:8, however, Isa. 51:1-8 must serve as the basis for Paul's comments. Because that passage, which speaks of the Gentiles acknowledging God, underlies this section of Romans, says Gaston, we can translate 9:31, "Israel, on the other hand, in pursuing the Torah of righteousness (for Israel alone) did not attain to (the goal of) the Torah" (p. 128). And the goal of the Torah, according to Isa. 51, is the inclusion of the Jews and the Gentiles in the people of God. The problem with this interpretation is that it rests on the conjecture that Paul had Isa. 51 in mind when he wrote. But since Paul did not quote the passage, it is impossible to verify the conjecture, and it seems imprudent to base exegesis on it. It is not clear from Gaston's argument, moreover, why Paul would need to pray for the *salvation* of Israel if her only "misstep" was a failure to fulfill her calling to be a light to the Gentiles.

When Gager and Gaston turn to Galatians they again argue that Paul's statements about the necessity of believing in Jesus Christ were meant for Gentiles alone. Appropriately, both scholars spend much exegetical energy on Gal. 2:15-21. Gager quotes Gaston's translation of 2:15-21, and verses 15-16 of that translation demonstrate clearly the exegetical decisions of both scholars:

> We who are Jews by birth and not sinners from the Gentiles knowing (therefore) that a (Gentile) human being is not justified from works of law, but (rather) through the faithfulness of Christ Jesus, we too became believers in Christ Jesus, in order that we might be justified from the faithfulness of Christ and not from works of law, because (as it is written:) by works of law "all" flesh "is not justified" (Psa. 143:2).

All Gager says about the insertion of "Gentile" before "human being" in v. 16 is that it is "clear enough from the context" that "*anthropos* in v. 16 must refer to Gentiles...for Paul's sole concern here is the Gentile Judaizers." Paul's overall concern in the letter is certainly with Gentiles who want to Judaize, but that is not his sole concern here. Also at issue is the hypocrisy of Peter, Barnabas, and other Jewish Christians at Antioch (2:11-14), hypocrisy based on the knowledge that what they required of the Gentiles they did not even believe themselves. From Paul's perspective Cephas was in the wrong because although Cephas lived like a Gentile himself he compelled Gentiles to live like Jews (2:14). In 2:15-17, then, Paul says that

we who are Jews by birth and not Gentile sinners—even we, because we know that
a person is not justified by works of law but through faith in (or the faith of) Jesus
Christ, have believed in Christ Jesus.

The argument runs from the greater to the lesser: if we Jews have agreed that justification by the law is impossible (as is evident from our conduct of living like
Gentiles) and therefore have believed in Jesus Christ for salvation, how much less
is it necessary for Gentiles to take on the yoke of the law in addition to faith in
Christ.

Gaston believes that 2:15-21 does not refer to Paul's disagreement with
Cephas in Antioch, but instead "sums up the whole narration...with special
reference to 1:15-16" (p. 68). Otherwise, says Gaston, Paul would be denying
that Jewish Christians could keep the law, and that would violate the agreement
with the Jerusalem "pillars" which Paul has just recounted. In 2:15-16, however,
Paul does not deny that Jewish Christians can keep the law but that the law is
more important than faith in Christ for salvation. The Jerusalem agreement,
moreover, was that James, Cephas, and John should go to the circumcised and
Peter and Barnabas should go to the uncircumcised; but Paul's argument in 2:15-
16 is against those who impose Jewish customs upon Gentiles even though they
know that faith in Christ, not Jewish customs, bring salvation. The two issues
are completely separate.

When Gager and Gaston turn to Galatians 3:1-4:20 they correctly realize that
any interpretation of the passage must come to terms with the meaning of "under
law," the phrase which Paul uses so frequently to describe the plight of those to
whom he is writing. Gager and Gaston agree that "under law" refers "to the
enslaved situation of Gentiles under the law" (Gager, p. 236, cf. Gaston, pp. 29-
31), that is to "those many and widely-attested Gentiles who undertook to observe
selected elements of the Mosaic commandments but stopped short of full
conversion" (Gager, pp. 236-37). But if this is true, then what would Paul mean
by his statement that "when the fullness of time came, God sent his Son, born of
a woman, born *under law*, in order that he might redeem those under law so that
we might receive adoption"? It is true, as the reference to adoption shows, that
Paul is thinking primarily of Gentiles in this passage; but it is also true that Paul
knew Jesus to be both "born under the law" and a Jew "born of the seed of David"
(Rom. 1:3). If Jesus, a Jew, was born "under law," it is impossible to maintain
that Paul reserved this phrase for so specific a group as Gentiles who were keeping part, but not all, of the Mosaic law.

Gager turns last in his treatment of Galatians to Paul's allegory in 4:21-31,
and again he relies heavily on Gaston's arguments and comes to Gaston's
conclusions. The thrust of the polemic at this point of Paul's argument, says
Gager, is against the Gentile Judaizers in Galatia, and Paul's point is that what is
right for Israel (circumcision) is wrong for the Gentiles. "...We can conclude," he
says, "that the Jews are absent from the entire passage" (p. 242). It is difficult to
see how the Jews can be absent from Paul's statement that "Hagar is Mount Sinai

in Arabia, and she corresponds to the present Jerusalem, for it is enslaved with her children" (4:25). Here is a place where Paul clearly describes non-Christian Judaism as "enslaved." He believes that if the Galatian Gentiles give in to the Judaizers in their midst they too will become enslaved to a law which, when elevated over faith in Christ, can only bring condemnation.

Gaston believes that Paul does not use the word "Jerusalem" in a negative sense here, for νῦν and ἄνω "are not really opposites" and Paul would not be likely to criticize Jerusalem in a letter meant to encourage the Galatians to contribute to his collection for Jerusalem (p. 89). The words "present" and "above" are opposites, however, in apocalyptic contexts. As I tried to show in chapter three, Paul's references to the "present" and the "heavenly" Jerusalems echo apocalyptic concepts of a present Jerusalem suffering for her sins which one day God would re-create on a glorious, heavenly scale. As for Gaston's second argument, it is difficult to give much weight to the idea that Galatians is concerned with the collection for Jerusalem, since that collection is never mentioned in the letter.

To these specific criticisms of the handling of Galatians in the work of Gager and Gaston can be added a more general criticism which nags the reader throughout. If Paul had no quarrel with salvation by Torah for Jews and Jewish proselytes (Gager, p. 236; Gaston, pp. 81-82), why was he so concerned about the Galatian situation in the first place? Gager of course argues that the Galatians were only observing part of the law, that they were not *full* proselytes, and that their readiness to combine partial obedience to the law and faith in Christ is what angered Paul. But the chief issue in Galatians was circumcision, usually the last step in becoming a full proselyte,[7] not food laws or festival keeping, although those elements are also mentioned. It seems likely that the Galatians were interested in combining their faith in Christ with full membership in Israel, and were becoming convinced that membership in Israel, not faith in Christ, was the most important element for salvation.

Romans and Galatians are the two letters which Gager and Gaston discuss most extensively; but they also comment on Phil. 3:7-11 and 2 Cor. 3. They believe that in Phil. 3:7-11 Paul's intention was not to commend his own experience to others; it was instead to describe his own unique call to be apostle to the Gentiles. 2 Cor. 3, they claim, clearly addresses a situation in which Paul opposes Jewish Christians; but Paul's objection to them involved their veneration of Moses as a "divine man" and an offensive idea of Christian ministry. Paul's remarks in this passage, therefore, cannot be construed as remarks against Judaism. Gaston and Gager may be correct, if not in the particulars of their exegesis at least in their main point, about 2 Cor. 3. Paul does not have Judaism and Torah in view in that passage (the word "law" does not even occur) but the way in which the Jewish Christian "pseudo-apostles" are conducting their min-

---

[7] See, for example, the discussion of Izates' conversion in Josephus, *Ant.* 20.42-44.

istry. As for Phil. 3:7-11, Paul says explicitly in that passage that his purpose in knowing Christ and "the power of his resurrection" is that he might "attain the resurrection of the dead." It is clear that for Paul—a Jew—participation in Christ was necessary for salvation on the day of resurrection.

SELECTED BIBLIOGRAPHY

Ancient Texts

A) Biblical

Christian Scriptures: *The New Oxford Annotated Bible with the Apocrypha.* Expanded edition. Edited by Herbert G. May and Bruce M. Metzger. New York: Oxford University Press, 1977.

New Testament: *H KAINH ΔIAΘHKH.* 2d ed. with revised critical apparatus. London: British and Foreign Bible Society, 1954.

Novum Testamentum Graece. 26th ed. Edited by Eberhard Nestle, Erwin Nestle, Kurt Aland, Matthew Black, et al. Stuttgart: Deutche Bibelstiftung, 1979.

Old Testament: *Biblia Hebraica Stuttgartensia.* Edited by R. Kittel, et al. Stuttgart: Bibelstiftung, 1977.

Septuagint: *Septuaginta Id est Vetus Testamentum graece iusta LXX interpretes.* Edited by Alfred Rahlfs. Stuttgart: Bibelgesellschaft, 1935.

Targums: *The Targums of Onkelos and Jonathan ben Uzziel on the Pentateuch with the Fragments of the Jerusalem Targum, from the Chaldee.* Trans. J. W. Etheridge. 2 vols. New York: KTAV, 1968.

B) Qumran

Lohse, Eduard. *Die Texte aus Qumran: Hebräisch und Deutsch mit masoretischer Punktation: Übersetzung, Einführung und Anmerkungen.* Munich: Kösel-Verlag, 1964.

Vermes, Geza. *The Dead Sea Scrolls in English.* 2d ed. Harmondsworth, Middlesex, England: Penguin, 1975.

C) Pseudepigraphical

Old Testament Pseudepigrapha: *The Old Testament Pseudepigrapha,* 2 vols. Edited by James H. Charlesworth. Garden City, New York: Doubleday, 1983-85.

The Apocryphal Old Testament. Edited by H. F. D. Sparks. Oxford: Clarendon Press, 1984.

Pseudo-Aristeas: *Aristeas to Philocrates (Letter of Aristeas).* Translated by Moses Hadas. Dropsie College Edition: Jewish Apocryphal Literature. New York: Harper & Brothers, 1951.

Testament of Abraham: *The Testament of Abraham: The Greek Recensions.* Translated
    by Michael E. Stone. Texts and Translations, 2; Pseudepigrapha Series, 2.
    Missoula, Mont.: Society of Biblical Literature, 1972.

D) Classical

Aristotle: *Aristotle, The Metaphysics, Books I-IX.* Loeb Classical Library.
    Translated by Hugh Tredennick. London: William Heinemann Ltd, 1933.

Arrian: *Epictetus, The Discourses as Reported by Arrian, the Manual, and Fragments,* 2
    vols. Loeb Classical Library. Translated by W. A. Oldfather. London: William
    Heinemann Ltd, 1928.

Cicero: *Cicero in Twenty Eight Volumes.* Loeb Classical Library. Vol. 1: *(Cicero), Ad
    C. Herennium, De Ratione Dicendi (Rhetorica Ad Herennium).* Translated by
    Harry Caplan. Cambridge Mass.: Harvard University Press, 1954.

Euripides: *Euripides, The Medea & Hippolytus with Introduction, Translations, and
    Notes.* Translated by Sydney Waterlow. London: J. M. Dent & Co., 1906.

Galen: Galen, *On the Doctrines of Hippocrates and Plato,* 3 parts. Translated and
    edited by Phillip De Lacy. Berlin: Akademi-Verlag, 1978.

Josephus: *Josephus. With English translations by H. St. J. Thackery, Ralph Marcus,
    Allen Wickgren, and Louis Feldman.* 9 vols. Loeb Classical Library.
    Cambridge, Mass.: Harvard University Press, 1926-65. London: William
    Heinemann, 1926-65.

Justin Martyr: *Justin Martyr: The Dialogue with Trypho.* Translation, introduction,
    and notes by A. Lukyn Williams. London: Society for Promoting Christian
    Knowledge, 1930.

Marcus Aurelius: *The Meditations of the Emperor Marcus Antoninus,* 2 vols. Edited
    and Translated by A. S. L. Farquharson. Oxford: Clarendon Press, 1944.

Ovid: *Ovid, Metamorphoses,* 2 vols. Translated by Frank Justus Miller. Loeb
    Classical Library. London: William Heinemann, 1925.

Philo: *Philo.* With English translations by F. H. Colson, G. H. Whitaker, and R.
    Marcus. Loeb Classical Library. Cambridge, Mass.: Harvard University Press,
    1029-53. London: William Heinemann, 1929-53.

Seneca: *Seneca's Tragedies,* 2 vols. Translated by Frank Justus Miller. Loeb Classical
    Library. London: William Heinemann, 1916.

Modern Works

Achtemeier, Paul J. "An Elusive Unity: Paul, Acts, and the Early Church." In *Catholic
    Biblical Quarterly* 48 (1986): 1-26.

Andrews, Mary E. *The Ethical Teaching of Paul: A Study of Origin.* Chapel Hill: University of North Carolina Press, 1934.

Aune, David Edward. *The Cultic Setting of Realized Eschatology in Early Christianity.* Supplements to Novum Testamentum, no. 28. Leiden: E. J. Brill, 1972.

Badenas, Robert. *Christ the End of the Law: Romans 10.4 in Pauline Perspective.* JSNT Studies, no. 10. Sheffield, Eng.: JSOT Press, 1985.

Bammel, Ernst. "NOMOS CHRISTOU." *Studia Evangelica* 3 (1964): 120-28.

Barrett, C. K. *The Epistle to the Romans.* Harper's New Testament Commentaries. New York: Harper & Row, 1957.

Bassler, Jouette M. *Divine Impartiality: Paul and a Theological Axiom.* Society of Biblical Literature Dissertation Series, no. 59. Chico, Calif.: Scholars Press, 1982.

Bauer, Walter. *A Greek-English Lexicon of the New Testament and Other Early Christian Literature.* Translated and adapted by William F. Arndt and F. Wilbur Gingrich. 2d ed., revised and adapted by Fredrick W. Danker and F. Wilbur Gingrich. Chicago: University of Chicago Press, 1979.

Beck, Fredrick A. G. *Greek Education, 450-350 B. C..* London: Methuen & Co Ltd, 1964.

Becker, Jürgen. *Das Heil Gottes: Heils—und Sündenbegriffe in den Qumrantexten und im Neuen Testament.* Studien zur Umwelt des Neuen Testaments, no. 3. Göttingen: Vandenhoeck & Ruprecht, 1964.

Beckwith, Roger. *The Old Testament Canon of the New Testament Church and Its Background in Early Judaism.* Grand Rapids: Wm. B. Eerdmans Publishing Co., 1985.

Beker, J. C. *Paul the Apostle: The Triumph of God in Life and Thought.* Philadelphia: Fortress Press, 1980.

Betz, Hans Dieter. *Galatians: A Commentary on Paul's Letter to the Churches in Galatia.* Hermeneia. Philadelphia: Fortress Press, 1979.

Bläser, Peter. *Das Gesetz bei Paulus.* Munster: Aschendorffsche Verlagsbuchhandlung, 1941.

Blank, Josef, "Erwägungen zum Schriftverständnis des Paulus." In *Rechfertigung: Festschrift für Ernst Käsemann zum 70. Geburtstag*, pp. 36-56. Edited by Johannes Friedrich, Wolfgang Pühlmann, and Peter Stuhlmacher. Tübingen: J.C.B. Mohr (Paul Siebeck), 1976.

Bligh, John. *Galatians: A Discussion of St. Paul's Epistle.* Householder Commentaries 1. London: St. Paul, 1969.

Borgen, Peder. *Philo, John and Paul: New Perspectives on Judaism and Early Christianity*. Brown Judaic Studies no. 131. Atlanta, Georgia: Scholars Press, 1987.

Bonner, Stanley F. *Education in Ancient Rome from the Elder Cato to the Younger Pliny*. Berkeley: University of California Press, 1977.

Bonhöffer, Adolf. *Epiktet und das Neue Testament. Religionsgeschichtliche Versuche und Vorarbeiten*, vol. 10. Gießen: Verlag von Alfred Töpelmann, 1911.

Bonsirven, J. *Le Judaïsme palestinien au temps de Jésus Christ: sa théologie*, 2 vols. Paris: Beauchesne, 1934-35.

Bornkamm, Günther. "Gesetz und Natur: Röm 2:14-16." In *Studien zu Antike und Urchristentum: Gesammelte Aufsätze*, vol. 2, pp. 93-118. 3d ed. Beiträge zur evangelishen Theologie, no. 28. Munich: Kaiser Verlag, 1970.

_____. "The Letter to the Romans as Paul's Last Will and Testament." In *The Romans Debate*, pp. 17-31. Edited by Karl Paul Donfried. Minneapolis, Minn.: Augsburg Publishing House, 1977.

_____. "Sünde, Gesetz und Tod: Exegetische Studien zu Röm 7:1." In *Das Ende des Gesetzes: Paulusstudien*, pp. 51-69. Munich: Chr. Kaiser Verlag, 1952.

Brandenburger, Egon. *Adam und Christus: Exegetisch-religiongeschichtliche Untersuchung zu Röm. 5.12-21 (1. Kor. 15)*. Wissenschaftliche Monographien zum Alten und Neuen Testament, no. 7. Neukirchen: Neukirchener Verlag, 1962.

Braun, Herbert. "Römer 7, 7-25 und das Selbstverständnis des Qumran-Frommen." In *Gesammelte Studien zum Neuen Testament und seiner Umwelt*, pp. 100-119. 2d ed. J. C. B. Mohr (Paul Siebeck), 1967.

Bring, Ragnar. *Commentary on Galatians*. Translated by Eric Wahlstrom. Philadelphia: Muhlenberg Press, 1961.

Bruce, F. F. "The Curse of the Law." In *Paul and Paulinism: Essays in Honour of C. K. Barrett*, pp. 27-36. Edited by Morna D. Hooker and S. G. Wilson. London: SPCK, 1982.

_____. *The Epistle of Paul to the Galatians: A Commentary on the Greek Text*. New International Greek Commentary. Grand Rapids: Wm. B. Eerdmans Publishing Co., 1982.

_____. *The Letter to the Romans: An Introduction and Commentary*. 2d ed. Leicester, Eng.: Inter-Varsity Press, 1985.

Bultmann, Rudolf. "Glossen im Römerbrief." In *Exegetica: Aufsätze zur Erforschung des Neuen Testaments*, pp. 278-84. Edited by Erich Dinkler. Tübingen: J. C. B. Mohr (Paul Siebeck), 1967.

_____. "Paul." In *Existence and Faith: Shorter Writings of Rudolf Bultmann*, pp. 111-146. Selected, translated, and edited by Schubert M. Ogden. New York: Meridian Books, Inc., 1960.

_____. *Primitive Christianity in Its Contemporary Setting*. Translated by R. H. Fuller. New York: World Publishing Company, 1956.

_____. "Prophecy and Fulfillment." In *Essays on Old Testament Hermeneutics*. 2d ed., pp. 50-75. Edited by Claus Westermann. Translated by James Luther Mays. Richmond, Va.: John Knox Press, 1964.

_____. "Romans 7 and the Anthropology of Paul." In *Existence and Faith: Shorter Writings of Rudolf Bultmann,* pp. 147-57. Selected, translated, and edited by Schubert M. Ogden. New York: Meridian Books, Inc., 1960

Burton, Ernest De Witt. *A Critical and Exegetical Commentary on the Epistle to the Galatians. International Critical Commentaries*, vol.10. Edinburgh: T & T Clark, 1921.

Caird, G. B. Review of *Paul and Palestinian Judaism* by E. P. Sanders. *Journal of Theological Studies* 29 (1978): 538-43.

Callan, Terrence. "Pauline Midrash: The Exegetical Background of Gal. 3:19b." *Journal of Biblical Literature* 99 (1980): 549-67.

Cambier, J. "Le jugement de tous les hommes." *Zeitschrift für die neutestamentliche Wissenschaft* 67 (1976-77): 187-213.

Cavallin, H. C. C. "'The Righteous Shall Live by Faith': A Decisive Argument for the Traditional Interpretation." *Studia theologica* 32 (1978): 33-43.

Charlesworth, James H. *The Old Testament Pseudepigrapha and the New Testament: Prolegomena for the Study of Christian Origins*. Cambridge: Cambridge University Press, 1985.

Clemen, Carl. "Die Auffassung des Alten Testaments bei Paulus." *Theologische Studien und Kritiken* 75 (1902): 176-80.

Clements, R. E. *Old Testament Theology*. Atlanta: John Knox, 1978.

_____. *Prophecy and Covenant*. Studies in Biblical Theology, no. 43. Naperville, Ill.: Alec R. Allenson, Inc., 1965.

Collins, J. J. *Between Athens and Jerusalem: Jewish Identity in the Hellenistic Diaspora*. New York: Crossroad, 1983.

Cosgrove, Charles H. "The Law and the Spirit: An Investigation into the Theology of Galatians." Ph.D. dissertation, Princeton Theological Seminary, 1985.

_____. "'What If Some Have Not Believed?' The Occasion and Thrust of Romans 3:1-8." *Zeitschrift für die neutestamentliche Wissenschaft* 78 (1987): 90-105.

Cranfield, C. E. B. *A Critical and Exegetical Commentary on the Epistle to the Romans*, 2 vols. International Critical Commentaries, vol. 7. Edinburgh, T & T Clark, 1975-79.

_____. "St. Paul and the Law." *Scottish Journal of Theology* 17 (1964): 43-68.

Dahl, Nils Alstrup. "Promise and Fulfillment." In *Studies in Paul: Theology for the Early Christian Mission*, pp. 121-36. Minneapolis, Minn.: Augsburg Publishing House, 1977.

_____. Review of *Paul and Palestinian Judaism* by E. P. Sanders. *Religious Studies Review* 4 (1978): 153-58.

Davies, W. D. "Paul and the People of Israel." In *Jewish and Pauline Studies*, pp. 123-52. Philadelphia: Fortress Press, 1980.

_____. *Paul and Rabbinic Judaism: Some Rabbinic Elements in Pauline Theology*. London: S. P. C. K., 1948.

_____. *Paul and Rabbinic Judaism: Some Rabbinic Elements in Pauline Theology*. 4th ed. Philadelphia: Fortress Press, 1980.

_____. Review of *Paulus: die Theologie des Apostles im Licht der jüdischen Religionsgeschichte*, by Hans Joachim Schoeps, *New Testament Studies* 10 (1963-64): 295-304.

_____. *Torah in the Messianic Age and/or the Age to Come*. Society of Biblical Literature Monograph Series, no. 7. Philadelphia: Society of Biblical Literature, 1952.

Delling, Gerhard. "στοιχεῖα" In *Theological Dictionary of the New Testament*, vol. 7, pp. 666-687. Edited by Gerhard Kittel and Gerhard Friedrich. Translated by G.W. Bromiley. 10 vols. Grand Rapids: Wm. B. Eerdmans Publishing Co., 1964-74.

Dibelius, Martin. *A Commentary on James*. Revised by Heinrich Greeven. Translated by Michael A. Williams. Hermeneia. Philadelphia: Fortress Press, 1975.

Dietzfelbinger, Christian. *Die Berufung des Paulus als Ursprung seiner Theologie*. Wissenschaftliche Monographien zum Alten und Neuen Testament, no. 58. Neukirchen-Vluyn: Neukirchener Verlag, 1985.

Dihle, Albrecht. *The Theory of Will in Classical Antiquity*. Sather Classical Lectures, vol. 48. Berkeley: University of California Press, 1982.

Dodd, C. H. *According to the Scriptures: The Substructure of New Testament Theology*. London: Nisbet & Co., Ltd. 1952.

_____. "The Mind of Paul: I." In *New Testament Studies*, pp. 67-82. Manchester: University of Manchester, 1953.

_____. "The Mind of Paul II." In *New Testament Studies*, pp. 83-128. Manchester: University of Manchester, 1953.

Doty, William G. *Letters in Primitive Christianity*. Philadelphia: Fortress Press, 1973.

Drane, John. *Paul: Libertine or Legalist? A Study in the Theology of the Major Pauline Epistles.* London: SPCK, 1975.

Dülmen, Andrea van. *Die Theologie des Gesetzes bei Paulus.* Stuttgarter biblische Monographien, no. 5. Stuttgart: Verlag Katholisches Bibelwerk, 1968.

Dunn, James D. G. "The Incident at Antioch." *Journal for the Study of the New Testament* 18 (1983): 2-57.

_____. "The New Perspective on Paul." *Bulletin of the John Rylands University Library of Manchester* 65 (1983): 95-122.

_____. "'Righteousness from the Law' and 'Righteousness from Faith': Paul's Interpretation of Scripture in Romans 10:1-10." In *Tradition and Interpretation in the New Testament: Essays in Honor of E. Earle Ellis,* pp. 216-228. Edited by Gerald F. Hawthorne with Otto Betz. Grand Rapids: Eerdmans, 1988.

_____. *Unity and Diversity in the New Testament: An Inquiry into the Character of Earliest Christianity.* London: SCM Press, 1977.

_____. "Works of the Law and the Curse of the Law (Galatians 3:10-14)," NTS 31 (1985): 523-42.

Enslin, Morton Scott. *The Ethics of Paul.* New York: Harper & Brothers Publishers, 1930.

Espy, John M. "Paul's 'Robust Conscience' Re-examined." *New Testament Studies* 31 (1985): 161-81.

Feuillet, A. "Loi de Dieu, loi du Christ et loi de l'Esprit d'après les épîtres pauliniennes: Les rapports de ces trois lois avec la Loi Mosaique." *Novum Testamentum* 22 (1980): 29-65.

Flückiger, Felix. "Die Werke des Gesetzes bei den Heiden (nach Röm 2, 14ff)." *Theologische Zeitschrift* 8 (1952): 17-42.

Freeman, Kenneth J. *Schools of Hellas, An Essay on the Practice and Theory of Ancient Greek Education from 600 B. C. to 300 B. C.* Edited by M. J. Rendall. London: Macmillan and Co., Limited, 1922.

Friedländer, M. "The 'Pauline' Emancipation from the Law a Product of the Pre-Christian Diaspora." *Jewish Quarterly Review* 14 (1902):265-301.

Fuller, Daniel P. "Paul and 'Works of the Law'." *Westminster Theological Journal* 38 (1975-76): 28-42.

Furnish, Victor Paul. *Theology and Ethics in Paul.* Nashville: Abingdon, 1968.

Garnet, Paul. *Salvation and Atonement in the Qumran Scrolls.* Wissenschaftliche Untersuchungen zum Neuen Testament, 2.3. Tübingen: J. C. B. Mohr (Paul Siebeck), 1977.

Gager, John G. *The Origins of Anti-Semitism: Attitudes toward Judaism in Pagan and Christian Antiquity.* New York: Oxford University Press, 1983.

Gaston, Lloyd. *Paul and the Torah.* Vancouver: University of British Columbia Press, 1987.

Gese, Harmut. "The Law." In *Essays on Biblical Theology,* pp. 60-92. Translated by Keith Crim. Minneapolis: Augsburg Publishing House, 1981.

Girard, Paul. *L'éducation athénienne au Ve et au IVe siècle avant J.-C.* Paris: Libraire Hachette et Cie., 1899.

Grönemeyer, Reimer. "Zur Frage nach dem paulinischen Antinomismus: Exegetisch-systematische Überlegungen mit besonderer Berücksichtigung der Forschunsgeschichte im 19. Jahrhundert." Dokotorwürde Dissertation, University of Hamburg, 1970.

Grundmann, W. "Gesetz, Rechtfertigung und Mystik bei Paulus: Zum Problem der Einheitlichkeit der paulinischen Verkundigung." *Zeitschrift für neutestamentliche Wissenschaft* 32 (1933): 52-65.

Gundry, Robert H. "The Moral Frustration of Paul before His Conversion: Sexual Lust in Romans 7:7-25." In *Pauline Studies: Essays Presented to F. F. Bruce on his 70th Birthday,* pp. 228-45. Edited by Donald A. Hagner and Murray J. Harris. Grand Rapids: Eerdmans, 1980.

Gutbrod, W. "νόμος." In *Theological Dictionary of the New Testament,* vol. 4, pp. 1036-1091. Edited by Gerhard Kittle and Gerhard Friedrich. Translated by G. W. Bromiley. 10 vols. Grand Rapids: Wm. B. Eerdmanns, 1964-74.

Hanson, A. T. "Abraham the Justified Sinner." In *Studies in Paul's Technique and Theology,* pp. 52-66. Grand Rapids: Wm. B. Eerdmans Publishing Co., 1974.

Harnack, Adolf von. *Marcion: Das Evangelium vom fremden Gott: Eine Monographie zur Geschichte der Grundlegung der katholischen Kirche.* 2d ed. Texte und Untersuchungen zur Geschichte der alterchristlichen Literatur, vol. 45. Leipzig: J. C. Hinrichs'sche Buchhandlung, 1924.

Hays, Richard B. "The Effects of Intertextual Echo in Romans: Preliminary Soundings." Paper given at the 1985 meeting of the Society of Biblical Literature, Pauline Epistles Section.

_____. *The Faith of Jesus Christ: An Investigation of the Narrative Substructure of Galatians 3:1-4:11.* Society of Biblical Literature Dissertation Series, no. 56. Chico, Calif.: Scholars Press, 1983.

Heiligenthal, Roman. "Soziologische Implikationen der paulinischen Rechtfertigungslehre im Galaterbrief am Beispiel der 'Werke des Gesetzes'." *Kairos* 26 (1984): 38-51.

_____. *Werke als Zeichen: Untersuchungen zur Bedeutung der menschlichen Taten im Frühjudentum, Neuen Testament und Frühchristentum.* Wissenschaftliche

Untersuchungen zum Neuen Testament, no. 2.9. Tübingen: J. C. B. Mohr (Paul Siebeck), 1983.

Hengel, Martin. *Jews, Greeks and Barbarians: Aspects of the Hellenization of Judaism in the Pre-Christian Period*. Translated by John Bowden. London: SCM Press, 1980.

_____. *Judaism and Hellenism: Studies in their Encounter in Palestine during the Early Hellenistic Period*, 2 vols. Translated by John Bowden. Philadelphia: Fortress Press, 1974.

Hommel, Hildebrecht. "Das 7. Kapitel des Römerbriefs im Licht antiker Überlieferung." In *Theologia Viatorum: Jahrbuch der Kirchlichen Hochschule Berlin*, 1961/62, pp. 90-116. Berlin: Walter de Gruyter & Co., 1962.

Horbury, W. "Paul and Judaism." *Expository Times* 89 (1977-78): 116-18.

Howard, George. *Crisis in Galatia: A Study in Early Christian Theology*. Society for New Testament Studies Monograph Series, no. 35 Cambridge: Cambridge University Press, 1979.

Hübner, Hans. "Das ganze und das eine Gesetz, zum Problem Paulus und die Stoa." *Kerygma und Dogma* 22 (1976): 250-76.

Janowski, Bernd and Hermann Lichtenberger."Enderwartung und Reinheitsidee: Zur eschatologische Deutung von Reinheit und Sühne in der Qumrangemeinde." *Journal of Jewish Studies* 34 (1983):31-62.

_____. *Gottes Ich und Israel: zum Schriftgebrauch des Paulus in Römer 9-11*. Forschungen zur Religion und Literatur des Alten und Neuen Testaments, no. 146. Göttingen: Vandenhoeck & Ruprecht, 1984.

_____. *Law in Paul's Thought*. Translated by James C. G. Greig. Edinburgh: T &T Clark, 1984.

_____. "Was heißt bei Paulus 'Werke des Gesetzes'?" In *Glaube und Eschatologie: Festschrift für Georg Kümmel zum 90. Geburtstag*, pp. 123-32. Edited by Erich Gräßer and Otto Merk. Tübingen: J. C. B. Mohr (Paul Siebeck), 1985.

Jaubert, Annie. *La notion d'alliance dans le Judaïsme aux abords de l'ère Chrétienne*. Paris: Editions du Seuil, 1963.

Jewett, Robert. "The Agitators and the Galatians Congregation." *New Testament Studies* 17 (1970-71): 198-212.

_____. *Paul's Anthropological Terms: A Study of Their use in Conflict Settings*. Arbeiten zur Geschichte des antiken Judentums und des Urchristentums, vol. 10. Leiden: E. J. Brill, 1971.

de Jonge, M. *Testamenta XII Patriarchum*. Pseudepigrapha Veteris Testamenti Graece, no. 1. Leiden: Brill, 1971.

Jungel, Eberhard. "Das Gesetz zwischen Adam und Christus: Eine theologische Studie zu Röm 5, 12-21." In *Unterwegs zur Sache: Theologische Bemerkungen*, pp. 42-74. Beiträge zur evangelischen Theologie, no. 61. Munich: Chr. Kaiser Verlag, 1972.

Käsemann, Ernst. *Commentary on Romans*. Translated by Geoffrey W. Bromiley. Grand Rapids: Wm. B. Eerdmans Publishing Co., 1980.

_____. "Paul and Early Catholicism." In *New Testament Questions for Today*, pp. 236-51. Translated by W. J. Montague. Philadelphia: Fortress Press, 1969.

_____. "The Righteousness of God in Paul." In *New Testament Questions of Today*, pp. 168-82. Translated by W. J. Montague. Philadelphia: Fortress Press, 1969.

Keck, Leander A. "The Function of Rom 3:10-18: Observation and Suggestions." In *God's Christ and his People: Studies in Honour of Nils Alstrup Dahl*, pp. 141-57. Edited by Jacob Jervell and Wayne A. Meeks. Oslo: Universitetsforlaget, 1977.

Kennedy, George A. *New Testament Interpretation through Rhetorical Criticism*. Chapel Hill: University of North Carolina Press, 1984.

Kertelge, Karl. "Gesetz und Freiheit im Galaterbrief." *New Testament Studies* 30 (1984): 382-94. Knox, W. L. *St. Paul and the Church of Jerusalem*. Cambridge: Cambridge University Press, 1925.

_____. *"Rechtfertigung" bei Paulus: Studien zur Struktur und zum Bedeutungsgehalt des paulinischen Rechtfertigungsbegriffs*. 2d ed. Neutestamentliche Abhandlungen, neue Folge, no. 3. Münster: Verlag Aschendorff, 1971.

Kim, Seyoon. *The Origin of Paul's Gospel*. Grand Rapids: Eerdmans, 1982.

Klein, Günther. "Individualgeschichte und Weltgeschichte bei Paulus: Eine Interpretation ihres Verhältnisses im Galaterbrief." *Evangelische Theologie* 24 (1964): 126-65.

_____. "Römer 4 und die Idee der Heilsgeschichte." *Evangelische Theologie* 23 (1963): 424-47.

König, A. "Gentiles or Gentile Christians: On the Meaning of Rom. 2:12-16." *Journal of Theology for South Africa* 15 (1976): 53-60.

Kümmel, Werner Georg. "Römer 7 und das Bekehrung des Paulus." In *Römer 7 und das Bild des Menschen im Neuen Testament*, pp. ix-160. 2d ed. Munich: Chr. Kaiser Verlag, 1974.

Kuhn, Heinz-Wolfgang. *Enderwartung und gegenwärtiges Heil: Untersuchungen von Qumran mit einem Anhang über Eschatologie und Gegenwart in der Verkündigung Jesu*. Studien zur Umwelt des Neuen Testaments, no. 4. Göttingen: Vandenhoek & Ruprecht, 1966.

Kuhn, Karl George. "New Light on Temptation, Sin and Flesh in the New Testament." In *The Scrolls and the New Testament*, pp. 94-113. Edited by Krister Stendahl. New York: Harper & Row, 1957.

Kuhr, Friedrich. "Römer 2:14f. und die Verheissung bei Jeremia 31:31ff. " *Zeitschrift für neutestamentliche Wissenschaft* 55 (1964): 243-61.

Kuss, Otto. *Der Römerbrief übersetzt und erklärt*, 3 vols. Regensburg: Verlag Friedrich Pustet, 1959-78.

Lambrecht, Jan. "The Line of Thought in Gal. 2.14b-21." *New Testament Studies* 24 (1977-78): 484-95.

Lang, Friedrich. "Gesetz und Bund bei Paulus." In *Rechfertigung: Festschrift für Ernst Käsemann*, pp. 305-320. Edited by Johannes Friedrich, Wolfgang Pohlmann, and Peter Stuhlmacher. Tübingen: J. C. B. Mohr (Paul Siebeck), 1976.

Leenhardt, Franz J. *The Epistle to the Romans: A Commentary*. Translated by Harold Knight. London: Lutterworth Press, 1961.

Lichtenberger, Hermann. "Enderwartung und Reinheitsidee: Zur eschatologischen Deutung von Reinheit und Sühne in der Qumrangemeinde," *Journal of Jewish Studies* 34 (1983): 31-59.

Liddell, H. G. and Scott, Robert. *A Greek-English Lexicon*. 9th ed. Revised by H. S. Jones with R. McKenzie. Oxford: Clarendon Press, 1940.

Lietzmann, Hans. *An Die Galater*. 3d ed. Handbuch zum Neuen Testament, vol. 10. Tübingen: J. C. B. Mohr (Paul Siebeck), 1932.

_____. *Einführung in die Textgeschichte der Paulusbriefe: An die Römer*. 4th ed. Handbuch zum Neuen Testament, vol. 8. Tübingen: Verlag von J. C. B. Mohr (Paul Siebeck), 1933.

Limbeck, Meinrad. *Die Ordnung des Heils: Untersuchungen zum Gesetzesverständnis des Frühjudentums*. Düsseldorf: Patmos-Verlag, 1971.

Lohmeyer, Ernst. "Gesetz und Werk." In *Grundlagen paulinischer Theologie*, pp. 5-61. Beiträge zur historischen Theologie no. 1. Tübingen: H. Kaupp, n.d.

Longenecker, Richard N. *Biblical Exegesis in the Apostolic Period*. Grand Rapids: Wm. B. Eerdmans Publishing Co., 1985.

_____. *Paul, the Apostle of Liberty: The Origin and Nature of Paul's Religion*. New York: Harper & Row Publishers, 1964.

Lührmann, Dieter. "Glaube." In *Reallexikon für Antike und Christentum: Sachwörterbuch zur Auseinandersetzung des Christentums mit der antikenWelt*, Lieferung 81, pp. 47-122. Edited by Theodor Klauser, Carsten Colpe, Ernst Dassmann, Albrecht Dihle, Bernhard Kötting, Wolfgang Speyer, and Jan Hendrik Waszink. Stuttgart: Anton Hiersemann, 1979.

_____. *Glaube im frühen Christentum*. Gütersloh: Gütersloh Verlagshaus, 1976.

Lull, David J. "'The Law Was Our Pedagogue': A Study of Galatians 3:19-25." *Journal of Biblical Literature* 105 (1986): 481-98.

Luther, Martin. *Commentary on Galatians.* Translated by Erasmus Middleton. Edited by John Prince Fallowes. Grand Rapids: Kregel Publishers, 1979.

Luz, Ulrich. *Das Geschichtsverständnis des Paulus.* Beiträge zur evangelischen Theologie no. 49. Munich: Chr. Kaiser Verlag, 1968.

Lyonnet, S. "L'histoire du salut sélon le ch. 7 de l'épître aux Romains." *Biblica* 43 (1962): 117-51.

_____. "Le Nouveau Testament à la lumière de l'Ancien. A propos du Rom 8,2-4." *La nouvelle revue théologique* 87 (1965): 561-87.

_____. "'Tu ne convoiteras pas' (Rom vii 7)." In *Neotestamentica et Patristica: Eine Freundesgabe, Herrn Professor Dr. Oscar Cullmann zu seinem 60. Geburtstag uberreicht,* pp. 157-65. Edited by W. C. van Unnik. Leiden: E. J. Brill, 1962.

Maccoby, Hyam. *The Mythmaker: Paul and the Invention of Christianity.* New York: Harper & Row, 1986.

Mansoor, Menahem. *The Thanksgiving Hymns Translated and Annotated with an Introduction.* Grand Rapids: Wm. B. Eerdmans Publishing Co., 1961.

Marrou, Henri Irenee. *Histoire de l'éducation dans l'antiquité* Paris: Éditions du Seuil, 1948.

Martyn, J. L. "Apocalyptic Antinomies in Paul's Epistle to the Galatians." *New Testament Studies* 31 (1985): 410-24.

van der Minde, Hans Jürgen. *Schrift und Tradition bei Paulus: Ihre Bedeutung und Funktion im Römerbrief.* Paderborner Theologische Studien, vol. 3. Munich: Verlag Ferdinand Schöningh, 1976.

Montefiore, Claude G. "First Impressions of Paul." *Jewish Quarterly Review* 6 (1894):428-74.

_____. *Judaism and St. Paul: Two Essays.* London: Max Goschen, Ltd., 1914.

_____. "Rabbinic Judaism and the Epistles of St. Paul." *Jewish Quarterly Review* 13 (1900-1901): 161-217.

Montefiore, C. G. and Lowe, H. *A Rabbinic Anthology, Selected and Arranged with Comments and Introductions.* New York: Schocken Books, 1974.

Moore, George Foot. *Judaism in the First Centuries of the Christian Era: The Age of the Tannaim.* 3 vols. Cambridge, Mass.: Harvard University Press, 1927- 30.

Mußner, Franz. *Der Galaterbrief.* Herders theologischer Kommentar zum Neuen Testament, vol. 9. Freiberg: Herder, 1974.

Neusner, Jacob. *Judaism in the Beginnings of Christianity.* Philadelphia: Fortress, 1984.

Nicklesburg, George W. E., Jr. *Jewish Literature between the Bible and the Mishnah: A Historical and Literary Introduction.* Philadelphia: Fortress Press, 1981.

_____. *Resurrection, Immortality, and Eternal Life in Intertestamental Judaism.* Harvard Theological Studies no. 26. Cambridge, Mass: Harvard University Press, 1972.

Noth, Martin. "'For All Who Rely on Works of the Law are under a Curse'." In *The Laws of the Pentateuch and Other Essays*, pp. 108-117. Translated by D. R. Ap-Thomas. Edinburgh and London: Oliver & Boyd, 1967.

_____. "The Laws in the Pentateuch: Their Assumptions and Meaning." In *The Laws in the Pentateuch and Other Essays*, pp. 1-107. Translated by D. R. Ap-Thomas. Edinburgh and London: Oliver & Boyd, 1967.

Nygren, Anders. *Commentary on Romans.* Translated by Carl C. Rasmussen. Philadelphia: Muhlenberg Press, 1949.

Oepke, Albrecht. *Der Brief des Paulus an die Galater.* Theologische Handkommentar zum Neuen Testament, vol. 9. Berlin: Evangelische Verlagsanstalt, 1957.

Parkes, James. *Jesus, Paul and the Jews.* London: Student Christian Movement Press, 1956.

Pagels, Elaine Hiesey. *The Gnostic Paul: Gnostic Exegesis of the Pauline Letters.* Philadelphia: Fortress Press, 1975.

Paulys Real-Encyclopädie der klassischen Altertumswissenschaft. 24 vols. Re-edited by Georg Wissowa. Stuttgart: J. B. Metzler, 1894-1963. S.v. "Paidagogos," by E. Shuppe.

Potter, Harry D. "The New Covenant in Jeremiah 31:31-34." *Vetus Testamentum* 33 (1983): 347-57.

von Rad, Gerhard. *Old Testament Theology*, 2 vols. Translated by D. M. G. Stalker. New York: Harper & Row, 1962.

_____. *Studies in Deuteronomy.* Studies in Biblical Theology, no. 9. Translated by David Stalker. London: SCM Press, 1953.

Räisänen, Heikki. "Galatians 2.16 and Paul's Break with Judaism." *New Testament Studies* 31 (1985): 543-53.

_____. *Paul and the Law.* Wissenschaftliche Untersuchungen zum Neuen Testament, no. 29. Tübingen: J. C. B. Mohr (Paul Siebeck), 1983.

Reinmuth, Eckart. *Geist und Gesetz: Studien zu Voraussetzungen und Inhalt der paulinischen Paränese.* Theologische Arbeiten, no. 44. Berlin: Evangelische Verlagsanstalt, 1985.

Rhyne, C. Thomas. *Faith Establishes the Law*. Society of Biblical Literature Dissertations Series, no. 55. Chico, Calif.: Scholars Press, 1981.

Riddle, Donald W. "The Jewishness of Paul." *Journal of Religion* 23 (1943): 240-44.

Rössler, D. *Gesetz und Geschichte: Eine Untersuchung zur Theologie der jüdischen Apocalyptik und der pharisaichen Orthodoxie*. Neukirchen Kreis Moers: Neukirchener Verlag, 1962.

Sand, A. *Der Begriff "Fleisch" in den paulinischen Hauptbriefen*. Biblische Untersuchungen, no. 2. Regensburg: Pustet, 1967.

Sanders, E. P. *Paul and Palestinian Judaism: A Comparison of Patterns of Religion*. Philadelphia: Fortress, 1977.

_____. *Paul, the Law, and the Jewish People*. Philadelphia: Fortress Press, 1983.

Sanders, James A. "Torah and Christ." *Interpretation* 29 (1975): 372-90.

Sandmel, Samuel. *The Genius of Paul: A Study of History*. New York: Farrar, Straus, and Cudahy, 1958.

Schlatter, Adolf. *Der Glaube im Neuen Testament*. 6th ed. Stuttgart: Calwer Verlag, 1927.

Schlier, Heinrich. *Der Brief an die Galater übersezt und erklärt*. Kritisch-exegetischer Kommentar (Meyer) vol. 7. Göttingen: Vandenhoeck & Ruprecht, 1949.

Schoeps, Hans Joachim. *Aus Frühchristlicher Zeit: Religionsgeschichtliche Untersuchungen*. Tübingen: Verlag J. C. B. Mohr (Paul Siebeck), 1950.

_____. *Paul: The Theology of the Apostle in the Light of Jewish Religious History*. Translated by Harold Knight. Philadelphia: Westminster Press, 1961.

Schreiner, Thomas R. "Paul and Perfect Obedience to the Law: An Evaluation of the View of E. P. Sanders." In *Westminster Theological Journal* 47 (1985): 245-78.

Schweitzer, Albert. *Paul and His Interpreters: A Critical History*. Translated by W. Montgomery. New York: Macmillan Publishing Company, 1951.

_____. *The Mysticism of Paul the Apostle*. Translated by W. Montgomery. New York: Seabury Press, 1968.

Schweizer, Eduard. "Slaves of the Elements and Worshipers of Angels." *Journal of Biblical Literature* 107 (1988): 455-68.

Segal, Alan F. *The Other Judaisms of Late Antiquity*. Brown Judaic Studies no. 127. Atlanta, Georgia, 1987.

Sieffert, F. *Der Brief an die Galater*. Dirtisch- exegetischer Kommentar über das Neuen Testament, vol. 7. Göttingen: Vandenhoeck & Ruprecht, 1899.

Slingerland, Dixon L. "The Nature of Nomos (Law) within the Testaments of the Twelve Patriarchs." *Journal of Biblical Literature* 105 (1986): 39-48.

_____. *The Testaments of the Twelve Patriarchs: A Critical History of Research.* Society of Biblical Literature Monograph Series, vol. 21. Missoula, Montana: 1977.

Smith, D. Moody, Jr. "Ο ΔΕ ΔΙΚΑΙΟΣ ΕΚ ΠΙΣΤΕΩΣ ΖΗΣΕΤΑΙ" In *Studies in the History and Text of the New Testament in Honor of Kenneth Willis Clark, Ph.D.*, pp. 13-35. Studies and Documents, no. 29. Edited by Boyd L. Daniels and M. Jack Suggs. Salt Lake City, Utah: University of Utah Press, 1967.

_____. "The Use of the Old Testament in the New." In *The Use of the Old Testament in the New and Other Essays: Studies in Honor of William Franklin Stinespring*, pp. 3-62. Edited by James M. Efird. Durham, N. C.: Duke University Press, 1972.

Snodgrass, Klyne R. "Justification by Grace—to the Doers: An Analysis of Romans 2 in the Theology of Paul." *New Testament Studies* 32 (1986): 72-93.

_____. "Spheres of Influence: A Possible Solution to the Problem of Paul and the Law." *Journal for the Study of the New Testament* 32 (1988): 93-113.

Stephens, Craig A. "Paul and the Hermeneutics of 'True Prophecy': A Study of Romans 9-11." *Biblica* 65 (1984): 560-70.

Stendahl, Krister. "Paul among Jews and Gentiles." In *Paul among Jews and Gentiles and Other Essays*, pp. 1-77. Philadelphia: Fortress, 1976.

_____. "Paul and the Introspective Conscience of the West." In *Paul among Jews and Gentiles and Other Essays*, pp. 78-96. Philadelphia. Fortress Press, 1976.

Stone, Michael E. "Coherence and Inconsistency in the Apocalypses: The Case of 'the End' in 4 Ezra." *Journal of Biblical Literature* 102 (1983): 229-43.

Strack, Herman L. and Billerbeck, Paul. *Kommentar zum Neuen Testament aus Talmud und Midrasch*, 4 vols. Munich: C. H. Beck'sche Verlagsbuchhandlung Oskar Beck, 1928.

Stuhlmacher, Peter. "The Apostle Paul's View of Righteousness." In *Reconciliation, Law and Righteousness*, pp. 68-93. Translated by Everett R. Kalin. Philadelphia: Fortress, 1986.

_____. "Paul's Understanding of the Law in the Letter to the Romans." *Svensk exegetisk årsbok* 50 (1985): 98-100.

_____. "The Law as a Topic of Biblical Theology." In *Reconciliation, Law and Righteousness*, pp. 110-33. Translated by Everett R. Kalin. Philadelphia: Fortress Press, 1986.

Theissen, Gerd. *Psychological Aspects of Pauline Theology.* Translated by John P. Galvin. Philadelphia: Fortress Press, 1987.

Thielman, Frank. Review of *Christ the End of the Law: Romans 10.4 in Pauline Perspective* by Robert Badenas. *Journal of Biblical Literature* 107 (1988):145-47.

Tyson, Joseph B. "'Works of the Law' in Galatians." In *Journal of Biblical Literature* 92 (1973): 423-41.

Vielhauer, P. "Paulus und das Alte Testament." In *Oikodome: Aufsätze zum Neuen Testament*, vol. 2, pp. 196-228. Theologische Bücherei, Neues Testament no. 65. Edited by Günther Klein. Munich: Chr. Kaiser Verlag, 1979.

Volz, Paul. *Jüdische Eschatologie*. Tübingen and Leipzig: J. C. B. Mohr (Paul Siebeck), 1903.

Watson, Francis. *Paul, Judaism and the Gentiles: A Sociological Approach*. Society for New Testament Studies Monograph Series, no. 56. Cambridge: Cambridge University Press, 1986.

Weder, Hans. "Gesetz und Sünde: Gedanken zu einem qualitative Sprung im Denken des Paulus." *New Testament Studies* 31 (1985): 357-76.

Wellhausen, Julius. *Prolegomena to the History of Ancient Israel with a Reprint of the Article "Israel" from the "Encyclopedia Britannica"*. Translated by Mr. Menzies and Mr. Black. Cleveland and New York: The World Publishing Company, 1957.

Westerholm, Stephen. *Israel's Law and the Church's Faith: Paul and His Recent Interpreters*. Grand Rapids: Eerdmans, 1988.

Westermann, Claus. *Elements of Old Testament Theology*. Translated by Douglas L.W. Stott. Atlanta: John Knox Press, 1982.

Wilckens, Ulrich. *Der Brief an die Römer*. 3 vols. Evangelisch-Katholischer Kommentar zum Neuen Testmanet, no. 6. Neukirchen-Vluyn: Benziger/Neukirchener Verlag, 1978-82.

_____. "Die Bekehrung des Paulus als religionsgeschichtliches Problem." In *Rechtfertigung als Freiheit: Paulusstudien*, pp. 11-32. Neukirchen-Vluyn: Neukirchener Verlag, 1974.

_____. "Statements on the Development of Paul's View of the Law." In *Paul and Paulinism: Essays in Honour of C. K. Barrett*, pp. 17-26. Edited by M. D. Hooker and S. G. Wilson. Cambridge: Cambridge University Press, 1982.

_____. "Was heißt bei Paulus: 'Aus Werken des Gesetzes wird kein Mensch gerecht'?" In *Rechtfertigung als Freiheit: Paulusstudien*, pp. 77-109. Neukirch: Neukirchener Verlag, 1974.

_____. "Zur Entwicklung des paulinischen Gesetzesverständnisses." *New Testament Studies* 28 (1982): 154-90.

Wilkins, A. S. *Roman Education*. Cambridge: Cambridge University Press, 1914.

Windisch, Hans. *Paulus und das Judentum*. Stuttgart: Verlag von W. Kolhammer, 1935.

Wolf, Hans Walter and Brueggemann, Walter. *The Vitality of the Old Testament Traditions*. Atlanta: John Knox, 1978.

Wolfson, Harry Austin. *Philo: Foundations of Religious Philosophy in Judaism, Christianity, and Islam*, 2 vols. 2d printing, revised. Cambridge, Mass.: Harvard University Press, 1948.

Wrede, William. *Paul*. Translated by Edward Lumis. London: Philip Green, 1907.

_____. *Paulus*. Tübingen: J. C. B. Mohr (Paul Siebeck),.1906.

Young, F. W. Review of *Paulus: die Theologie des Apostles im Licht der jüdischen Religionsgeschichte*, by Hans Joachim Schoeps, *Theology Today* 20 (1963-64): 555.

Ziesler, John. *The Meaning of Righteousness in Paul*. Society for New Testament Studies Monograph Series, no. 20. Cambridge: Cambridge University Press, 1972.

Zimmerli, Walther. *A Commentary on the Book of the Prophet Ezekiel*. Translated by Ronald E. Clements. Vol. 1: Chapters 1-24. Philadelphia: Fortress Press, 1969.

_____. *The Law and the Prophets: A Study of the Meaning of the Old Testament*. Translated by R. E. Clements. Oxford: Basil Blackwell, 1965.

_____. *Old Testament Theology in Outline*. Translated by David E. Green. Atlanta: John Knox Press, 1978.

INDEX OF AUTHORS

INDEX OF REFERENCES

1. OLD TESTAMENT

2. NEW TESTAMENT

3. APOCRYPHA

4. PSEUDEPIGRAPHICAL AND PATRISTIC TEXTS

5. DEAD SEA SCROLLS AND RELATED TEXTS

6. TARGUMIC, MISHNAIC, AND RELATED LITERATURE

7. CLASSICAL TEXTS